Armies and

of the

Crusades

1096–1291

by Ian Heath

SECOND EDITION 2019

CONTENTS

FOREWORD TO THE 2019 EDITION

Although it's a great delight to see this book being reissued – not least because it means all those versions that people have illegally downloaded onto and from the Internet are no longer correct – I have to concede that, even in this corrected and revised Second Edition format, it is not as comprehensive as I would like.

So many new books have been published about the Crusades and Crusading warfare in the past 40 years that I doubt I'd live long enough to read them all! The bibliography therefore remains substantially unaltered, and people wishing to learn more about this fascinating and continuingly relevant theatre of medieval conflict must therefore peruse the many online booklists and publishers' catalogues to be found on the Internet.

Ian Heath, March 2019

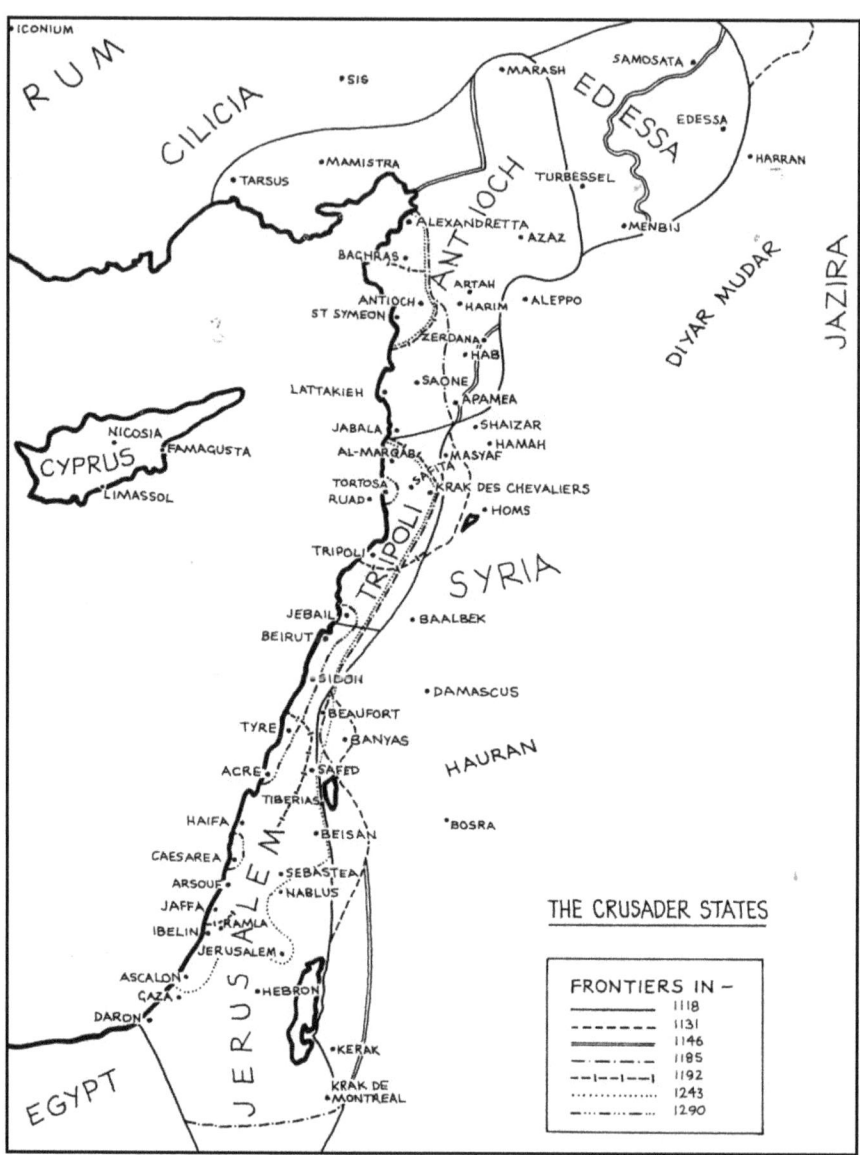

ICONIUM

RUM

CILICIA

·SIS

·MARASH

SAMOSATA

EDESSA

EDESSA

·TARSUS

·MAMISTRA

ANTIOCH

TURBESSEL

·HARRAN

·ALEXANDRETTA

·AZAZ

·MENBIJ

BAGHRAS·

·ARTAH

·ALEPPO

ANTIOCH·

·HARIM

ST SYMEON·

ZERDANA·

·HAB

·SAONE

·APAMEA

LATTAKIEH

JABALA·

·SHAIZAR

·HAMAH

NICOSIA

AL-MARQAB·

·MASYAF

CYPRUS

·FAMAGUSTA

TORTOSA·

SAFITA·

·KRAK DES CHEVALIERS

·LIMASSOL

RUAD·

·HOMS

TRIPOLI·

TRIPOLI

SYRIA

JEBAIL·

·BAALBEK

BEIRUT·

·SIDON

·DAMASCUS

DIYAR MUDAR

JAZIRA

BEAUFORT

TYRE·

·BANYAS

HAURAN

ACRE·

·SAFED

TIBERIAS·

HAIFA·

·BOSRA

·BEISAN

CAESAREA·

ARSOUF·

·SEBASTEA

JAFFA·

·NABLUS

IBELIN·

·RAMLA

JERUSALEM

JERUSALEM·

ASCALON·

·HEBRON

GAZA·

DARON·

·KERAK

EGYPT

KRAK DE
·MONTREAL

THE CRUSADER STATES

FRONTIERS IN —

——————— 1118
- - - - - - - 1131
═══════ 1146
·—·—·—· 1185
—1—1—1—1 1192
·············· 1243
·—··—··—·· 1290

INTRODUCTION TO THE 1978 EDITION

Although many books have been written on the Crusades over the years they mostly approach the subject from a political or social viewpoint, and with the exception of R.C. Smail's workmanlike *'Crusading Warfare 1097-1193'* few or none have ventured to describe in any detail the warriors and armies with which Muslim and Christian vied for control of the Holy Land. The aim of this book, therefore, is to fill this gap and add a little flesh to the bones of crusading history, by not only describing but also illustrating the myriad warrior-types of Outremer and the lands of Islam and Byzantium, so that together with the notes on organisation and tactics an entire picture can be built up of warfare in the Middle East in the two centuries between the fateful Battle of Manzikert in 1071 and the fall of the city of Acre to the Mamluks 220 years later.

A few notes on terminology. I have used the term 'Frank' throughout to describe crusaders of European origin or extraction, though the Byzantines tended to refer to them more often as 'Latins'. Where their ethnic origins are mixed or uncertain Muslims I have usually called by that name, though where applicable I have sometimes substituted 'Turks' or 'Arabs' and on occasion have even lapsed into using the popular term 'Saracen' (a corruption of 'Sharkeein', meaning Easterner or Levantine). Following convention, natives of the Eastern Empire are referred to as Byzantines, or sometimes as Greeks, which term they were beginning to apply to themselves during the course of this era, although they more often persisted in calling themselves 'Romans' even in the 12th and 13th centuries. 'The Holy Land', although it refers specifically to the Kingdom of Jerusalem, I have generally used (interchangeably with Palestine, Frankish Syria and 'Outremer') as a collective term for the mainland crusader states of Jerusalem, Tripoli, Antioch and Edessa; no modern geographical boundaries are intended by any of these terms, and if this should at times cause confusion I crave your indulgence. European Crusades of this same era, such as were fought in Spain, Southern France and Prussia, are not covered here, the participating armies of these campaigns having already been described in *'Armies of Feudal Europe 1066-1300'*.

The third and final part of what was once envisaged as a single book, I think I can safely say that this is the part which I have most enjoyed preparing. I hope you will find it equally enjoyable to read, and that it will encourage further interest in one of the most neglected, and yet at the same time most fascinating, theatres of mediaeval warfare.

Ian Heath, February 1978

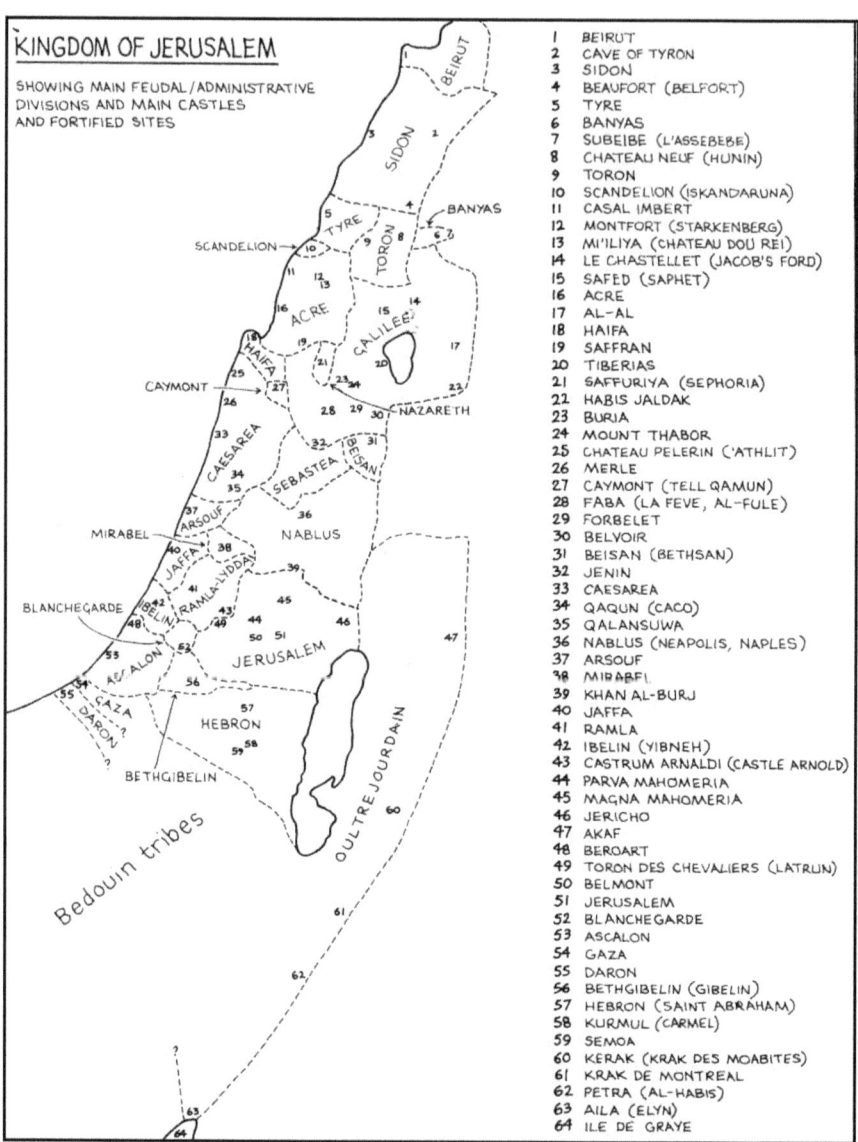

KINGDOM OF JERUSALEM

SHOWING MAIN FEUDAL/ADMINISTRATIVE
DIVISIONS AND MAIN CASTLES
AND FORTIFIED SITES

1	BEIRUT
2	CAVE OF TYRON
3	SIDON
4	BEAUFORT (BELFORT)
5	TYRE
6	BANYAS
7	SUBEIBE (L'ASSEBEBE)
8	CHATEAU NEUF (HUNIN)
9	TORON
10	SCANDELION (ISKANDARUNA)
11	CASAL IMBERT
12	MONTFORT (STARKENBERG)
13	MI'ILIYA (CHATEAU DOU REI)
14	LE CHASTELLET (JACOB'S FORD)
15	SAFED (SAPHET)
16	ACRE
17	AL-AL
18	HAIFA
19	SAFFRAN
20	TIBERIAS
21	SAFFURIYA (SEPHORIA)
22	HABIS JALDAK
23	BURJA
24	MOUNT THABOR
25	CHATEAU PELERIN ('ATHLIT)
26	MERLE
27	CAYMONT (TELL QAMUN)
28	FABA (LA FEVE, AL-FULE)
29	FORBELET
30	BELVOIR
31	BEISAN (BETHSAN)
32	JENIN
33	CAESAREA
34	QAQUN (CACO)
35	QALANSUWA
36	NABLUS (NEAPOLIS, NAPLES)
37	ARSOUF
38	MIRABEL
39	KHAN AL-BURJ
40	JAFFA
41	RAMLA
42	IBELIN (YIBNEH)
43	CASTRUM ARNALDI (CASTLE ARNOLD)
44	PARVA MAHOMERIA
45	MAGNA MAHOMERIA
46	JERICHO
47	AKAF
48	BEROART
49	TORON DES CHEVALIERS (LATRUN)
50	BELMONT
51	JERUSALEM
52	BLANCHEGARDE
53	ASCALON
54	GAZA
55	DARON
56	BETHGIBELIN (GIBELIN)
57	HEBRON (SAINT ABRAHAM)
58	KURMUL (CARMEL)
59	SEMOA
60	KERAK (KRAK DES MOABITES)
61	KRAK DE MONTREAL
62	PETRA (AL-HABIS)
63	AILA (ELYN)
64	ILE DE GRAYE

ORGANISATION

THE CRUSADER STATES

European feudalism was introduced into Syria by the crusaders, who founded the Principality of Antioch (1098-1263), the Counties of Edessa (1098-1144) and Tripoli (1109-1289, incorporating Antioch after 1219), the Kingdom of Cyprus (1191-1489, thereafter a Venetian colony until 1571) and the Kingdom of Jerusalem (1100-1187, thereafter in reality the Kingdom of Acre rather than Jerusalem until the final extinction of the state in 1291).

Feudal contingents

Since there was a constant shortage of manpower, and the survival of Frankish Syria depended entirely on its military capabilities, general knight service was subject to far fewer restrictions than in Europe. For instance, there seems to have been no time-limit on the length of service that might be required even up to a full year, though it is not clear whether this was at the expense of the vassal or the tenant-in-chief; either way it was not at the king's expense unless it took place outside of the kingdom.

Each vassal was a vassal of the king, irrespective of whose lands he was enfeoffed upon (with the exception of the lands of the church and the Military Orders), and so long as he was under 60 years of age he was expected to serve mounted and fully-armed anywhere within the realm and within 15 days whenever the king summoned him. In addition the vassal would be accompanied by whatever knights, sergeants, esquires or mercenaries his terms of enfeoffment might demand (it should be noted, however, that a vassal was not allowed to subinfeudate more of his fief than he himself held, which effectively restricted the size of personal retinues[1]).

The principal limitation on feudal service to the crown was that Edessa, Tripoli and Antioch were not considered part of the realm, and military assistance from these principalities was only to be expected when the king was strong enough to enforce it. When the crowns of Jerusalem and Cyprus were united in 1268 this problem became more complicated, Cypriote knights insisting that they owed no military service to the king save on the island of Cyprus itself; but in 1273 agreement was reached that Cypriote knights owed service in Jerusalem too – or wherever else the king might have need of them – for four months every year. However, even prior to this date, as early as the reign of Amalric II (1194-1205), Cypriote feudal troops had

---

[1] By the mid-13th century there was considerable dispute as to whether this meant that the vassal must (a) hold at least 51% of the fief himself, or (b) that he need only hold more than was subinfeudated to his greatest vassal.

appeared in mainland armies on a number of occasions; 100 Cypriote knights took part in the Fifth Crusade under the Constable of Cyprus, and in an attack on Hamah in 1233, while perhaps 300 Cypriotes were killed at La Forbie in 1244 and at least 200 Cypriote knights and 500 infantry took part in the final defence of Acre in 1291. (The Estoire d'Eracles informs us that when feudal tenure was established on Cyprus by Guy de Lusignan, 1192-1194, vassals 'came from the Kingdom of Jerusalem, from Tripoli, from Antioch, and from Armenia [i.e. Cilicia]. And there were established fiefs worth 400 white bezants for a knight and worth 300 for a Turcopole with two horses and a coat-of-mail.' In all 300 knight's fees were parcelled out and 200 Turcopole's fees, leaving Guy with scarcely enough land or revenue to maintain a familia of 20 – one source says 70 – knights.)

Because of the shortage of land many vassals received money-fiefs in exchange for service (especially in the Principality of Antioch), usually from the revenues of specific towns and cities; Frankish mercenaries were also paid with money-fiefs (see below). Some of the knights owed by the towns (see Appendix I), and perhaps by the church as well, were probably also supplied in exchange for money- fiefs.

Though often complicated by the presence of crusading European kings and magnates overall command was usually in the hands of the king himself or his bailli (regent), though in reality a council of the chief men of the army decided strategy and policy (as Beha ed-Din puts it, 'it is their custom, when it is a question of war, to take counsel together on horseback'). In the absence of king or bailli the Constable of the Kingdom led the army assisted by his lieutenant, the Marshal. Supplies and justice were responsibilities of the Constable, as was the employment and fair payment of mercenaries, both the king's and those hired independently by the feudal lords, from whom he collected the appropriate payments; but the Marshal actually commanded the mercenaries in the field. In battle the Constable commanded a double-strength troop (he had the first choice of men after the king's own troop had been made up) and marched in the vanguard, immediately behind the Turcopoles, with the Marshal's troop, then the king's, behind him. Antioch, Edessa and Tripoli had their own constables and marshals (two marshals could hold office simultaneously in Antioch), as did the great barons of Jaffa, Sidon, Galilee and possibly Oultrejourdain and Caesarea. The Seneschal was senior to the Constable but he was a court official rather than a military commander. In the Principality of Antioch there were additional officers (in Antioch, Jabala and Lattakieh) called 'duces' or Dukes.

Frankish mercenaries

Mercenaries, called 'sodeers' or soldiers, were of great importance from the very beginning of the crusader states' existence, at least partially compensating for the critical shortage of feudal manpower. They became even more important over the years as the steady reconquest of land by the Saracens further reduced the numbers of feudal troops available. Some were provided on a feudal basis by vassals who owed 'service de compaignons' (which required that the vassal should raise and pay a specified number of mercenaries), others being provided by Frankish knights and sergeants who stayed on in the East after visiting the holy places.

They were contracted month by month (from the 1st of the month), breach of such a contract being regarded as a very serious offence; in the case of a knight it was punishable by confiscation of his fief if he had one (presumably land or money) or his armour and equipment if he did not, while an ordinary soldier might have his hands mutilated with a hot iron. On the other hand mercenaries were paid at a very high rate (though probably not at 100 times the rate of a Muslim warrior as is suggested in one of Usamah ibn Munqidh's anecdotes; evidence suggests, in fact, that Franks were paid 2-5 times as much as their Muslim counterparts). Many – knights, sergeants and infantry – tended to be hired outright, but mercenary knights were often paid for with money-fiefs, usually from the revenues of some town, city or trade specified in their contracts. The revenues varied from 300 bezants per annum to 600 or even 1,000 depending on how secure the revenues were and how many men were needed – the more men needed, the lower the revenue. However, because of almost constant warfare and the frequent loss of towns and lands it was not uncommon for mercenaries' pay to be well overdue, and under such circumstances they could sell their equipment and live off the proceeds, owing no service until the outstanding debt had been paid off. On other occasions they were paid for by special taxes (as in 1183), or by gifts of money from European rulers in lieu of actual troops; the Historia Regni Hierosolymitani records that as many as 1200 mercenary knights and 7,000 mercenary infantry were hired prior to the Battle of Hattin in 1187, explaining that they were paid for by a money gift from Henry II of England (in atonement for the murder of Thomas á Becket), but these figures are somewhat on the high side, while in his will of 1222 Philip II of France left 155,000 silver marks to the king of Jerusalem and the Orders of the Temple and Hospital for the maintenance of 100 mercenary knights each for a period of 3 years. Likewise, money sent out to Outremer by the Pope seems to have been largely used to hire mercenaries throughout the 13th century.

Examples of Frankish knights staying on in Outremer in exchange for pay are provided by the 40 knights left with a year's pay by Walter d'Avesnes on his return to Europe in 1218, and the French regiment of 100 knights established in Acre by Louis IX (St Louis) prior to his own departure in 1254 and continuously maintained by gifts of money until the fall of the city in 1291. Although not strictly mercenary, the units of French and German knights maintained by the baillis of Charles of Anjou and Frederick II should probably also be mentioned here.

Native soldiers and mercenaries: Syrians, Maronites, Turcopoles and Armenians

Far from all mercenaries were of Frankish origin. As mentioned above, crusaders from Europe often did stay on for pay, but the majority of mercenaries were hired from amongst the native Christians – the Syrians, Armenians and Maronites. These would be hired outright rather than being granted money-fiefs.

It has been suggested that Syrians may have supplied the bulk of the kingdom's infantry, and though there is little evidence to support this rather sweeping statement it is undeniable that Syrians are to be occasionally found in Frankish armies; some, for instance, helped Raymond de Saint-Gilles in the conquest of Tripoli. Undoubtedly others would take up arms in an emergency, as some did in 1124, and passages in William of Tyre and Fulcher of Chartres indicate that they might sometimes perform garrison duties. However, William also points out that in general they were of a timorous nature, 'a race which is regarded by us as weak and effeminate', in which assessment he is backed up by Jacques de Vitry, Bishop of Acre, who wrote in the 13th century that 'they are altogether unwarlike and in battle are as helpless as women, save for some of them who use bows and arrows but are unarmoured and ready for running away. These men are known as Syrians ... For the most part they are untrustworthy, two-faced cunning foxes just like the Greeks [Byzantines], liars and turncoats, lovers of success, traitors, easily won over with bribes, men who say one thing and mean another, and think nothing of theft and robbery. For a small sum of money they become spies and tell the Christians' secrets to the Saracens.' Hardly reliable allies!

The principal native Christian element in the County of Tripoli was provided by the Maronites of Lebanon, settled principally in Gibbat Bsarri, Kisrawan and round Jebail. They appear to have numbered about 30-40,000. William of Tyre praised the military skill of the Maronites, 'a stalwart race, valiant fighters, and of great service to the Christians in the difficult engagements which they so frequently had', to which de Vitry adds 'they are numerous, use bows and arrows, and are swift and skilful in battle.' They served in most Tripolitanian armies, fighting under their own chieftains (called by the Arabic title Muqaddam), some of whom even received fiefs (which would indicate that a few were actually knights; other native Christian knights are also to be found in the sources, with surnames such as Arrabi, Qelbe Arab, Elteffaha, etc., while in Antioch many knights bore Greek names). Between 1192 and 1194 Guy de Lusignan is reported to have even introduced a large number of Maronites into Cyprus (the figure of 30,000 is given), these subsequently serving as a sort of militia. The larger part of Krak des Chevaliers' garrison in 1271 were Maronites, and some may have later accompanied the Hospitallers to Rhodes, and later still to Malta.

The most numerous, reliable and efficient Syrian element in Frankish armies, however, was provided by the Turcopoles. The term Turcopole itself, meaning literally 'son of the Turks', had been borrowed from the Byzantines, who used the name Turcopouloi for their own mercenary Turkish regulars (Raymond d'Aguilers states that 'Turcopoles were so named because they were either reared with Turks or were the offspring of a Christian mother and a Turkish father'). The Franks applied the term rather more loosely to Syrians, natives of mixed parentage (Turkish fathers and Greek mothers according to Albert of Aix), and converted Turks serving in their own armies. By the mid-12th century, however, judging from the evidence of names recorded for Turcopoles in written sources it would seem possible that at least some, and possibly a great many, may have actually been Franks born and raised in Outremer (Poulains) or even European Franks, probably equipped to fight in Turkish fashion. (In support of this last theory it is interesting to note that Turcopouloi employed by the Catalans in Greece in the early 14th century included native Greeks who had shaved their heads Turkish-fashion in order to be employed in this capacity.) Although it has been suggested that some Turcopoles were foot-soldiers the sources seem to indicate that they fought principally if not exclusively as light cavalry (see also note 14 in the dress and equipment section). They had their own officers called Turcopoliers (probably Franks) but like all other mercenaries came under the overall command of the Marshal of the Kingdom.

There were 1,500 Turcopoles in the army which campaigned in the Jezreel valley in 1183 and the army at Hattin may have included as many as 4,000; Usamah records a single nobleman (William-Jordan, regent of Tripoli) having as many as 200 'Turkubuli' (from Latin 'Turcopoli') in his employ in 1107. Turcopoles served in addition in Tunisia (during Louis IX's Eighth Crusade) and Cyprus and were employed in considerable numbers by the Military Orders – the Hospitallers supplied 500 in 1168 while the Hospitallers and Templars together lost over 500 at La Forbie in 1244.

The other most important group of native Christians were the warlike Armenians of Cilicia (Lesser Armenia). These were numerous in the Principality of Antioch and composed most of the population of the County of Edessa, and they are to be found serving variously as subjects, mercenaries and allies under their own chieftains, supplying both cavalry and infantry, particularly under Count Joscelyn II (1131-1150). In 1108 the Armenian prince of Kesoun, Kogh Vasil (Vasil the Robber), supplied Baldwin of Edessa with an army of as many as 1-2,000 cavalry and 2,000 infantry, including a number of Seljuk renegades, while the chronicler Matthew of Edessa records that there were 500 Armenian cavalry in Roger of Antioch's army at Ager Sanguinus in 1119 and a similar number at 'Azaz in 1125. When Edessa fell in 1144 many of its mercenary defenders were Armenians, and some Armenians were even present at the siege of Acre in 1191.

It should be noted, however, that the Armenians (and very occasionally the Maronites) could also be found fighting against the Franks. Armenians seem to have played a particularly important role in some Seljuk armies of the late 11th century, notably that of Tutush of Damascus (1079-1095), and they were to be found too in the various Turkish armies which opposed the First Crusade. In addition the Fatimids employed Armenian archers in the 12th century. Sometimes too open warfare could flare up between Cilicia and neighbouring Antioch.

The fleet: the Italian communes

Though Antioch and Tripoli both developed small fleets the Kingdom of Jerusalem itself had no permanent fleet of its own (though it maintained arsenals at Tyre and Acre, raising 33 ships from these at short notice in 1182, probably including Italian merchant vessels in port at the time, while in 1232 money-fiefs were paid out to Poulains of the coastal cities for fitting out armed ships). Instead the kings of Jerusalem depended principally on the Italian communes and the Military Orders for naval support (the Orders maintaining both transports and galleys; in a naval engagement during the siege of Tyre in 1187 we find as many as 17 galleys manned by Hospitallers and Templars). 13th-century Cyprus similarly relied on Italian ships, usually Genoese.

The Italian communes (second in importance only to the Military Orders in 13th-century Outremer) had mostly been established in the early years of the 12th century in exchange for the services rendered by Italian fleets in the capture of the coastal cities, which, with the exception of Tyre and Ascalon, all fell between 1100 and 1111. For example, 40 Genoese ships had attended the siege of Jebail in 1103, 70 were at Acre in 1104, 60 at Tripoli in 1109, 40 Genoese and Pisan ships at Beirut in 1110, and later as many as 100-130 Venetian ships at the siege of Tyre in 1124. Such fleets had been supplied principally by the city-states of Genoa, Pisa and (at first to a lesser extent) Venice, generally in exchange for pay, trading concessions or loot, or often all three; usually they were promised part of the besieged city too, often a third. The end product was the establishment of self-governing Italian communes in all the coastal cities, each under a consul or viscount (vicomte) appointed by its parent city in Italy. Genoa possessed such communes in Acre, Antioch, Arsuf, Beirut, Caesarea, Jaffa, Jebail, Lattakieh, Saint Symeon, Tyre and Tripoli, and Venice had its own communes in the larger of these cities, both having quarters in Jerusalem too. Pisa had communes in Acre, Antioch, Botrun, Lattakieh, Tripoli and Tyre. In addition there were Amalfitan communes in Acre and Lattakieh and Marseillais communes in Acre, Jaffa, Jebail and Tyre, there even being a Barcelonese commune in the latter. Except for Acre few of these could have mustered more than about 500 men.

Though the communes were under no obligation to serve in the king's army they could be called upon to help defend the cities in which they had their quarters and to lend naval support (usually in exchange for extra privileges) in defence of the coastal towns. Italian contingents also often went along as 'allies' in many offensive campaigns, and as mercenaries in others.

Unfortunately for the kingdom, however, the Venetian, Pisan, Genoese and other Italian contingents were mutually hostile, and Jacques de Vitry remarks dryly that 'they would be very terrible to the Saracens if they would cease from their jealousy and avarice and would not continually fight and quarrel with each other. But they more often join battle against one another than against the treacherous infidel.' One of the worst of these bloody civil wars was the War of Saint Sabas in Acre in 1259, in which allegedly (but improbably) 20,000 Venetians, Genoese and others died.

Other sources of troops

Church lands and the towns of the kingdom were obliged to supply contingents of sergeants. Those contingents on record (listed by Jean d'Ibelin – see Appendix 1) varied between 25 and 500 each, the lists apparently recording the state of affairs as it existed in the reign of Baldwin IV (1174-1185). D'Ibelin gives a total of 5,025 sergeants being available from these sources, though his figures are probably incomplete and reflect the service of the kingdom of Jerusalem only, exclusive of Antioch and Tripoli (Edessa had fallen in 1144). These sergeants were not a militia, serving rather in exchange for sergeants' fees. They were probably infantry. Though there were also mounted sergeants these were more usually in the retinues of knights.

On occasion the Arrière-Ban – the levy of all able-bodied freemen – might be summoned to supplement the feudal and mercenary contingents, either locally as, for example, at Jaffa in 1122 and Acre in 1218, or to relieve the siege of Ba'rin in 1137; or on a national scale as at the siege of Acre in 1104, for a war against Damascus in 1126, at Ascalon in 1153 (where in addition some pilgrims were hired temporarily), at Montgisard in 1177, or for the Hattin campaign of 1187. Pilgrims also appeared in exchange for pay on other occasions, as at Ramla in 1102, Sennabra in 1113, and in the 'Ain Jalut campaign of 1183, but it is clear that such service was not always performed willingly. Crusading knights constantly arriving from Europe also supplemented the kingdom's army for the duration of their stay, often staying on as mercenaries (as mentioned above).

Muslims and Mongols

In the first half of the 12th century Turkish amirs, fearful of losing their independence to more powerful neighbours or even to the Sultan, could be found allied to the crusader states and supplying troops, such as the 600

Aleppene cavalry and more than 1,000 Turks and Bedouins who fought for Tancred of Antioch and Baldwin II of Edessa respectively at Tell Bashir in 1108, and the 5,000 from Aleppo, Mardin and Damascus who served during the 1115 campaign. The Frankish army besieging Aleppo in 1124 is recorded to have included as many as 100 'Muslim tents' (Bedouins under the amir Dubays), comprising one-third of the total force, Bedouin spies and scouts being recorded in addition on other occasions. Assassins were also to be found allied to the Franks on occasion (there were some in Raymond of Antioch's army defeated at Fons Muratus), while Egyptian troops too appeared in Frankish armies, notably during the struggle with Nur ed-Din for control of Egypt in 1167, but they were regarded as poor soldiers of little military significance. There were also some Saracen archers introduced from Sicily in 1113; more accompanied Frederick II during the Sixth Crusade of 1228-1229 and probably the 300 'Turcopoles' reported in the fleet despatched by William II of Sicily in 1187 were also Saracens.

Even the Mongols (in this case the Nestorian or Christian-influenced Ilkhanids of Persia) sometimes fought for the Frankish cause, and in this context appear some of the most unlikely armies of this era, such as the mixed bag of Mongols, Turks, Franks (under Bohemond VI of Antioch), Armenians and Georgians which campaigned in Syria in 1259 and 1260 under the Ilkhan Hulagu. In 1281, under his successor Abaqa, an army of similar composition, chiefly Mongols, Georgians and Armenians but including Hospitallers from the garrison of al-Marqab, fought the Mamluks at Homs. Ten years earlier, in 1271, Abaqa had allegedly despatched as many as 10,000 Mongols against the Mamluks in Syria in response to an appeal from the English prince Edward (later King Edward I), then involved in what transpired to be a very minor crusading enterprise.

Total strength

In the autumn of 1099 Godfrey de Bouillon could muster 3,000 men in Jerusalem, but Albert of Aix records that by the spring of 1100 this had declined to only 200 knights and 1,000 infantry. The next year Fulcher of Chartres records that King Baldwin 1 had barely 300 cavalry and 300 infantry with which to garrison Jerusalem, Ramla, Jaffa and Haifa, and even at the First Battle of Ramla there were as few as 260 cavalry and 900 infantry present. Baldwin found it necessary, in fact, to establish a mercenary force to garrison both Jerusalem and Jaffa at least as early as 1101, and in 1108 we hear of a force of as many as 200 mercenary knights and 500 mercenary infantry from the garrison of Jerusalem.

700 knights and 4,000 infantry gathered by Baldwin in 1111 probably represented the total feudal strength of the kingdom at that time (though here as elsewhere an unknown number of mounted sergeants should probably be added to the total number of knights); the contingents of Bertrand of Tripoli,

Tancred of Antioch, Baldwin of Edessa (200 knights and 100 infantry), Joscelyn of Turbessel (100 knights and 50 infantry), Richard of Marash (60 knights and 100 infantry) and others, plus Armenian contingents, brought this force up to a total strength of some 16,000 men.

For a campaign in 1115 Baldwin supplied 1,000 infantry and 500 knights, Antioch mustering 2,000 cavalry and infantry and Tripoli 2,000 infantry and 200 knights. To these were added 5,000 Seljuk auxiliary cavalry. Another Antiochene force, recorded at Ager Sanguinus in 1119, consisted of 700 knights and 3-4,000 infantry and this possibly represents the principality's total strength in knights and sergeants respectively, the latter including a number of Syrians and Armenians. The total number of knights actually available to Antioch or Tripoli was probably about the same as in the kingdom of Jerusalem. The number of knights in Edessa was probably somewhat less but appears to have been at least 500. In 1138 a force recorded marching from Samosata to the relief of Edessa itself is recorded as numbering 300 knights and about 4,000 infantry.

In 1183 an army of over 15,000 'truly excellent armed foot-soldiers' and 1,300 knights is recorded by William of Tyre, while Imad ad-Din gives 15-20,000 infantry and 1,500 knights plus in addition 1,500 Turcopoles. Either way, at that time it was the largest army to have been mustered in Frankish Syria, though it included some European crusaders. But the largest army ever mustered by the kingdom was the force of 20-63,000 recorded in the Hattin campaign of 1187. The only detailed set of figures for this army gives us a breakdown of 1,000 knights, 1,200 mercenary knights, 4,000 Turcopoles, 25,000 infantry, and 7,000 mercenary infantry, totalling 48,200 men. However, on the evidence of the Itinerarium Regis Ricardi, which reckons more than 1,000 knights and 20,000 infantry; the Libellus de Expugnatio, which gives 1,200 knights, many Turcopoles and over 18,000 infantry; the Brevis Historia, which gives 25,000; and the Muslim author Abu Shamah, who reckons at least 23,000 men, it seems a reasonable assumption that the army was about 20-25,000 strong, probably including 1,200 knights of whom about 200 were mercenaries. Another source, the Hospitallers' letter, records the army to have been 30,000 strong including some 1,200 knights. The lowest figure given in the sources is 5,000, which is as improbable as the 63,000 given in one Muslim source.

It is from lists of just a few years earlier than this date that Jean d'Ibelin compiled his record of feudal service owed to the Kingdom of Jerusalem, full details of which are given in Appendix 1. Contingents ranged in size from the 100 knights each due from the three great baronies of Sidon, Galilee and Jaffa and Ascalon, right down to the service of single knights. D'Ibelin adds up his figures to a total of 577 knights, but his arithmetic appears to be at fault, the actual total being at the most 749 and at the least 636 if certain discrepancies are taken into account. Nor are d'Ibelin's figures complete, his list omitting the service due to the kingdom from Tripoli (from which he elsewhere records the service of 100 knights being potentially available) and Antioch, as well as certain known fiefs for which he probably had no information. It seems reasonable to assume that if these unknown contingents were added a total strength in the region of 1,000 knights would probably be arrived at. Even then mercenaries and the Military Orders are not included. During the 13th-century Cyprus too could raise 1,000 knights.

The last large army raised by the crusader states was that which fought, and was destroyed, at La Forbie in 1244. Figures vary and are not altogether reliable, but it would appear that this totalled 6,000 men including, according to the Estoire d'Eracles, 600 knights from Acre, Jaffa, Antioch-Tripoli, Cyprus, and the Military Orders of Temple, Hospital, Teutonic Knights and St Lazarus. One chronicler, Salimbene de Adam, says that Cyprus and Antioch-Tripoli lost as many as 300 knights each, which is almost certainly an exaggeration. However, the casualties suffered by the Military Orders would tend to suggest that the Eracles' 600, if it is an accurate figure, refers only to lay knights. The Patriarch of Jerusalem wrote a letter reporting the loss of 312 Templar brethren and 324 Turcopoles in their employ, 325 Hospitaller brethren and 200 Turcopoles, 297 out of an improbable 300 Teutonic Knights, and the total destruction of the Lazar contingent. Frederick II received reports that the Hospitallers lost 200 brethren and the Templars 300, perhaps their whole Convent, while Matthew Paris records that these two Orders together mustered 500 brethren for the battle. (In all these figures no differentiation is made between brother knights and brother sergeants.) All in all the inference is that there were about 1,000-1,200 knights in total, possibly more, with probably about half supplied by the Military Orders.

THE MILITARY ORDERS

These were without doubt the most important source of troops in the crusader states. Unlike the transitory bands of crusading knights who came and went with every spring and autumn, they provided a permanent, ready source of experienced fighting men in a state of permanent mobilisation, the Orders' very existence being based on the premise of war. 'In addition,' as Joshua Prawer observed in his 'Latin Kingdom of Jerusalem' in 1972, 'training formed part of their daily schedule and the continuity of their existence turned them into a repository of military tradition and experience. No European host on a Crusade could dispense with the advice of the Orders. They knew the East and the Muslim foe, with all his strategies and weaknesses.' Contingents of Templars and/or Hospitallers consequently appeared in every army mustered by the king of Jerusalem from the mid-12th century onwards. Their military services, however, were not obligatory, the great Orders of Temple, Hospital and Teutonic Knights being answerable directly - and only – to the Pope (they even drew up their own treaties and alliances independently of the crown, often motivated by financial considerations), and the king often felt obliged to encourage their military assistance by promising extra-large shares of the spoils, or other allurements; in 1220, for example, John de Brienne promised the Teutonic Knights as much as half of all the plunder of Damietta. R.C. Smail, however, remarks in his *'Crusading Warfare'* that the presence of Military Order contingents 'cost the feudal rulers full military command of their forces in the field.'

On occasion the Orders even drew up their own treaties and alliances independently of the crown, their own interests always being placed first, even at the risk of endangering the peace of the kingdom. Immune even from sentences of excommunication issued by clergymen outside of the Order, and with the Pope their only suzerain, there was no real limit to their power and they became a law unto themselves. Almost inevitably, a bitter rivalry also developed between the Templars and Hospitallers, the two most powerful Orders, which astonishingly sometimes even led to bloodshed.

The heavy reliance which the king was obliged to place on their troops effectively increased the power and independence of the Orders, which the granting to them of fortresses for their defence against Muslim incursions (starting with Gibelin or Bethgeblin, near Ascalon, granted to the Hospitallers in 1136) did much to encourage; at one stage the Templars held some 18 fortresses in the crusader states, while Dr. Jonathan Riley-Smith estimates that the Hospitallers probably held 25 fortresses in 1180 and 29 in 1244. (It should be noted, however, that none of the smaller Orders held fortresses, with the possible exception of one tower held by the Lazars at Bethany.) Large frontier estates were also purchased from lords no longer able to maintain or defend them, and even some towns, such as Safed, Tortosa and Ascalon, came into their possession. The Orders were also entrusted with the defence of some royal fortresses and assisted in the defence of others.

In addition to their territorial possessions in the East they also received estates throughout Europe from large numbers of benefactors, eventually holding property in England, Ireland, Scotland, France, Spain, Portugal, Italy, Sicily, Germany, Scandinavia, Hungary, Cyprus and, after the Fourth Crusade, Greece and Romania. Matthew Paris estimated the property of the Hospital in the mid-13th century at 19,000 manors, and of the Temple at 9,000 manors, and though improbable such figures are certainly representative of the way contemporaries perceived the wealth of the Orders. It was from their European commanderies that the Convents of Outremer drew their supplies (transported to Outremer in their own ships), as well as reinforcements in times of great need, such as after the disaster of Hattin in 1187 and the fall of the key Hospitaller fortress of Arsuf in 1265.

Their smallest administrative unit was the commandery, common to the organisation of all the Orders. This comprised a unit of brother knights and brother sergeants, usually totalling 12 or more brethren – the knights generally outnumbering the sergeants – under an officer called a commander (a Pfleger or Hauskomtur in the case of the Teutonic Knights, and a Comendadore in the case of Montjoie). The headquarters of each Order was its Convent in Jerusalem under the Grand Master himself, with lesser Convents in Antioch and Tripoli under provincial commanders. The Temple and Hospital had 14 and 12 commanderies respectively in Syria, plus others in Cilicia and Cyprus, in addition to fortress garrisons that, though they had a nucleus of brethren, were by necessity largely mercenary, the Orders being the most important employers of mercenaries in Outremer.

There were three main Orders active in Outremer – the Hospitallers, the Templars and, to a lesser extent, the Teutonic Knights – plus several of much less significance. These we shall now consider individually.

The Hospitallers

The Hospitallers were so named because of their original foundation c.1070 as an order of nursing brethren who cared for pilgrims in the monastery hospital of St Mary of the Latin in Jerusalem. They were granted Papal protection in 1113 as the Order of the Hospital of St John. The nursing role of the Order predominated initially and remained important throughout this era (750 men wounded at the Battle of Montgisard in 1177, for instance, were treated at the Hospital in Jerusalem). Membership was largely French but included many Englishmen and Italians.

Military brethren may have been present in the Order as early as 1126, when a Constable is recorded; 1130, when a papal Bull refers to the Hospitallers as a fighting body; or, at the very latest, by 1137, when the Order was granted the fortress of Bethgeblin. However, a brother knight does not occur in any Hospitaller document until 1148, and prior to the mid-12th century it is probable that the majority of whatever armed forces it maintained were supplied by mercenaries – possibly even including Templars. Thereafter their military responsibilities steadily increased, and statutes of 1204-1206 indicate that the Order's organisation was by then based on its military brethren, both knights and sergeants.

Their military hierarchy, probably modelled on that of the more militaristic Templars, was headed by the Marshal, though inevitably the Order's Master himself had supreme command. The Marshal only first appears in the 1160s, though as already mentioned a Constable is recorded as early as 1126 and this post lasted until at least 1169, probably as the Marshal's lieutenant. Immediately beneath the Marshal came the Gonfanonier (the Order's standard-bearer), the Commander of the Knights, and the Master Esquire of the Convent. Of these the Commander, first recorded in 1220, was an officer appointed by the Marshal to lead a force in his absence, while the Master

Esquire was a brother sergeant responsible for all the esquires and grooms Three other officers known to have existed were mercenaries, these being the Master Crossbowman, the Master Sergeant and the Turcopolier. The last was commander of the Turcopole light cavalry employed by the Order, regularly referred to in their service, such as in the invasion of Egypt in 1168, at the Battle of Arsuf in 1191, and at La Forbie in 1244; by 1206 they were even being assigned to the retinues of the senior Hospitaller officers. The importance of the Order's turcopoles resulted in the turcopolier becoming a brother sergeant by 1248 and a brother knight after 1303.

The brethren-at-arms of the Order consisted of knights and sergeants (the latter invariably outnumbered by the former), though this distinction is only first made in 1206, at which date each brother knight was accompanied by four horses and probably two esquires, each brother sergeant having only two horses and a single esquire, the esquires being drawn from amongst the serving brethren as was customary in all the Military Orders. At the end of the 13th century the knight's complement of horses was reduced to three. Perhaps surprisingly, brother sergeants of both Hospital and Temple included converted Arabs.

As well as the Turcopoles mentioned above additional troops were supplied by confratre or confrère knights and donats (terms used to describe non-brethren affiliated to or permitted to join the Order for a limited period of time under special conditions, such as a donation of property). There were also feudal vassals raised from the Order's estates, allied contingents (sometimes including Muslims) and mercenary knights, sergeants and infantry.

Unfortunately contemporary chroniclers[2] usually fail to distinguish between actual brethren-at-arms and these various types of auxiliary, so it is hard to judge with any accuracy exactly what the full strength of the Order in Outremer might have been at any one time. However, figures can be found scattered in contemporary sources that provide some idea of its potential.

The earliest large force recorded, in 1168, consisted of 500 knights and 500 Turcopoles promised to King Amalric I for his invasion of Egypt, this was probably composed chiefly of mercenaries (or so we can assume from the fact that the Master, Gilbert d'Assailly, raised huge loans to finance this force). Four years earlier a visitor to Jerusalem wrote that the Hospital was capable of housing 400 knights in addition to pilgrims and the sick. During the Fifth Crusade of 1217-1221 the Order appears to have provided 700

---

[2] Some indication of proportions may possibly be given by the Templar garrison of Safed, recorded c.1243 to have consisted of 50 brother knights, 30 brother sergeants, 50 Turcopoles, 300 crossbowmen, 820 esquires, workmen and others (largely natives) and 400 slaves.

knights (or, more probably, horsemen, therefore including Turcopoles, sergeants and mercenaries) and 2,000 'persons', presumably other soldiers, while for an attack on Hamah in 1233 a force of 100 knights, 300 mounted sergeants and 500 (or 1,500) infantry sergeants was mustered, which appears to have represented almost the full strength of the Convent of Antioch at that date. In 1244 some 200-325 Hospitaller brethren were killed at the Battle of La Forbie, while 5, 15 or 26 escaped and others were taken captive, which suggests an overall total possibly greater than 350; 200 Hospitaller Turcopoles were also killed, while in addition the total of 350 may have included other non-brethren. Most of the Convent of Jerusalem's brethren-at-arms appear to have been lost when Arsuf fell in 1265, 80-90 being killed and 180 captured (of a garrison totalling about 1,000 men). A further 45 brethren were killed at Caroublier the following year, while at the fall of Tripoli in 1289 40 brethren and 100 horses were lost, which was considered so grave a crisis that steps were taken to bring in reinforcements from Europe.

Garrison strengths where recorded are often considerably greater than field-army contingents, though these were certainly largely mercenary and the proportion of brethren-at-arms must always have been small, probably comprising a complement of no more than 50 or 60 men. In 1203 the Hospitaller garrisons of Krak des Chevaliers and al-Marqab together mustered an army of as many as 4-500 cavalry and 1,100-1,400 infantry, plus Turcopoles, while in 1212 the same two fortresses are recorded to have been garrisoned by 2,000 and 1,000 men respectively even in peacetime. By 1271 Krak des Chevaliers' garrison included 200 brother-knights and brother-sergeants under the Marshal, and in 1280 al-Marqab was held by 600 horsemen (obviously not all brethren), presumably supplemented by infantry in both instances. Bar Hebraeus records more than 200 cavalry and 500 infantry at al-Marqab at the same date, while in 1281 200 cavalry and 200 infantry are recorded in a sortie against the Mamluks; but in all these figures only about 25-60 would have been brother knights.

Perhaps the most reliable evidence of all for the total strength of the Hospitallers in Outremer is a letter written by the Order's Master Hugh Revel in 1268, in which it is specifically stated that by that date the Order could muster only 300 brother knights in the whole of Syria (i.e. including the Convents of Antioch and Tripoli). Even more revealing is another statement in the same letter where it is claimed that in the past the Order had been able to muster 10,000 men. Allowing for vassals, Turcopoles, mercenaries, serving brethren and so on this claim is not altogether impossible.

Following the fall of Acre in 1291 the Hospitallers removed their headquarters to Cyprus, and in 1301 the strength of their Convent on the island totalled 70 brother knights and 10 brother sergeants, though the proportion changed slightly in 1302 to 65 knights and 15 sergeants; in addition they were still augmented by Turcopoles and other auxiliaries.

Once established in Cyprus it became obvious that to maintain their struggle against the Muslims the Order was going to have to henceforth concentrate on naval operations, and it was as a maritime power that the Hospitallers were to earn their fame in the later Middle Ages. They had ships even in the 12th century but these were chiefly transports, and it was not until towards the end of the 13th century that they began to concentrate on building up their fleet of war-galleys. As early as 1300 their small fleet launched a naval attack on the Nile delta.

In 1310 the Order again shifted its headquarters, this time to the island of Rhodes (captured from the Byzantines in a series of campaigns which had commenced in 1306), where in 1311 it was declared that the Order needed to maintain 1,000 infantry and 500 cavalry for the island's future defence.

The Templars

Unlike the Hospitallers, or for that matter the Teutonic Knights, the Templars were from the outset a purely military Order, and in fact the Hospitallers' military organisation was to a great extent based upon the military institutions of the Temple. It is even possible that in the first half of the 12th century the Hospital actually employed Templar knights to fulfil certain military functions.

The aggressiveness, belligerence and military importance of the Templars, 'the new Maccabees', is well documented by contemporaries such as Jacques de Vitry, who wrote c.1225 that 'When the Templars were called to arms they did not ask how many the enemy were, only *where* they were'. King Amalric II of Jerusalem, writing to the King of France, said of the Templars that 'in them indeed, after God, is placed the entire reliance of all in the East,' and even the Byzantine chronicler Cinnamus believed that 'the man in command of [all] the knights in Palestine' was he 'whom the Latins call the Master of the Temple.'

The Order's origins, however, were humble. It was initially founded in Palestine in about 1118 by two French knights, Hugh de Payens and Godfrey de St Omer, for the protection of pilgrims on the road from Jaffa to Jerusalem. At first its handful of knights, nine in number, relied on gifts and cast-offs for their clothes and keep and were called the Poor Knights of Christ as a result; but King Baldwin II, suitably impressed by their devotion, very soon granted them lodging in a section of the royal palace of Jerusalem which was supposed to have been the site of the Temple of Solomon, whence the Order's full title, 'the Poor Knights of Christ and the Temple of Solomon'. They were granted Papal protection as a Military Order in 1128.

Military command was basically as per that described above for the Hospitallers, officers including the Marshal, Commander of the Knights, Gonfanonier, Master Esquire, Turcopolier and others. Likewise, in addition to brethren their forces included vassals, mercenaries, allies (sometimes Saracens) and the inevitable Turcopoles, there apparently being a Turcopolier in each commandery. The Templar garrison of Safed has already been cited as a possible indication of proportions. The number of Turcopoles in Templar service would appear to have been similar to those of the Hospitallers, basically on a level with the number of brethren; for example at La Forbie in 1244, where the Templars may have lost as many as 312 brethren, they also lost 324 Turcopoles. Foot-soldiers in the Order's employ were apparently organised in companies of 50 men, Muslim sources recording 15 such infantry companies in the garrison of Le Chastellet. Military brethren again consisted of knights and sergeants, with the latter in existence at least as early as 1147. The distinction between them was almost inevitably more noticeable than amongst the less militaristic Hospitallers, and by 1250 an initiate seeking entry into the Order as a brother knight had first to prove that he was the son or descendant of a knight, a qualification which was likewise requested by the Hospitallers and the Spanish Orders too within the next two decades.

Again, the full strength of the Order in Outremer is unknown and can only be surmised from fleeting references to be found amongst contemporary records. In 1152 a letter records that the Order could 'only gather 120 knights and 1,000 serving brethren and hired soldiers' to fight in Antioch, while in the kingdom of Jerusalem as early as 1157 85-88 Templars were captured and allegedly 300 killed in an engagement with Nur ed-Din, these figures possibly including various auxiliaries. Conversely at Montgisard in 1177 there were as few as 80 brethren present, despite the Convent having summoned all its available knights for the campaign; the figure would seem to indicate that the Templars' full strength had not yet assembled when the army marched, particularly since at about the same date William of Tyre records that 'there are in the Order about 300 knights ... and an almost countless number of lesser brethren.' In the disastrous year of 1187 we hear of 90 Templars being killed in the skirmish at Cresson and of a further 260 (perhaps including some Hospitallers) being executed after Hattin, from which battle a number of others escaped, which would imply that their total strength at the latter battle was in the region of 300, as opposed to perhaps 250 Hospitallers. During the Templar occupation of Cyprus a few years later (1191-1192) we hear of about 120 Templar cavalry, plus infantry, being shipped to the island; of the horsemen 15 were knights, 74 were sergeants and 29 were Turcopoles.

In the early-13th century Jacques de Vitry records that the Convent of Jerusalem still comprised about 300 brother knights (supplemented by the usual auxiliaries). Another source of similar date records their stables in Jerusalem holding up to 2,000 horses which, allowing for those of mercenaries and auxiliaries as well as spare mounts, etc (Templar knights being accompanied by 2 horses, as well as 2 esquires), seems to support de Vitry's figure. The garrisons of frontier fortresses were as large or even larger. When Le Chastellet fell in 1179 its Templar garrison appears to have comprised 80 knights (and sergeants?) and 750 infantry plus servants and craftsmen, while in 1230 the garrison of Tortosa, together with the Hospitallers of Krak des Chevaliers, raised as many as 500 cavalry and 2,700 infantry, of whom at least 200 cavalry and about 1,000 infantry were probably supplied by the Templars. An anonymous 13th-century source records the garrison of Safed as 1,700 men in peacetime, rising to a wartime strength of 2,200.

The Temple, like the Hospital, appears to have supplied 700 'knights' and 2,000 others during the Fifth Crusade, probably chiefly composed of mercenaries, while at Darbsaq in 1237 100 brethren and 300 crossbowmen in the employ of the Order are reported to have been killed, there possibly being in all about 200 brethren in the Principality of Antioch's Convent at this time. As already mentioned, 312 brethren were killed at La Forbie in 1244 and between four and 36 more escaped, though Matthew Paris records that the whole Convent (the figure of 300 brother knights again appears) was lost. Six years later 285 Templars, probably including a fair number of mercenaries, were killed in the main battle at El Mansurah, others being killed or captured in earlier and subsequent engagements. There were perhaps 240 at the fall of Acre in 1291, compared to possibly 140 Hospitallers, only 15 Teutonic Knights, and 25 brethren and 9 brethren respectively from the Orders of the Hospitals of St Lazarus and St Thomas Acon (for which see below). Finally, the waterless island of Ruad off Tortosa was garrisoned by as many as 120 Templar knights and 500 Syrian archers (i.e. Turcopoles) at the time of its capture by the Mamluks in 1303.

After the fall of the kingdom the Templars withdrew first to Cyprus, then to France, where after a few years the Order came to an ignominious end. Its great wealth had aroused the jealousy of the avaricious King Philip the Fair of France, who with Papal support and trumped-up charges of heresy and worse instigated the arrest of the Order's members on an international scale in 1307-1308. Following a series of prejudiced trials backed up by 'confessions' extracted under torture the Order was officially suppressed in 1312, the last Grand Master, Jacques de Molay, being burnt at the stake as a heretic in 1314.

The Teutonic Knights

The sinister reputation of the Teutonic Knights resulted not from their brief Levantine career but rather from their notorious, even infamous, activities in

Prussia, Lithuania and Poland, the early stages of which have been briefly outlined in '*Armies of Feudal Europe*'. Nevertheless, the Order was actually founded in Outremer in 1190 when, during the Third Crusade, merchants of Bremen and Lubeck established a hospital for the care of German pilgrims at the siege of Acre. It turned military in 1198 when many German knights joined following the abortive German crusade of 1197. The Order went under a variety of names until 1220, when it adopted its full title of 'the Hospital of St Mary of the House of the Teutons of Jerusalem'. It was always exclusively German and, except for Romania, the Baltic lands and (briefly) Hungary, outside of Outremer it held estates only in Germany itself.

Officially the Order's headquarters was always at Acre, despite the fact that the Templars drove them out of the city on one occasion, but their chief stronghold from 1229 until 1271 was actually Montfort, which they renamed Starkenberg. However, in Syria the Order was always overshadowed by the Temple and the Hospital, and it instead concentrated most of its attentions in the Levant on enterprises in Cilicia, where the main fortresses amongst its many possessions were Adamadana and Harunia. Even so, Teutonic contingents were present at most major engagements of the 13th century including Bahr Ashmun (1221), La Forbie (1244) and El Mansurah (1250). Fifteen brethren were present at the fall of Acre in 1291, of whom only the Order's Hochmeister or Grand Master escaped alive. The Order thereafter transferred its headquarters to Venice before moving on to Marienburg in Prussia in 1308.

Like the Templars and Hospitallers, the Teutonic Knights employed large numbers of Turcopoles, these probably supplying the bulk of the allegedly 300-strong Teutonic contingent at La Forbie and certainly comprising the greatest part of Starkenberg's garrison at its fall in 1271. They also had brother sergeants, confrère brethren (called 'half-brothers', *halbbruders*), mercenaries, and the vassals of the Order's estates (the Order held, for instance, the Seignory of Count Joscelyn after 1220).

The Hospitallers of St Lazarus

After the Temple and the Hospital the Order of St Lazarus or St Ladre was the third Military Order to be established in Outremer. Like the two main Orders it also had commanderies in Europe (e.g. Burton Lazars in Leicestershire) as well as Syria, where it had houses in Jerusalem, Acre, Ascalon, Tiberias, Caesarea and Beirut.

This was basically a Hospital Order concentrating on the treatment of leprosy, and was probably established as an offshoot by the Hospitallers themselves during the second decade of the 12th century, turning military by mid-century (one authority says c.1123). Templar brethren who contracted leprosy were transferred to the Lazars, as probably were Hospitallers. Even lay knights who contracted leprosy had to join the Order (though they had first to provide substitutes to render the requisite military service owed for their fiefs).

The Master of the Order was said to have himself been a leper, as were many brethren-at-arms, but as well as these 'unclean' brethren there were also non-lepers. However, the actual number of military brethren was never particularly high, and Jean Sire de Joinville's statement about the Master of St Lazarus 'who held no rank in the army' best sums up their military importance. Nevertheless, a contingent of Lazar brethren was present, and wiped out, at La Forbie, while in 1253 Lazars formed part of the army under St Louis which encamped before Jaffa, where an impetuous attack led by the Lazar Master saw all but four of the brethren killed. In 1291 25 brethren were present at Acre, all of whom were killed in the course of the siege. The Order basically ceased to involve itself in military activities from the early 14th century.

The Hospitallers of St Thomas Acon

The Hospitallers of St Thomas of Canterbury at Acre, usually called the Knights of St Thomas Acon, were established in Acre as a nursing Order after the capture of the city by Richard I of England and Philip II of France in 1191. Membership was restricted to Englishmen. It was always a small Order and probably did not turn military until the Fifth Crusade of 1217-1221, or possibly even as late as Prince Edward's Crusade of 1271.

The nine brethren present and killed at Acre in 1291 bear adequate testimony to the Order's minimal military potential; even with mercenaries and Turcopoles it is improbable that it ever mustered even 40 men in Outremer. After the fall of Acre the Order established a preceptory in Cyprus, and along with the Hospitallers and Templars held some fortresses there, but thereafter it underwent a gradual military decline. No brother knights are recorded after 1357.

The Knights of Our Lady of Montjoie

Named after a hill outside Jerusalem, this Order was established in Spain in 1175 by an ex-Santiagan knight. The following year it received its first grants of land in Outremer from King Baldwin IV. The Order held property in Spain and Italy but was of minimal significance in the Levant, though Sibylla (later Queen Sibylla) assigned them four towers in Ascalon in 1177. However, the Order did not prosper in Outremer and withdrew to its commanderies in Aragon after the defeat at Hattin in 1187, where according to one authority a small contingent of brethren was present. In Spain they became known as the Order of Trufac.

ROMANIA: THE LATIN EMPIRE

After the fall of Constantinople in 1204 the Franks divided the Byzantine Empire amongst themselves, the Latin Emperor (yet another Baldwin) receiving one-quarter and the Venetian and Frankish crusaders the remaining three-quarters, probably three-eighths each. These lands were then divided up and parcelled out in groups of 200, 100, 70, 60, 40, 20, 10, 7 or 6 knights' fees each, to be distributed by the vassals amongst their retainers. The greater vassals each received their fiefs in two parts – one within the Emperor's own lands near Constantinople, and the other in the provinces.

The basis of military service, drawn up in 1205, was that when the Emperor and his senior Venetian and Frankish vassals decided that a campaign was necessary all knights – Venetians as well as Franks – were automatically obliged to serve for a period of four months, from 1 June to 29 September. In the case of invasion this service could be required for as long as the Emperor and nobility deemed necessary.

But of all the Frankish conquests that resulted from the Fourth Crusade, precise details of organisation are known for only one of the states thereby established within the old Byzantine territories – the Principality of Achaia, also known as Morea.

As with all other Frankish conquests in the East, organisation involved the application to the conquered territories of current feudal practices. The Principality of Achaia was no exception, being divided up into 12 baronies with estates varying from four knights' fees right up to 24 (chiefly in multiples of four), with many lesser estates of one fee or a half-fee each, some held by Greeks. There were also seven ecclesiastical baronies, 6l of four fees held by bishops and one, Achaia itself, of eight fees held by an archbishop, as well as three estates belonging to the Military Orders, with Templars, Hospitallers and Teutonic Knights holding four fees each.

The service from the larger estates was based on the holding of four fees, which was obliged to supply 14 horsemen consisting of the vassal (i.e. the banneret), a second knight, and 12 sergeants. Estates over **four** fees had to supply an extra knight or two sergeants for each additional fee. In the case of a single fee or half-fee the vassal (knight or sergeant respectively) served alone and in person. As in the kingdom of Jerusalem, all vassals were expected to serve in person up to the age of 60, after which a son or tenant might substitute.

In addition to the standard four months' service garrison duty was required for a further four months a year (though the Church and Military Orders were exempt from the latter). Even in the remaining four months of the year there might be a further summons from the Prince if the need should arise. This service could also be demanded overseas; Prince William was certainly accompanied by 400 Achaian knights in Cyprus in 1249 and in Italy in 1268.

This permitted the maintenance of an almost permanent feudal army, and the number of troops that could be thus summoned was quite considerable; at Bodonitsa in 1250 William was accompanied by 800 knights, and up to 1,000 are recorded on other occasions, these probably representing the full feudal muster. As many as 8,000 Achaians are recorded in a campaign of 1246, while at Pelagonia there were allegedly 12,000 infantry in addition to an improbable 8,000 horsemen (of whom in any case very few would have actually been knights).

Throughout the Empire auxiliary troops were supplied by the indigenous population, both Greeks and Slavs; in Achaia the latter were principally from the Peloponnesian Melingi tribe, still favoured by the Catalans in the 14th century. An army raised in the Duchy of Athens in 1302 contained as many as 6,000 Thessalian and Bulgarian cavalry[3] under 18 Greek nobles (possibly organised in allaghia – see Byzantine organisation), plus some 30,000 mixed infantry, chiefly Greeks and Slavs; up to 24,000 Greek infantry are recorded in the Athenian army at Kephissos in 1311. The Slavs usually supplied archers and spearmen, and these are certainly the types specifically mentioned in an Achaian army of 1296.

Many such troops were supplied to the Frankish army by Byzantine archontes (noblemen) whom the Franks had confirmed in their possessions, probably pronoiai (see Byzantine organisation). The contingents they provided were probably the same as they had been obliged to supply to the Byzantine army in pre-Conquest days so must have varied considerably in numbers, but in one instance in 1205 a certain Theodore Branas agreed to supply as many as 500 men. In fact the ease with which many Byzantines and Byzantine subjects shifted their loyalty from Byzantine to Frankish rule is noteworthy, for without such obvious disaffection on their part it is unlikely that these Frankish conquests would have lasted for as long as they did or even, perhaps, have succeeded at all. But the discontent was there and it proved a very real ally of the Franks; the incorporation into his army in 1211 of Nicaean prisoners-of-war under their own officers by the second Latin Emperor, Henry of Flanders, was without doubt far from being an isolated incident, and such troops clearly helped to compensate for the constant and often critical shortage of manpower in Frankish Greece and Romania. However, it was not long before the greed and general cruelty of the Franks turned the native population against them.

---

[3] Bulgarian mercenaries also frequently appeared in Cyprus during the 14th century.

Other auxiliaries included Turks and Cumans, the latter to be found in alliance with the Empire from 1239; there were apparently Cumans present in the Achaian army defeated at Pelagonia in 1259. Some Turks settled in Achaia after 1262 and some were even knighted and granted fiefs! After the ascent of Charles of Anjou to the Achaian throne in 1278 there was a marked increase in the use of Turkish and Bulgarian auxiliaries, and in addition Saracen archers were imported from his Sicilian kingdom to serve principally as garrison troops.

Frankish mercenaries were also employed quite often, an army of allegedly 60,000 recorded under Emperor Baldwin II in 1239 containing Frenchmen, Venetians and Franks of various other nationalities in addition to Greeks, Muslims and Cumans. If this army really was 60,000 strong then it is hardly surprising to find that it consisted almost entirely of foreign mercenaries and auxiliaries, since Romanian armies were in general ridiculously small; at Philippopolis in 1208 Henry had only 2,000 men including about 390 knights (of whom one-sixth were Greeks), and as few as 260 knights (plus sergeants and infantry, presumably) at Lake Apollonia in 1211, Henry drawing up the knights in 18 and 15 'battles' respectively with his own being of 50 men in each instance. In 1206 he had raised a somewhat larger feudal army of 600 knights in addition to 10,000 infantry.

Although Frankish Greece lasted until long after the close of this period the Latin Empire of Romania itself survived only until 1261, when Constantinople fell to the Nicaean Byzantines (it would appear that the establishment in 1260 of a full-time, regularly-paid garrison of 1,000 men for the city could have met with little success!). Thereafter titular Latin Emperors drifted about Europe in search of military aid for the reconquest of 'their' Empire. In 1267, for instance, Charles of Anjou promised to provide the titular Emperor Baldwin II with 2,000 knights for a year's service towards the recovery of Constantinople, while by a treaty of 1281 he and the titular Emperor Charles de Courtenay were to provide 8,000 knights for another expedition planned for 1283, to which Venice promised to contribute 40 or more galleys. Gradually, however, the concept of even a titular Latin Empire faltered and died.

SYRIA AND ANATOLIA: THE SELJUK TURKS

Under Sultan Alp Arslan and his son and successor Malik Shah the Seljuks ruled a vast territory stretching from Anatolia as far east as Khwarizmia and Afghanistan, north to the Caucasus and the Aral Sea, and south to Syria, the Red Sea and the Persian Gulf, and although this great Empire began to break up into a plethora of lesser states towards the end of the 11th century the Eastern Seljuk Sultans retained supremacy – albeit in many instances only nominal – until the death in 1157 of Sanjar, the last great Sultan, after which the remnants of the once great Sultanate collapsed entirely.

Even prior to that date the Sultan's influence in Syria had declined considerably; Transoxiana, conquered in 1073, had fallen in 1141 to the Qarakhitai; and the Sultanate of Merv had begun to collapse into total anarchy as a result of a series of revolts by Ghuzz (Turcoman) tribes after 1153.

In 1194 the Sultanate of Hamadan fell to the Khwarizmians, leaving the Sultanate of Rum in Anatolia (conquered in the years after Manzikert) as the only remaining major Seljuk state, since the Syrian Seljuk provinces, long-since autonomous, had by that time passed to the Ayyubid Sultanate of Egypt. It is these western Seljuk states, of Rum and Syria, which are our concern here, since the interests of the other major Seljuk powers were always in the East and so technically lie beyond the scope of this book.

The strength of all Turkish armies lay in their bow-armed cavalry, backed by smaller numbers of heavy but otherwise similarly armed horsemen. Infantry were provided chiefly by volunteer town militias, called Ahdath – literally 'young men' – in Syria (often based on the Futuwwah, quasi-political factions, and comparable to the 'Ayyarun and Fityan of Iraq), plus foreign auxiliaries (notably Daylamis) and tribal irregulars, though sometimes better-trained foot-soldiers who may be professionals appear in contemporary sources; certainly it seems probable that the naptha-throwers and crossbowmen recorded in the 12th and 13th centuries must have been regulars. The militias served most frequently in the vicinity of their cities, often being used for siege and camp duties.

As in contemporary Fatimid armies, actual organisation was basically decimal where it existed, based on units and multiples of 10, 100 and 1,000.

Iqta'at

Lacking great wealth and therefore unable to pay their men in cash, the Seljuks adopted and perfected a quasi-feudal system of military land tenure previously utilised by their Ghaznavid and Buyid predecessors. This was the iqta' (plural iqta'at) established initially by the Buyids in the mid-10th century when it was a grant of confiscated or uncultivated land. However, iqta'at had remained rare until the Seljuk conquests of the mid-11th century, and were only fully regularised under Nizam al-Mulk, the celebrated vizier of Alp Arslan and Malik Shah, so that his claim that previous rulers had never distributed grants of land but paid their soldiers only in money is probably a reasonably accurate statement. However, the iqta' could be a payment in cash and the Ghaznavids were still paying their iqta'at exclusively in money even in Nizam's time, so that the payment of troops only in money by the Seljuks' predecessors probably indicates no more than that iqta'at were paid in cash rather than land.

There were two types of iqta' – the qati'a and the tu'ma, the hereditary benefice and the lifetime benefice respectively. Either was transferable from district to district, since unlike the Frankish fief the military iqta' represented not a personal estate but a payment in land revenues for services rendered; and since as a soldier the holder – the iqta'dar or muqta' – might need to be posted from one area to another then his iqta' could likewise be transferred with him. The other main difference from Frankish feudalism was that the iqta'dar was permitted to levy only a specific sum (in cash and/or kind) from the populace of his iqta' – his actual pay – and other than this usually had no further authority over them (an exception being the iqta'at granted by the Zengids). The fact that the iqta'dar had to collect his pay personally at the due time was probably contributory to the inability of Muslim armies to remain in the field for extended periods.

The granting of an iqta' involved in return the military service of the iqta'dar, who was usually an amir, with a specific number of soldiers – usually mamluk slave-soldiers (see Egyptian organisation) – depending on the size of the iqta'. (Later, under the Ayyubids, iqta'at appeared in Syria which were specifically called iqta'at of 10, iqta'at of 20, etc., the figures referring to the number of troops to be supplied.) Parts of the iqta' might even be granted to lower-ranking amirs by the iqta'dar, by a process comparable to subinfeudation. Under the Mamluks as much as two-thirds of each amir's iqta' had to be divided amongst his own mamluks as pay, though under the Ayyubids each amir received two land grants, one (the khassa) for his personal needs, the other (the actual iqta', or khubz) for the maintenance of his troops. Certainly by the mid-12th century Seljuk mamluks were being granted their own lands under a similar system.

'Askaris and auxiliaries

Early Seljuk armies consisted of two major elements – the 'askar of the Sultan, a full-time force paid in cash or iqta'at and composed chiefly of mamluk slave-soldiers; and the provincial contingents of the amirs, who had 'askars of their own, together with auxiliaries supplied by Turcomans, Bedouins, Kurds and other tribesmen. The provincial 'askars numbered from a few hundred to several thousand dependent on the size of the city or district – Damascus had an 'askar of 1,000, Antioch apparently 2,000, and so on. As mentioned above, the 'askaris were largely mamluks but could also include freemen, the chronicler Usamah ibn Munqidh himself serving as a paid freemen in the 'askars of Zengi, Damascus, Egypt and Nur ed-Din (the 'askaris included Kurds, Armenians and Arabs as well as Turks). Organisation was clearly on a decimal basis.

In his famous written work the Siyaset-Nameh, the Seljuk vizier Nizam al-Mulk records the Sultan's standing army to be as large as 400,000 men in the reign of Malik Shah (1072-1092), all paid with iqta'at: a courtier is reputed to have advised that this total should be cut back to 70,000 since peace then reigned, though Nizam advocated an increase in strength to a total of 700,000 men. These figures, if credible, probably represent the total strength of all the 'askars, both royal and provincial, over the whole, vast Sultanate, especially since another source records the royal 'askar under Malik Shah on one occasion as consisting of 46,000 cavalry. Before the accession of his successor Barkiyaruq (1092-1105) this had declined to only 20,000.

Nizam himself advised the maintenance of an elite unit of 1,000 Hasham (Guards) from amongst the mamluks of the Sultan, which should be increased in strength to 5-10,000 in wartime; these particular mamluks were to be trained from Daylamis, Khorasanians, Georgians and young Turcomans. Much later, towards the end of the 13th century, Ibn Bibi-Duda records mamluks in Rum (Anatolia) as being chiefly of Byzantine, Cilician, Georgian and Crimean extraction, the largest number being Byzantine Greeks or Cilician Armenians (the mamluk who captured the Byzantine Emperor Romanus IV at Manzikert was, by a twist of fate, a Byzantine!). These were obtained by war, purchase or gift, or recruited by levy within the Seljuk state itself.

After the death of Malik Shah in 1092 and the subsequent disintegration of centralised Seljuk power, the second of the afore-mentioned elements (the provincial 'askars and various auxiliaries) assumed the leading role as the provinces became practically and then totally independent. Only in the mid-12th century under Nur ed-Din, following in the footsteps of his father Zengi, were the Syrian provinces forcibly reunited, Nur ed-Din adding Egypt to his domains in 1169 and thereby setting the stage for Saladin's rise to power by making him governor, from which position it proved to be but a short step to the Sultanate, thereby succeeding to the Syrian provinces and more besides.

Prior to these events command of the Syrian provincial armies was usually entrusted to the more powerful amirs, frequently the amir of Mosul. But unfortunately the amirs did not like taking orders from each other and frequently this led to dissention and a lack of unity in Syrian armies; deliberate desertion was often carried out by jealous amirs in the face of the enemy so as to bring about the downfall of particularly powerful rivals. Such dissent, all too common, together with the somewhat tribal composition of Turkish armies, meant that the combined forces of a district or province could take months to muster and even then the amirs often required liberal bribes to guarantee their continued presence and support.

Both Rumi and Syrian Seljuks relied heavily on Turcoman auxiliaries, and these Turcoman tribesmen – who were fierce though unreliable soldiers – were the nucleus of Seljuk military strength throughout the whole of this period. They did not readily accept any form of authority or discipline and served mainly in the hope of plunder coming their way; if none was forthcoming they were more than likely to abandon the army. Otherwise their pay often took the form of ransom money taken by their employer in exchange for high-ranking prisoners; sometimes when the Turcomans indiscriminately massacred their prisoners they were therefore depriving themselves of their own pay! Some chieftains were paid with extremely large iqta'at that seem to have been intended as a substitute for the grazing lands essential to such nomadic herdsmen. They fought in tribal units under their own standards and chieftains. Modern estimates have reckoned Turcoman strength in Anatolia at some 30,000 men in the late 11th century, but this figure is clearly far too low. Frankish chroniclers, though undoubtedly going to the opposite extreme, claim that during the First Crusade the Sultan of Rum, Kilij Arslan I, mustered some 200-360,000 cavalry, and by far the majority of such a force would have been Turcomans. Certainly in the early 12th century it was possible to raise 20-50,000 Turcomans from the Jazira alone

Other auxiliaries were principally supplied by Bedouins and Kurds. The Kurds were a hill-people from the mountainous districts of north-west Iran, according to Marco Polo 'lusty fighters and lawless men, very fond of robbing merchants'; they often featured in Seljuk armies (there were as many as 10,000 at Manzikert), but, like the Turcomans, lacked organisation and fought principally for loot, so were disheartened by long or unsuccessful campaigns. Kurds were particularly prominent in the armies of Nur ed-Din, Saladin and other Zengid, Ortoqid and Ayyubid princes, serving both as auxiliaries and paid 'askaris. In Rum other auxiliaries were of Persian, Arab and even Russian origin by the 13th century. Frankish adventurers also appeared on occasion in Syrian and Anatolian armies (see below).

The Syrian army present at Harran in 1104 may help to give some idea of the proportion of auxiliaries in their forces; of 10,000 men 7,000 were Turcomans, while the remaining 3,000 included Bedouins and Kurds as well as Seljuks.

Rum in the 13th century

Under Sultans Kai Kobad I (1220-1237) and Kai Khosrou II (1237-1246) a brief revival of Seljuk power took place in Anatolia, both Cilician Armenia and the Byzantine Empire of Trebizond becoming vassal states of the Sultanate of Rum. Simon de St Quentin, a Frankish visitor to Rum in the 1240s, recorded that Kai Khosrou was owed the service of 1,400 lances by the Cilician Armenians for four months a year, 1,000 lances by the Sultan of Aleppo, 400 lances by the Emperor of Nicaea, and 200 lances by the Emperor of Trebizond; these may have all served for pay since Bar Hebraeus records Kai Khosrou taking Aleppene and Byzantine cavalry as well as Bedouins into his army 'for gold' in 1243. Whether the figures of lances are to be taken as the total number of men involved is unknown, but it seems improbable; the numbers are otherwise insignificantly low when compared to the Sultanate's regular mamluk units, which perhaps totalled 60,000 men at this time.

In addition Frankish mercenaries were employed, particularly under Kai Kaus I, Kai Kobad I and Kai Khosrou II, though even as early as 1148 apparently 3,000 Franks captured at Attaleia during the Second Crusade had taken service with Sultan Masud I. Kai Kaus even formed a bodyguard unit from Franks he had liberated by victories over rival Muslim chieftains. There were at least 1,000 Frankish cavalry in Kai Khosrou II's army at the commencement of his reign (1237) and it was principally thanks to 300 of them that a serious Turcoman revolt was put down in 1241; in 1243 he employed 2,000 more and these were present in his army at Kuzadagh. The latter contingent consisted chiefly of Cypriotes, Cyprus also owing service to the Sultanate at about this date, but otherwise such mercenaries were mainly French, German and Italian. Their commander held the rank of Kondistabl (Constable) but he was not always a Frank (for instance a Georgian named Zahiruddaula held this office at one point in the 13th century, and the future Byzantine Emperor Michael VIII was Kondistabl under Sultan Kai Kaus II). In fact 'Frankish' or 'Firenk' troops appear to have often included Greek elements, both mercenaries employed from the Archontes and Akritai of the Empire and troops levied from the Sultan's own Greek subjects (see note 51 in the dress and equipment section).

During Kai Kobad's reign the threat of the Mongols first became a reality, when over 10,000 fleeing Khwarizmian troops entered the Sultanate. Kai Kobad took them into his service, granting them a number of extensive iqta'at, but they abandoned these during the civil strife that followed his death in 1237 and fled across the Euphrates to take service with the Ayyubids; already the Mongols were raiding eastern Rum, and this was the reason for the Khwarizmians' earlier flight from certain frontier iqta'at. The abrupt departure of such a large number of auxiliaries must have been a blow to the Seljuks, who knew that it was only a matter of time before a showdown with the Mongols should prove unavoidable.

Following the almost inevitable defeat of Kai Khosrou II at the Battle of Kuzadagh in 1243 the Sultanate of Rum became a vassal state of the Mongols, and the Seljuk army and administration underwent a rapid decline. Constant financial depression led to a growing need to grant ever-larger iqta'at to soldiers in lieu of payment, which led only to a further loss of revenue to the state and encouraged the independence of provincial amirs. Nor did the Sultan any longer have the money to employ foreign mercenaries, even if his Mongol overlords had been willing to permit it, which seems unlikely, and he was therefore obliged to depend on the provincial armies and the undisciplined Turcomans.

There was, however, a Mongol garrison force stationed in the Sultanate after 1256 which steadily grew in numbers, its members settling principally in the eastern provinces where they were nearer to their own seat of power (the Persian Ilkhanate) and to the frontiers of their Mamluk enemies. The presence of these Mongol troops was another reason for the abrupt decline of the Seljuk army since they satisfied most of the Sultanate's remaining military requirements. They were maintained by payments of tribute (one of the reasons why the Seljuks were in financial straits) and grants of grazing lands, some of which ultimately became the independent property of Mongol chieftains.

By the end of the 13th century, and particularly after the capture of Iconium by Karamanli Turcomans in 1276, the power of the Sultanate of Rum had collapsed entirely as Mongol administration gradually replaced Seljuk; by this time the Mongols had a fairly firm hold on eastern Anatolia, but in the western provinces a number of autonomous Turcoman amirates arose, of which the Karamanli was the most powerful and the Osmanli (Ottoman) the most important to the course of subsequent history. Though they relied heavily on their tribesmen all of these successor amirates employed mamluks of their own.

THE EGYPTIANS: FATIMIDS AND AYYUBIDS

The Fatimids

From the mid-9th century Arab armies had gradually become dependent for regular troops on their contingents of slave-soldiers, the ghulams. Of these the white slaves, largely Turks, were properly called mamluks (deriving from the Arabic word for 'owned'), the name under which they rose to their greatest power. Such troops were purchased as slaves and trained and kept at their master's personal expense, which theoretically ensured their undivided loyalty to him. When they became competent soldiers they were legally freed and, by the late-Fatimid era, each given an iqta' on which to support themselves; these iqta'at usually reverted to the mamluks' master on their holder's death (though in the mid-12th century Nur ed-Din made those of his personal mamluks hereditary and this became the norm under the later Zengids and the Ayyubids).

The senior mamluks held the rank of amir and were expected to supply a number of troops from their iqta'at, these too being usually – though not necessarily – slave-soldiers, maintained by a process comparable to feudal subinfeudation. The occasional description of larger iqta'at as iqta' of 10, iqta' of 25, iqta' of 100 and the like reflects this practice, the figures indicating the strength of the iqta'dar's 'idda, his contingent of horsemen. However, prior to the Mamluk era iqta'dars were not required to maintain specific numbers of men, their charters only demanding that each support as many as possible.

More often than not the more powerful iqta'dars commanded even larger numbers in the field because the contingents of lesser amirs would be added to their own.

The central corps of both Fatimid and later armies was the Royal Mamluks. Under the late Fatimids these numbered about 5,000, together with an elite 'Young Guard', the Sibyan al-Khass, of about 500. The Royal Mamluks and other regular regiments were backed up in wartime by the personal mamluks of the amirs. These personal mamluks of each successive Caliph, sultan or amir were not disbanded after his death, but retained his name[4] and continued to exist as part of the regular army until their members found employment elsewhere or died out; Shirkuh's regiment, the Asadiyyah (originally 500 strong according to Abu Shamah) were still fighting in the Egyptian army in 1192, despite the fact that Shirkuh himself had died over 20 years earlier, in 1169. Usually such units were absorbed into the standing regiments of the Caliph, sultan or amirs, though under the Ayyubids they were sometimes attached to the al-Halqa (see Mamluk organisation).

Arabs and Egyptians were not permitted to become mamluks. Under the Fatimid Caliphate (909-1171) slave-soldiers were mostly Sudanese, Berbers and Turks. The Sudanese units, known collectively as the 'Abid al-Shira or 'Purchased Slaves', consisted principally of the Rayhaniyyah, Juyushiyyah, Farahiyyah and Alexandrian regiments by the mid-12th century, the Juyushiyyah alone possibly numbering 10,000 men; they generally served as infantry, both spearmen and archers but principally the latter. (Sometimes Sudanese cavalry are to be found in contemporary sources – Saladin's Qaraghulams may have included some such – but these were rare.)

In addition Turcoman and even Seljuk auxiliaries were sometimes to be found in Fatimid armies, as more often were Bedouin and Berber tribesmen, while additional infantry might be supplied by volunteer irregulars. Turcomans were first employed by the Fatimids in 1072. Even prior to their unification with Egypt under the Zengids and Ayyubids, Syrian units sometimes appeared in Egyptian armies – there were, for example, 1,000-1,300 Damascenes at the Third Battle of Ramla in 1105 and an unrecorded number of Seljuks at the Battle of Ascalon in 1099.

As an indication of Fatimid field-army strength, at Ascalon there were probably 20,000 cavalry and infantry altogether (the latter including volunteers and militia levies), while at the First and Second Battles of Ramla in 1101 and 1102 the Egyptian forces are recorded as 11,000 cavalry and

---

[4] Now as earlier each regiment was usually named after its owner, for example Juyushiyyah (Vizier Amir al-Juyush), Hafiziyyah (Caliph al-Hafiz), Asadiyyah (Asad ad-Din Shirkuh), Nuriyyah (Sultan Nur ed-Din), Salahiyyah (Saladin), Adiliyyah (Sultan al-Adil), Kamiliyyah (Sultan al-Kamil), etc.

21,000 Sudanese infantry, and 20,000 cavalry and 10,000 Sudanese infantry respectively, both armies consisting largely of ghulams. At least 7,000 men are recorded by Ibn al-Athir in a raid of 1118 (other sources claiming 15,000 cavalry and 20,000 infantry), and there were 16,000 Fatimids at Yibneh in 1123. We also frequently hear of the frontier garrison of Ascalon (500 cavalry and 1,000 infantry) launching its own raids into Frankish Syria.

During this period command of the Fatimid army was generally in the hands of the Vizier who, like the Caliph, maintained a large body of personal mamluks; for instance, the Vizier Bahram (1134-1137) had at least 2,000 Armenian soldiers in his service, and his successor 'Abbas 3,000 Armenians in 1154. (Armenian infantry, principally archers, still constituted an important element of the Fatimid army as late as 1169.)

Saladin's armies, 1169-1193

By 1169, when Saladin succeeded Nur ed-Din's appointee Asad ad-Din Shirkuh as governor of Egypt under the last Fatimid Caliph, the Egyptian army consisted of 40,000 cavalry and 30-50,000 Sudanese infantry, the cavalry probably including Qaraghulams (literally 'Black Slaves', probably Sudanese and Berber slave cavalry) and Bedouin and Turcoman auxiliaries as well as mamluks.

Al-Maqrizi, recording an earlier writer's notes on a review of Saladin's cavalry in 1171 (the year which saw the final demise of the Fatimid Caliphate) notes that the standard unit at this date was the Tulb, apparently a Kurdish or possibly a Ghuzz institution. The Tulb is the only unit commonly mentioned in this era, under both Ayyubids and Mamluks, but it was of a very loose character and varied considerably in strength, those recorded in the review comprising either 70, 100 or 200 men; basically any company led by an amir in wartime was a Tulb, as too was the entire body of Royal Mamluks.

The amir was perhaps assisted by an 'NCO' called a Jawish. 174 Tulbs were present at the review of 1171 and a further 20 were absent. Those present are recorded to have numbered some 14,000 men excluding Bedouin auxiliaries. William of Tyre repeats the earlier figure of 40,000, and the difference of 26,000 possibly accounts for absent Tulbs (1,400- 4,000 men), the Bedouins (of whom al-Maqrizi records 7,000 including 1,300 'regulars'), the Turcomans and the remnants of the Fatimid mamluk units such as the Ascalon (Asaqila) regiments.

The Fatimid Sudanese infantry, meanwhile, had revolted against Saladin; they were crushed in 'The Battle of the Blacks' in Cairo in 1169, the survivors being disbanded and driven out of Egypt. The Sudanese present in Saladin's army at Arsuf in 1191 were undoubtedly from new regiments raised after that date, and Sudanese infantry were still an important element of the Ayyubid army in 1221 when they harassed King John's withdrawal from Damietta during the Fifth Crusade. However, their numbers were much smaller than before and continued to dwindle so that by the time the Bahriyyah Mamluk dynasty came to power in 1250 they had apparently disappeared altogether.

By 1177 18,000 Qaraghulams and 8,000 Toassin or Tawashis (elite, fully-armed cavalry), including the 1,000 Royal Mamluks, could be raised for a raid on Ascalon and Gaza according to William of Tyre, who describes them all as 'light-armed' (they were defeated at Montgisard). Muslim sources record maximum figures of 8,000 Toassin and only 7,000 Qaraghulams during the period 1171-1181, though in addition there were the usual Kurdish, Bedouin and Turcoman auxiliaries, as well as Muttawwi'a (Ghazis, and volunteers paid less than the regulars and only for the duration of a campaign) and Arab and Sudanese infantry. Saladin, a Kurd himself, employed a considerable number of Kurds, though he disbanded many of them after his defeat at Montgisard, for which disaster he held them responsible (William of Tyre's figure of 18,000 Qaraghulams therefore probably includes auxiliaries since he does not mention Kurds individually).

The Egyptian 'askar as reorganised by Saladin in 1181 consisted of 111 amirs, 6,976 Toassin, and 1,553 Qaraghulams, giving a total of 8,640 men but not including un-beneficed troops, auxiliaries, or the remaining Fatimid mamluks (the ex-Fatimid element was by this time very small, receiving perhaps less than 2% of the army's total pay). It will be noticed that these figures make no provision for regular infantry, though these are known to have existed, which has led to the suggestion that perhaps the Qaraghulams should be assumed to represent such troops. However this seems improbable.

The army reviewed prior to the Battle of Hattin in 1187 consisted of 12,000 Egyptian and Syrian regular cavalry and perhaps a similar number of volunteers and auxiliaries. H.A.R. Gibb in his article 'The Armies of Saladin' calculates that the regulars were probably:-

　　　1,000 Royal Mamluks

　　　1,000 from the Damascene 'askar

　　　1,000 from northern Syria and the Aleppene 'askar

　　　4,000 from the Egyptian 'askar

　　　5,000 from the Jazira (Mesopotamia) and the 'askars of Mosul　　and Diyar Bekr

The estimated strength of the 'askars of Damascus and Aleppo at 1,000 men each is based on sound evidence. Gibb similarly estimates the 'askars of Homs and Hamah at 500 and 1,000 or somewhat less respectively; certainly Shirkuh's Asadiyyah regiment of 500 men had once constituted the 'askar of Homs. The figure for the Jazira, Mosul and Diyar Bekr is based on a statement by Ibn al-Athir, who records some 6,500 cavalry for Mosul, Diyar Bekr and the Jazira in 1176, specifically refuting Imad ad-Din's statement that they numbered 20,000. Gibb calculates that of the 6,500 approximately 2,000 would have been supplied by Mosul. At the same time it seems likely that Diyar Bekr, Mardin and Harran would have maintained 'askars of 1,000 men each – Harran certainly had an 'askar of 1,000 (officially) in 1242. It must be remembered, however, that these forces only represent regular cavalry, not total available strength; as examples of the latter it is only necessary to quote the combined force of 6,000 cavalry from Damascus and Aleppo recorded in 1149, which could undoubtedly be supplemented by a liberal number of infantry.

Although no accurate breakdown is available for Saladin's army as it appeared at the Battle of Arsuf in 1191, Ambroise and the Itinerarium Regis Ricardi (apparently Old French and Latin editions of the same eyewitness account) give a good idea of the heterogeneous nature of Egyptian armies at this date, recording Bedouins and Sudanese infantry, Syrian and Turcoman light cavalry (at least 2,000 and possibly 10,000, armed with bows and javelins), and perhaps 20,000 (Ambroise records 30,000) heavy cavalry, both Saladin's and those of his provincial 'askars, 'clothed and equipped splendidly'; the figure of 20,000, though high, does tally with the alleged strength of Saladin's forces at Belvoir in 1182 and probably includes Qaraghulams. At Jaffa in 1192 there appear to have been 7,000 cavalry present.

The later Ayyubids

Kipchak Turks (i.e. Cumans) formed the bulk of the mamluk troops under Saladin 's descendants. There was an influx of Kipchak mamluks under Sultan as-Salih (1240-1249) in particular, as a result of the steadily growing pressure of the Mongols on their eastern frontier, and from amongst them the elite bodyguard unit of the Bahriyyah as-Saliyyah was formed, some 800-1,000 men, usually incorrectly referred to as the 'River' regiment. It was this regiment which laid the foundations of the Mamluk state in 1250 when some of its officers, led by Aybek and the future Mamluk sultan Baibars, assassinated Sultan Turan-Shah. The Royal Mamluks appear to have totalled 8,000 under al-Aziz (1193-1198) and 10,000 under both as-Salih and his father Sultan al-Kamil (1218-1238).

Bedouin and Turcoman light cavalry continued to supplement the mamluk regiments of the 'askars. Kurds also continued to feature in many armies, the Kurdish Qaimariyyah regiment being a particularly powerful element at the close of the Ayyubid era. In 1258 an-Nasir of Damascus employed as many as 3,000 Shahrazuriyyah Kurds.

Other auxiliaries employed under al-Kamil and as-Salih were the Khwarizmians who had fled from Rum. As many as 10,000 (one source says more than 12,000) under a certain Barbeh Khan were taken into service in 1244, receiving in exchange the lands of Diyar Mudar as an iqta', and these featured prominently in the capture of Jerusalem and the Battle of La Forbie the same year. They were at first a powerful element amidst the political chaos which prevailed in Egypt and Syria at that time, but their semi-independent existence was ended abruptly by a devastating defeat at Homs in 1246 at the hands of Sultan as-Salih, after which some of the survivors again took service in the royal and various provincial 'askars, though in considerably smaller numbers than before. A few hundred (300 or more) were present at the Battle of El Mansurah in 1250, while their final appearance was in 1260 in the Mamluk army which defeated the Mongols at 'Ain Jalut.

Frankish mercenaries

Frankish mercenaries sometimes appeared in Egyptian armies in the 12th and 13th centuries, but although there are many allusions to them there is very little concrete evidence. One clearly recorded instance of Franks in Fatimid employ, where in 1111 Shams al-Khilafah, the governor of Ascalon, employed 300 knights as his bodyguard, is more apparent than real since Shams was planning to hand the city over to King Baldwin.

A somewhat later indication of the apparent desirability of Frankish mercenaries dates to 1191 when, during negotiations with King Richard I of England, Saladin is alleged to have proposed that in exchange for considerable territorial concessions he should receive the services for one year of as many as 2,000 knights and 5,000 infantry for use against the Zengids of Mosul; bearing in mind the military potential of the kingdom of Jerusalem at this date these are very high figures indeed.

Later in the Ayyubid period we have one of the few certain references to the employment of such Frankish mercenaries, several knights being recorded in Damascus in 1227. Later still al-Maqrizi records even the Mamluk sultan Baibars employing Frankish knights after the fall of Caesarea and Haifa in 1265, even granting them feudal estates!

THE MAMLUKS

Under the Mamluk Sultans the regular army consisted of 3 major elements – the Royal Mamluks, the mamluk troops of the amirs, and the al-Halqa.

The Royal Mamluks consisted of the reigning sultan's own guards (the Khassakiyyah), who were selected from the Julban ('Imported', Turkish mamluks purchased from the steppes, Caucasus or elsewhere), plus the mamluk units of former sultans (the Sultaniyyah) and the units of deceased amirs (the Saifiyyah). Under Baibars (1260-1277) the Royal Mamluks were 12-16,000 strong. One source claims the unlikely total of 40,000, though elsewhere giving the figure of 4,000; al-Maqrizi records 12,000, 4,000 each being posted in Cairo, Damascus and Aleppo. Qalaun (1279-1290) had at the most 7-12,000 and apparently only 6,000 by the close of his reign; if, as Muslim sources claim, his mamluks exceeded in number those of any preceding sultan then Baibars must have had considerably less than 12,000, let alone 16-40,000. In addition Qalaun justifiably distrusted the Bahriyyah regiment and raised instead a new elite unit of 3,700 men which came to be known as the Burjiyyah ('Tower') regiment; these were Circassians and Mongols as opposed to Kipchaks, and they eventually displaced the Bahriyyah sultans from the throne in 1390. Under Qalaun's successors Khalil (1290-1293) and Mohammed (1293-1341, with interruptions) al-Maqrizi records that the Royal Mamluks numbered 12,000, though elsewhere he implies that Khalil actually had less than 10,000. Another source suggests that Mohammed had 10,000 in 1299 and it seems that in reality he probably had even less, perhaps as few as 2,000 by 1315. In peacetime most of the Royal Mamluks were stationed in Cairo itself.

The amirs were mostly, if not exclusively, drawn from among the Royal Mamluks. They were graded according to the actual number of horsemen and/or mamluks they employed, giving rise to the titles amir of 5, amir of 10, amir of 40 (usually called amir al-tablkhanah, 'amir with band') and amir of 100, and to rank as an amir at all one had to command 5 or more mamluks or horsemen. This was basically the same system as had been employed by the Ayyubids except that under the Mamluks the previously highly variable numbers of horsemen had been stratified into just the 4 or 5 formal ranks as listed above and below. The titles themselves are a little misleading, however, since contemporary sources state that the amir of 10 could command up to 20 mamluks (the title amir of 20 also appears), the amir of 40 up to 70-80 mamluks, and the amir of 100 up to 110-120. Even these official figures were often surpassed, totals of up to 5-700, 1,500 and in one case even 3,000 horsemen sometimes being recorded in the employ of a single amir, though such instances were exceptional. Yet they indicate that the official quotas were often exceeded.

Amirs of 100 also theoretically commanded a regiment of 1,000 al-Halqa in wartime, giving rise to the alternative and equally inaccurate rank amir of 1,000; the inaccuracy of this title is best demonstrated by the fact that although in 1315 only 8,932 men and 204 officers of the al-Halqa are recorded in Egypt, there were under the first Mamluk sultans as many as 24 amirs of 1,000 in Egypt, so that the average al-Halqa command of each amir could not have much exceeded approximately 380 men. Possibly the numbers were made up with auxiliaries.

By 1315 there were 200 amirs of 40 and 200 amirs of 10 in addition to the 24 amirs of 100. A later authority, Zahiri, quoting a source of unknown date, gives the lower figures of 24 amirs of 100, 40 amirs of 40, 20 amirs of 20, 50 amirs of 10 and 30 amirs of 5 in Egypt, while Damascus had 12 amirs of 100, 20 amirs of 40 and 60 amirs of 10, and Aleppo 6-9 amirs of 100, 10 amirs of 40 and 20 amirs of 10. The smallest Mamluk province, Gaza, had only 2 amirs of 40.

The al-Halqa itself first appeared in 1174 and consisted of an elite of non-mamluk cavalry, mainly Arabs, native Egyptians and mamluks' sons born in Egypt. The last, the Awl'ad al-nas, were regarded as second-class because they had not been born on the steppes as true Turks, while Arabs and Egyptians were not permitted to become mamluks. When chronicler and crusader Jean de Joinville describes the al-Halqa as the Sultan's bodyguard, and mamluks to boot, he is therefore undoubtedly confused in his terminology (though their name al-Halqa, meaning 'Ring', does tend to imply a bodyguard function). However, the al-Halqa often, if not always, outnumbered the Royal Mamluks, but were generally posted in the provinces as opposed to Cairo. It has already been mentioned that there were over 9,000 al-Halqa in Egypt in 1315. Zahiri, who appears to be speaking of the 14th or the beginning of the 15th century, records that there were as many as 24,000 al-Halqa in Egypt (which tallies with 24 amirs of 100), 12,000 in Damascus, 6,000 in Aleppo, and 9-11,000 spread over five out of the remaining six provinces, and this is despite the al-Halqa having undergone a decline in importance since the early 14th century; however, since these figures were recorded in response to a Mongol threat one should allow for exaggeration and take them all with a pinch of salt, even though al-Maqrizi also implies the improbable figure of 24,000 Egyptian al-Halqa at one point. An alternative account says the al- Halqa numbered only 12,000, this figure later being reduced. 4,000 al-Halqa are recorded to have been present in the army that fought at Homs in 1281, in comparison to only 800 Royal Mamluks. In addition some of the al-Halqa themselves employed 1-4 personal mamluks.

Every 40 al-Halqa were commanded by an officer with the title Muqaddam al-Halqa (literally 'Commander of al-Halqa', equivalent in rank to an amir of 10), every 100 by a Bash, assisted by a Naqib, and every 1,000, as already stated, by an Amir of 100. Unlike the amirs the al-Halqa officers held their rank only during wartime. The organisation of the actual mamluks was probably likewise based on a 40 or 50-man unit, with companies of 100 (or possibly 200) and regiments of 1,000. Amirs and officers were not included in these totals. However, a much later author, Ibn Iyas, states that the Royal Mamluks at least were not organised into regular units and sub-units until they set out on campaign, and even then it was the sultan who decided the sizes of the units.

The overall strength of these regular Mamluk troops is not easy to resolve, but certainly 40,000 are recorded on campaign against the Sudan in 1289 and 10-19,000 at the siege of Tripoli the same year, while 60,000, though including some auxiliary cavalry, were present at the siege of Acre in 1291. Gibbon, in his *'Decline and Fall of the Roman Empire'*, records only 25,000 Mamluk cavalry, though he does not cite a source, or date, for this information. Whether any of these figures include al-Halqa units is unknown.

Auxiliaries and infantry

In addition to the mamluks and al-Halqa large numbers of auxiliary troops could be raised from amongst the Turcoman, Kurd, Bedouin, Syro-Palestinian and Lebanese tribesmen. Such auxiliaries were sometimes called Khasseki (cf. Russian 'Kazaks', meaning freebooters or nomad vagabonds).

The Turcomans and Kurds were settled on grants of land as military colonists by the Mamluks, chieftains being given the titles amir of 10, amir of 20 or amir of 40 depending on their importance. However, these chieftains remained inferior in rank to Mamluk amirs of the same grade.

The Bedouins were under no obligations whatsoever and supplied auxiliary cavalry in emergencies only; nor were they consistently reliable. Their chieftains were therefore graded lower than those of the Turcomans and Kurds, being ranked as amirs only if they were powerful, otherwise being classified as al-Halqa.

The semi-nomadic al-'Ashair, the Syro-Palestinian and Lebanese tribesmen, appear to have been hired principally as bow and sling armed mercenary infantry during this period, though they sometimes supplied cavalry. After 1289 most officially became regular soldiers of sorts when the tribal chieftains came to hold their lands as direct grants from the sultan. Their infantry probably resembled figure 15 in the dress and equipment section.

Zahiri records that the auxiliary contingents available from these sources numbered 180,000 Turcomans, 20,000 Kurds (he says 'formerly' 20,000), 93,000 Bedouins (29,000 from Syria and Palestine, 33,000 from Egypt, and 31,000 from the Hijaz and Mesopotamia; their contingents ranged from 100 to 2,000 men), and 35,000 Syro-Palestinians and Lebanese. In addition Zahiri records that every village in the Mamluk state was required to supply 2 horsemen, and he gives the figure of 33,000 villages; these possibly represent the Awl'ad al-nas. These auxiliaries were all cavalry, no infantry figures being given.

However, Gibbon mentions auxiliary troops consisting of a 'provincial militia' of 107,000 infantry, almost certainly including the Syro-Palestinians and Lebanese, in addition to 66,000 Bedouin cavalry, while Frankish sources record 100,000 and Muslim sources 100-160,000 irregular infantry at the sieges of Tripoli (1289) and Acre (1291) respectively.

Though the infantry were nearly always irregulars (foot-soldiers played only a minor role in Mamluk warfare) a description of the siege of al-Marqab in 1285 mentions a regiment of 1,000 infantry called the Aqjiyyah forming part of the garrison installed by the Mamluks after its capture; the regiment is otherwise unknown, but they were quite clearly non-mamluk regulars of some kind, perhaps Lebanese. Somewhat earlier, in 1279, an army composed of 4,000 infantry and 9,000 cavalry attacked Qal'at Rhomaita on the Euphrates, and certainly so far from home such infantry could hardly have been supplied by irregular militia. In addition the axe-armed Tabardariyyah regiment was clearly regular.

Another band of infantry irregulars in the Mamluk army were the Hadjis, light-armed religious fanatics comparable to the Iaylars of the later Ottoman period. At the siege of Acre they are recorded throwing themselves into the ditch before the walls so that their own infantry could advance across their bodies!

Engineers were also irregulars, though naptha troops may have been employed full-time since naptha, siphons and other incendiary equipment was kept exclusively in royal arsenals and must have required specialist knowledge in order to utilise them safely and effectively.

The Wafidiya

In addition to the usual auxiliaries some Mongols were to be found serving in Mamluk armies after 1262, as many as 3,000 taking service during Baibar's reign. These were generally called by the names Wafidiya or Musta'mina, meaning 'immigrants' or 'those who seek asylum' respectively. Like the Turcomans, Bedouins and Kurds they retained their status as free men but, unlike other auxiliaries, some actually served within regular Mamluk units, usually those of the amirs though some even served alongside the Royal Mamluks and even in the Khassakiyyah, the Sultan's personal bodyguard. Most, however, were enrolled in the aj-Halqa and nearly all ranked lower than the Mamluks themselves, their chieftains being given only low ranks, usually Muqaddam al-Halqa and rarely higher than an amir of 40 during this era (this relatively low rank was even given to the Ilkhan Hulagu's son-in-law, Turghay, who entered Mamluk service in 1297 with as many as 10,000 or 18,000 Kalmuks! Later, however, in Mohammed's reign when the days of such mass immigrations were past, higher ranks were sometimes assigned to Wafidiya chieftains.)

THE ASSASSINS

The Assassins were founded in the late-11th century by a Persian, Hasan as-Sabah, who in 1090 set up his headquarters at Alamut in the Daylam mountains. They were an extremist group of a Shi'ite Muslim sect, the Isma'ilites, their name of Assassins (Arabic Hashishiyun) deriving from a corruption of the Latin word for hashish, to which substance they were allegedly (but highly improbably) addicted. The Muslims more often called them Batinis or Nazaris.

Their existence as an independent political entity under their Grand Master was mainly a result of the inaccessibility of their mountain fortresses – Alamut itself means 'Eagle's Nest' – of which there were perhaps 60 or more in the region of Alamut alone by the mid-13th century. In addition from the early 12th century there was a large Syrian offshoot of 10 fortresses, with its headquarters at Masyaf after 1141, the most famous leader of whom was Rashid ad-Din Sinan (1169-1193) known as Sheikh al-Djabel, 'The Old Man of the Mountain', a title thereafter borne by his successors.

Their most notable contribution to this era – and all eras since – was the gentle art of political assassination, to which they gave their name. The sectaries were blindly obedient to the Grand Master or the Old Man of the Mountain and were even prepared to kill themselves if ordered to do so, so they did not fear capture or death in the course of executing their duty, which was a good job since more often than not they did not return from their assignments; as Bar Hebraeus graphically puts it, 'killing they were killed'. (Those of their brethren actually responsible for the majority of assassinations were the Fida'is or Fidawis, meaning 'those ready to offer their lives for a cause'.) Celebrities removed from the course of history by Assassin activity included Nizam al-Mulk (1092), the Fatimid vizier al-Afdal (1122), il-Bursuqi of Mosul (1126), Conrad of Montferrat (1192), and Genghis Khan's second son Jagatai (1242) to name but a few. Even Saladin came close to having his career abbreviated on more than one occasion, while Prince Edward, later Edward I of England, narrowly escaped death when he was wounded by a poisoned Assassin dagger in 1271. There are even stories that Assassins were actually sent as far afield as Europe, and that some tried to murder Louis IX of France prior to his departure on the Seventh Crusade.

Quite often such assassinations were motivated by outsiders – the murder of the Patriarch of Jerusalem in 1214, for example, was instigated by the Hospitallers of all people – but equally, if not more, often they were aimed at controlling the balance of power amongst the Assassins' enemies. For the same reason Assassins might be found allied to either Franks or Muslims as the needs of the moment dictated. During the 13th century the Syrian Assassins were almost permanently subject to the Hospitallers.

The strength of the sect was effectively broken when its headquarters at Alamut was destroyed by the Mongols in 1256, the nucleus of the Persian sectaries being all but exterminated by 1257. The Syrian Assassins lasted a little longer, though the Mamluk Sultan Baibars achieved their final destruction by 1273, ending their political power for ever. Nevertheless, Assassins still occasionally appear thereafter, in 1275 even recapturing and holding Alamut for a few months, and though the remaining sectaries were gradually absorbed by other Isma'ilite groups they continued to be employed as political assassins under the Mamluks, Ibn Battuta recording how during the 14th century they were normally paid at a fixed rate per murder.

Scattered as the communities of the sect were it is impossible to establish their military potential, but William of Tyre states that the Syrian Assassins numbered 60,000 and Burchard of Mount Sion that they numbered 40,000; the Syrian Assassins are recorded to have fielded perhaps as many as 10,000 men against the Franks as early as 1128. They relied on volunteer civic militias for both infantry and cavalry; these were of a high standard and received pay for the duration of their service, usually in the form of booty, horsemen being paid twice as much as foot-soldiers.

THE BYZANTINE EMPIRE

The traditional army described in *'Armies of the Dark Ages'* was defeated and all but destroyed by the Seljuk Turks at the disastrous Battle of Manzikert in 1071, and the succeeding centuries saw the final demise of classical military organisation. The subsequent changes in Byzantine organisation can be fairly accurately summarised as a decline in the importance of the provincial forces of the Themata accompanied by an increased reliance on mercenaries and the contingents of the landowning aristocracy.

Mercenaries and the Regular army

Though they had always been an outstanding feature of Byzantine armies, from the practical point of view, and certainly as a successful solution to the Empire's immediate needs, the principal result of Manzikert was a considerable and ever-increasing reliance on mercenaries. It was undoubtedly this which led to the final disappearance amongst many of the native Greek[5] population of any kind of military potential, steadily on the decline since the 10th century. It was inevitable, therefore, that the Comneni Emperors and their successors should show a marked preference for mercenary troops.

Anna Comnena describes the mercenaries in the army of her father Alexius I as 'horsemen and footmen from all lands'; by the end of the 11th century they included Colbingians (Kolbingoi = Kolbyagy? Germanic inhabitants of the southern Baltic coastline), Cumans, Seljuks, Patzinaks (Pechenegs), Uzes (Torks), Alani, Macedonians (Slavs and Bulgars, employed extensively under the early Comneni), Serbs, Georgians, Armenians, Nemitzoi or Alamanoi (Germans and possibly Flemings; just to confuse the issue Frenchmen are

---

[5] Although even after 1204 the Byzantines continued to generally call themselves 'Rhomaioi' (i.e. Romans) they seem to have gradually adopted a preference for the term Hellene or 'Greek' so as to avoid any confusion between themselves and the hated Franks.

sometimes referred to as 'Germans' in Byzantine sources), Latins (a blanket term for Frenchmen, Normans and Italians), Englishmen, Saracens, Russians and Varangians, and on the whole these elements continued to serve throughout the 12th and 13th centuries. (Some, however, served as vassals rather than as mercenaries; the Serbs, for instance, supplied 500 cavalry for campaigns in Asia and 2,000 for campaigns in Europe during Manuel I's reign.) Niketas Choniates, writing in the early 13th century, says that each different tribe or race formed a different regiment, which must have helped to minimise what would have otherwise undoubtedly been a disastrous communication problem!

Alongside these irregular units of mercenaries and auxiliaries there were a number of full-time mercenary units that, throughout most of this era, constituted the bulk of the regular army, the old elite regiments of the Tagmata having been practically destroyed at Manzikert. Though the Excubitae are recorded at Durazzo in 1081, the Hetaeria and Ikanatoi elsewhere, and though the Scholae apparently survived at least as an institution, these units were merely shadows of their former selves and as elite army units fade into oblivion before the close of the 11th century. For a brief period during the reign of Alexius I (1081-1118) the restored army nucleus was based on the following units:

- the Vardariots, a cavalry unit of Christianised Turks, probably Uzes, from Macedonia.

- Frankish mercenaries, later called the Latinikon, at this date mainly of Norman or French extraction, commanded by an officer with the feudal European title of Konostablos or 'constable'. (The Maniaketes regiment, which features in late 11th-century sources, also appears to have consisted of Franks, descendants of the mercenaries employed by the general Maniakes in the 1030s and 1040s.)

– the Skythikon, at the beginning of this era consisting mainly of Pechenegs, for whom the Byzantines generally reserved the archaic term 'Scyth'.

– the Turcopouloi, 'Sons of Turks', composed of the sons of Christianised Turks and Seljuk and Turcoman mercenaries.

– a number of native Greek regiments which all vanished after only short careers. These comprised the Immortals, a large unit (10,000 men according to Bryennius) formed by Nicephoros III in 1078 from remnants of the Eastern Themata supplemented with new recruits; the Chomatenoi, a cavalry regiment raised in Choma in Phrygia, also by Nicephoros, apparently numbering as few as 300 men in 1081 but probably about 1,000 when at full strength; the Archontopouloi ('Sons of Leaders'), a unit of 2,000 cavalry raised by Alexius from officers' orphans in the 1080s; and the Vestiaritae, household troops who perhaps included in addition -

– the famous Varangian Guard, founded in the late 10th century by Basil II from Scandinavian and Russian mercenaries. There were in addition other Varangian regiments, which by the end of the 11th century also included English mercenaries.

Franks (otherwise referred to in Byzantine sources as Latins or 'Kelts') were employed in large numbers by the end of the 11th century, and it may have been a request made to the West by Alexius for mercenaries in 1091 or 1095 that inadvertently resulted in the First Crusade! At the beginning of this era, in 1071, when they were commanded by the unscrupulous adventurer Roussel de Bailleul, their strength is recorded as 3,000. A few years later there appear to have been as many as 8,000. Their numbers were increased considerably by the Latinophile Emperor Manuel I (1143-1180) under whom Franks, particularly Frenchmen, Germans and Italians, became the predominant mercenary element of the army after the Turks.

Most of the native, and some of the mercenary, regiments mentioned above had disappeared by as early as the end of the 11th century, apparently being disbanded by Alexius; the disappearance of others was possibly the result of having suffered heavy casualties throughout the 12th century, particularly at the Battle of Myriokephalon in 1176, which left the army in an even worse state comparatively than had Manzikert a century earlier. However, the Archontopouloi are still recorded in the Nicaean period in court circles; in 1261 there were only 52 of them, which would seem to indicate that they had earlier become some type of inner bodyguard and had declined considerably in strength and importance. Others of the old regiments may, like the Scholae and Archontopouloi, have gone through a similar process of gradual deterioration.

The regular mercenary regiments, however, thrived. Only the Turcopouloi – a name which appears regularly in Byzantine sources from the late 11th century through to the 14th century – seem to have undergone any kind of decline, and this appears to have been in status rather than strength. Alexius I seems to have relied heavily on the Turcopouloi; they feature prominently in the events of the Crusade of 1101, and he had as many as 7,000 Seljuk Turks in his employ as early as 1083. It is also worth remarking here that under the Comneni a large number of senior Byzantine officers were either Byzantinised Turks or of Turkish descent.

The other 4 regiments – Varangians, Vardariots, Skythikon and Latinikon – continued to form the nucleus of the regular army, changing only in their ethnic composition. The Skythikon, for instance, which had since 1122 recruited its members principally from amongst Pecheneg prisoners-of-war settled in the European provinces after the decisive defeat of Eski Zagra, had begun to include Cumans during the reign of John II (1118-1143) at the latest, and though the Pecheneg colonies continued to flourish until the Latin

Conquest of 1204 the Cumans seem to have become predominant by the end of the 12th century; militarily, in fact, the Pecheneg element was probably on the decline by the mid-12th century and it seems likely that inter-marriage and the introduction of reinforcements from other Turkish peoples brought about the gradual change of composition from Pecheneg to Cuman. Uzes also appear in large numbers during this century, and some at least found their way into the Skythikon; Byzantine sources even seem to imply that they formed the largest percentage of Turkish mercenaries at the time of Myriokephalon.

Likewise the composition of the Varangians, though still principally Scandinavian at the beginning of this period, gradually changed over ye course of time, acquiring a larger and larger percentage of Englishmen. In the late 1070s the Strategicon of Cecaumenus makes the first mention of Englishmen in an apparently military context, but they are only first mentioned in official Byzantine sources in 1080 and 1088, where they are nevertheless specifically mentioned separately from the Varangians. Ordericus Vitalis, writing c.1130, clearly records Englishmen serving the Emperor, and there were certainly English troops present at Myriokephalon in 1176 (they are mentioned in a letter from Manuel to King Henry II). Though important (being apparently the most trusted element of the Guard under Alexius I) their numbers were obviously still small in the early 12th century, Saxo Grammaticus (writing c.1102) stating that the Emperor's guard was composed of 'men of Danish tongue', and Snorri Sturlusson recording 'a great many Northmen' taking service with Alexius in 1112. The English element, however, steadily increased until by c.1180 the Byzantine chronicler Cinnamus could state quite specifically that the Varangians were 'of British race'. Even so, Sverrir's Saga records that as late as 1195 envoys were sent to the Scandinavian kings to request 1,200 men for the Guard, while Villehardouin records Danish as well as English guardsmen in 1204, alongside other units composed of men of many nationalities.

After the fall of Constantinople to the Franks in that year the Empire devolved into three principal states, Nicaea, Epirus and Trebizond, of which Nicaea appears to have inherited the main remnants of the Imperial army. Theodore II (1254-1258) reorganised the army nucleus, now called the Allaghion or Taxis and at least 27 Allaghia strong by 1259, under an officer called the Archon, later titled the Megas Archon. The Varangians and Vardariots were the mainstay of the Taxis while the Latinikon and Skythikon were loosely associated with it. Pseudo-Codinus records that after 1261 the full strength of the Taxis proper was 6,000 men, consisting of 12 Allaghia of 500 men each, which would seem to suggest that the Vardariots and Varangians probably numbered about 3,000 men each. By this time the Scandinavian element of the latter had practically disappeared, and in a document of 1272 Michael VIII refers to the Varangians as *Englinvarrhangoi* which, if it needs translation, is 'English Varangians'. In other sources the name is abbreviated to Englinoi, 'Englishmen'.

One of Theodore's other reforms was a reduction of the wages and privileges granted to Frankish mercenaries, since he thought that the large-scale reliance on foreigners was a principal weakness of the Byzantine army and had a preference for native Greek soldiers. Nevertheless, the Latinikon seems to have been as strong at the end of his reign as it had been at the beginning, so his measures probably had little or no effect. The Frankish mercenaries constituting the Latinikon were chiefly drawn from the Syrian crusader states and Romania by this time (and probably had been since the mid-12th century), though they also included Sicilians, Italians, Venetians and Achaian Franks. Their commander's title had changed to Megas Konostablos, 'Grand Constable', under Theodore II though, like the earlier Konostablos, he was not always himself a Frank – the future Emperor Michael VIII, for instance, held the rank of Megas Konostablos under Theodore.

The Skythikon now consisted chiefly of Cumans, recruited after 1241 from some 10,000 who had been settled on land grants in Anatolia and Thrace. Many of them, together with other regular mercenaries, were detached to serve as garrison troops at strategic points or under provincial commanders, this being particularly true of the Cumans and, earlier, the Pechenegs, these often serving as a kind of provincial police. These detached units were called Megalon Allaghia or Stratopeda and their officers Stratopedarchs. Even the Varangians appear to have sometimes been used in this way, for detachments are found at Kalaura in Thrace, Cibetot on the Anatolian coastline, and possibly even at Cherson in the Crimea.

The irregular mercenary units who backed up the regular field army also contained large numbers of Franks. Theodore I's army of 2,000 men at Antioch-in-Pisidia in 1211, for example, contained 800 Frankish mercenaries, principally Italians. Three years later, in 1214, his army is described as consisting of Germans, Romanians, Armenians and Turks, and his successor John III Vatatzes (1222-1254) is recorded to have employed particularly large numbers of Frankish mercenaries. The Nicaean army at Pelagonia in 1259 included 300 German cavalry, 1,500 Hungarian cavalry, 600, 1,000 or 5,000 Serbian cavalry (apparently including horse-archers, probably Turks or Cumans), 500-1,500 Turkish horse-archers, 4,000 Cumans and Alans and an unknown number of Bulgarian horse-archers.

One early Ottoman source even records Mongol auxiliaries in a Nicaean army defeated by Kai Khosrou II of Rum in the 1240s. The Mongols sometimes supplied troops during Michael VIII's reign as well, for example in 1282 when 4,000 were sent to his assistance by the Golden Horde, while Andronikos II was promised 40,000 by the Ilkhan Oljeitu in 1305. Pachymeres records that 20,000 of these actually advanced as far as Iconium, while in 1308 he records another 30,000 being sent into Bithynia by the Ilkhan to recapture certain places recently seized from the Byzantines by the Turks. Even as late as 1402 5,000 Mongols are recorded fighting for the Byzantines against the Ottomans.

Under Michael VIII (1259-1282) there was an increased intake of Turkish mercenaries, Michael having a minimum of 5,000 regulars in his employ by 1262, and Turks and Turcopouloi, both infantry and cavalry, continued to be a major element in the army of his son and successor Andronikos II. However, the most memorable mercenaries of Andronikos' reign were undoubtedly the Catalans and Almughavari of Roger de Flor's Catalan Grand Company, whose career is described in Appendix 2 here and in *'Armies of the Middle Ages, volume 2'*. In addition to the Turks and Catalans the other principal mercenary elements of his army are recorded by Pachymeres as Gazmouloi, Cretans and Alans, 10-16,000 of the latter being employed as late as 1302.

Provincial troops: Themata and Stratiotes

In addition to the regular central army based in Constantinople there were subsidiary armies scattered throughout the Empire's various provinces. These semi-regular provincial troops, however, were usually relatively few in number, and to face any large-scale incursion it was necessary for the armies of several provinces to be gathered into one large force, often reinforced in addition by the central army and laced with liberal quantities of mercenaries. However, it should be noted that most provincial troops continued to be largely of native stock; certainly, despite the preponderance of mercenaries, native troops continued to serve in Byzantine forces in large numbers, notably under Alexius I, Manuel I and Isaac II. Even when the Asiatic provincial regiments underwent a decline in the 1190s and were replaced with entirely new and rigorously trained regiments they were recruited again from the native peasant-farmers. In the course of the 13th century many such provincial troops were drafted into the regular army, notably in the reign of Theodore II Lascaris, though by this time the distinction between central and provincial armies was becoming somewhat blurred. As early as Manuel I's reign we even find the central army itself being billeted throughout the provinces in winter so as to ease the strain on the Imperial treasury, and this practice appears to have persisted throughout the remainder of this era.

Another large part of the Empire's provincial troops was composed of the contingents of the Dynatoi and Archontes, the land-owning magnates. Even before Manzikert (and at the battle itself) such noblemen are to be found leading their personal retinues, and after 1071 this element became prevalent, the old provincial levies of the Themata at the same time undergoing a dramatic decline in most parts of the Empire. The last general muster of the Eastern Themata was in 1073, and the ease with which they were defeated by some 3,000 rebel Norman mercenaries would indicate that they were inadequate in quality and few in number. Even so, evidence suggests that the military obligations of the Themata continued to survive; certainly when Andronikos I marched on Constantinople in 1182 the bulk of his army was composed of the Thematic forces of Thracesion, Paphlagonia and Nicaea, while the military Theme structure of Chaldia, complete with its Banda of semi-regular cavalry, survived right up to 1461.

After 1071, however, many native troops were being raised in return for an alternative type of land grant to that held by the Thematic farmers. This was the Pronoia (literally 'Provision'), which may possibly have originally evolved from the Muslim iqta'. Though it was then chiefly a civilian holding there is some evidence of military service occasionally being performed in exchange for Pronoiai as early as the mid-10th century, and certainly in the immediate post-Manzikert era Michael VII made increasing use of such grants to pay his troops. The main difference of the Pronoia from the old Thematic grant was that the owner of the latter was a self-supporting farmer who received his land as payment for performed military service, while the former was an estate held by a quasi-feudal tenant who performed military service in exchange for the grant, which was usually supplemented by payments in cash and/or kind. But, unlike the Thematic grant, the Pronoia was not hereditable until the reign of Michael VIII (1259-1282), usually being made only for a specific number of years (most commonly the holder's lifetime). During that time the taxes and revenues of the estate were payable to the holder rather than the Imperial treasury, while the holder himself – known either as a Pronoiarios or Pronoetes or, more usually, a Stratiotes ('Soldier')[6] – paid no tax at all. Instead he was obliged to perform mounted military service, almost certainly (though this is a much debated point) with a predetermined number of men in the case of the larger estates – in the mid-13th century a Lombard received the island of Euboea in exchange for the service of himself and 200 knights, but whether such troops were ever obligatory or merely represent the personal attendants of the greater Stratiotai is unknown. Most Stratiotai, however, obviously would have held only small estates and served alone and in person.

Although some members of such contingents as did follow the Stratiotai were probably similarly armoured and equipped as heavy cavalry others were equally probably lighter-armed or served as infantry; certainly as early as Alexius I's reign church and monastery lands were obliged to raise levies of light infantry, and some lesser landowners also appear to have served as

---

[6] This term, somewhat corrupted, appears in the West in the 15th and 16th centuries as 'Stradiot', the name under which Albanians and Greeks served in Venetian employ after the fall of Constantinople in 1453 and the subsequent conquest of Albania by the Ottomans.

infantry, though under what obligation is unclear (possibly they were local Thematic troops). Clearly, however, Pronoiai were regarded principally as a source of heavy cavalry, and more and more Pronoiai were granted to this end in the course of the 12th century, the Stratiotai rapidly evolving into a quasi-feudal military aristocracy as their numbers grew. In fact the general resemblance of this system to European feudalism is striking and becomes even more so when we learn that by the beginning of the 13th century at the latest some such land grants were actually called Fiefs, and when the Franks conquered vast tracts of Byzantine territory after 1204 they found the existing conditions of land-tenure so similar to those of feudal Europe that little administrative change (in some cases none whatsoever) was necessary.

Under Manuel I Pronoiai were first granted to 'half-barbarians', probably Cumans or Turks in Byzantine employ, though they had been used as payment for other mercenaries, chiefly Franks such as the Normans mentioned above, even in the 11th century and during the 12th century had become the generally accepted means of maintaining the regular army as well as provincial units. In this form Pronoiai survived right down to the fall of Constantinople in 1453, although – in total contradiction to the purpose for which they had been established – some were receiving exemption from the obligation of military service by the middle to late-13th century.

Likewise many of the remaining Thematic soldiers customarily exempted themselves from service by cash payments by the end of the 11th century. However, as noted above, such Thematic troops still served in the 13th century, some performing garrison duties in local frontier fortresses under officers called Tzaousioi and Kastrophylakes. These garrison troops included foreign mercenaries as well as native farmers, all being granted Pronoiai in the vicinity of whichever fortress they defended. These garrisons, of vital importance in Anatolia, declined considerably under Andronikos II at the very end of this era.

Unit sizes

Although the old Byzantine unit organisation described in *'Armies of the Dark Ages'* survived, by the 12th century at the latest and probably as early as the late 11th century the standard unit of the Byzantine army consisted of some 300-500 men, comparable to the old Bandon or Tagma but by this later date generally called by the name Allaghion (this term having clearly derived a new meaning since the days of Leo VI's Tactica, when it had referred to a unit of only 50 men). It is logical to assume that the unit's strength was technically 400 but, like the earlier Bandon, this could vary depending on whether the unit was under or over the official strength. At the siege of Constantinople in 1204, for example, the French chronicler Robert de Clari speaks of the Byzantines mustering 17 'battles' for an engagement before the Palace of Blachernae; of nine of these he says 'there was no one of these nine

Battles in which there were not 3,000 knights, or four or five in some', and allowing for de Clari's tendency towards exaggeration these 'battles' probably represent such units of 300, 400 or 500 cavalry.

The term Moira (a unit consisting of a number of Banda in the old system) is also still used occasionally in the sources (as are Bandon and Tagma), but in general the Allaghion appears to have now been the largest unit; for instance, a force of 6,000 cavalry recorded in 1263 including a minimum of 1,500 Turks was organised as 18 Allaghia. Smaller units of 40-60 and 100 men also appear to have existed, probably indicating that the Allaghion was subdivided into four units of 100 (official strength), each of two units of 50 men. The smallest cavalry unit was still of ten men. Infantry may still have been organised in 16-man sub-units.

It should also be noted that units of a rather more 'feudal' character are to be sometimes found in the sources. Cinnamus, for instance, records a regiment under the Emperor Manuel 'consisting of those nearest him in blood, among whom were many of his most intimate associates and those who had wedded his sisters'; undoubtedly the size of such a unit would, like its Frankish counterpart, adhere to no regulation standard whatsoever.

Servants

Paid servants accompanied Byzantine soldiers now as in the earlier period. By the 13th century they are generally referred to as the Tzouloukonae. Like their earlier counterparts they were on occasion expected to fight, as at Serrhae in 1246, but they were lightly, if not poorly, armed and probably served chiefly as slingers and archers.

The Navy

As in the crusader states of Palestine, Byzantine naval power throughout most of this era depended heavily on the contingents of the Italian maritime republics, particularly Venice and Genoa but also on occasion Pisa, which served in exchange for pay and favourable trading concessions within the Empire. Venetian colonists were present in Constantinople from 1084, though the Pisan and Genoese colonies were only established in 1111 and 1155 respectively and on an inferior scale. By 1171 there were some 20,000 Venetians settled within the Empire, 10,000 of them in Constantinople itself, while Bar Hebraeus records as many as 30,000 Frankish merchants (probably chiefly Pisans and Genoese) in Constantinople by 1204.

An agreement made with the Venetians in 1187 is fairly typical of the arrangements by which such auxiliaries served. By the conditions of this treaty the republic of Venice agreed to supply 40-100 galleys equipped at the Emperor's expense, on which three out of every four Venetian colonists were to serve. They had their own officers, though these had to follow the orders of the Byzantine admiral. In emergencies such as a sudden attack by 40 or more enemy ships, in which situation no time would have been available to await the arrival of the galleys from Venice, the colonists were obliged to serve instead on Byzantine ships. On the conclusion of peace auxiliary galleys could return to Venice but had to be kept ready for further service. By a later agreement the Genoese, in exchange for their re-establishment in Galata in 1261 (following the reconquest of Constantinople) agreed to supply 100 galleys for defensive warfare, 50 of them manned and fully armed, the other 50 unmanned. In addition further galleys were often hired on a purely mercenary basis

The Byzantine navy proper continued a steady decline. The Thematic fleets and Imperial fleet were combined under the command of a Megas Dux during the reign of Alexius I, but although the fleet underwent a brief revival at this time even Alexius found it expedient to employ Venetian ships and their numbers steadily increased until the mid-12th century, when Manuel I temporarily rectified the balance by constructing a fleet of considerable proportions; as many as 200 ships, including galleys and horse-transports, are recorded in 1169. Quite what resources Manuel employed to maintain this fleet, however, is not clear, since it was during his reign that many of the coastal districts and islands exempted themselves from naval service by payments in cash. Not surprisingly, therefore, the fleet declined again under his successors so that by 1196 only 30 galleys remained. When the fleet of the Fourth Crusade appeared before Constantinople in 1203 not a single large ship remained serviceable in the whole Byzantine fleet, which by that time consisted of only 20 worm-eaten hulks, and the Megas Dux – when he did appear – was in command of a detachment of cavalry!

Even so, after Constantinople fell the Nicaean Despot Theodore I Lascaris is recorded to have possessed a fleet of 30 galleys as early as 1205. In the same year Leo Gabalas, the Despot of Rhodes, could muster 20-30 galleys. 33 ships are recorded under the Nicaean Megas Dux in 1230, and ten years later John Vatatzes had 30 galleys.

The fleet had increased to some 80 galleys by 1283 when, shortly after his succession, Andronikos II disbanded it altogether, instead placing total reliance on Genoese auxiliary vessels, 50-60 of these being employed by 1291. This was principally a financial cutback which increased taxation revenue was intended to rectify c.1320 by the establishment of a Byzantine fleet of 20 galleys; however, this plan may never have been carried out.

The Gazmouloi

These were mixed-blood Franko-Greeks (of Frankish fathers and Greek mothers), regarded by the Byzantines as particularly good soldiers because their parentage gave them, according to Pachymeres, both the wild, reckless courage of the Franks and the calculating caution of the Byzantines. Together with the Tzakones (Peloponnesians – Pachymeres plausibly identifies them with the descendants of the classical Laconians. the Spartans) they supplied a large part of the Byzantines' naval manpower. Andronikos II disbanded them when he abolished the fleet, which was a mistake since thereafter a number of them took service with the Empire's Frankish enemies, others even going over to the Turks!

In the 13th century a large number of pirates – particularly Genoese pirates – also operated under the Byzantine flag against the Franks, and two successive Byzantine Megas Duces of the last quarter of the century (Licario and John de lo Cavo) were themselves corsairs. (Some Syrian and Romanian Franks also employed pirate ships, such as the 15 in the pay of Gerard of Sidon at the siege of Ascalon in 1153.)

GEORGIA

The state of Georgia, founded through the union of Abasgia and Iberia in 1008 (the name derives not from any special association with St George but rather from their Arabic/Persian name, Gurj or Kurj), underwent mixed fortunes during this period, growing to considerable dimensions before being defeated in 1221 and reduced to vassalage in 1239 by the Mongols. Though Christians, the Georgians had no special liking for the Franks of Outremer, but their country was strategically situated on the flank of the Muslim world and at least one Frankish writer, Anseau, observed that 'the land and kingdom [of Georgia] are for us like a rampart against the Medes and Persians'.

A feudal system, called Patronqmoba, prevailed in Georgia from the 11th century onwards and most Georgian armies were composed chiefly of the 'feudal' contingents of the nobility. The ruling class were the Patroni, composed of Eristavt-Eristavni, who led the provincial contingents in wartime under their own banners; Eristavni, 'commanders of armies', equivalent to the Byzantine Strategoi; Didebulni, literally 'the Great', subject to the local Eristavt-Eristavi (not to the Ersitavi); Spasalari (cf. the Arabic Sipahsalar); Atassistavni, commanders of 1,000 (organisation in Georgia was decimal); and Aznauri, the basic 'knightly' class. Many aznauri had their own fortresses (sometimes no more than a fortified house), and many installed castellans, called Tsikistavni or 'heads of fortresses'. Their 'feudal' contingents consisted of the Qmani, clients resident on their estates, numbers depending on the size of the estate; those Qmani who served well were given their own lands and improved status in return. The elite troops were those from the region of Karatli, and it was from amongst these that the king maintained a personal cavalry retinue, a sort of Familia, apparently 200-strong under King Dimitri in the late 13th century.

No regular military force was formally established until the reign of David II Aghmashenbeli (1089-1125), who recruited a standing army of mercenaries from amongst the Kipchaks (Cumans) and Ossetians (Alans). The Kipchaks, settled in large numbers in depopulated parts of the kingdom, could muster

40,000 men on demand, as well as an elite guard unit of 5,000. In fact it was a new wave of these Kipchak mercenaries who were largely responsible for Georgia's rapid, but short-lived, growth to military greatness in the late 12th century under Giorgi III (1156-1184) and the celebrated Queen Thamar (1184-1213), when they were led by a certain Qubasar. In addition to these troops a large force of regular, paid garrison troops was maintained in Tiflis, the capital, and in many provincial fortresses (David II maintained as many as 60,000 men in this capacity, of whom at least some if not the greater proportion are certain to have been foreign mercenaries.)

In fact most Georgian kings appear to have maintained such foreign troops, Bagrat IV of Karatli (1027-1072) even having a contingent of 3,000 Varangians in his employ (chiefly Russians but possibly including some Scandinavians), as too did Queen Thamar. In addition to Ossetians and Kipchaks, David II was even employing several hundred Frankish mercenary knights as early as 1121, and Seljuks and Turcomans were employed on other occasions. All such troops were responsible for supplying their own armour and equipment.

A good idea of the mixed nature of Georgian armies can be taken from an army of 40,000 recorded in 1228 to have consisted of Georgians, Armenians (from Greater Armenia, not Cilicia), various nomads (Serirs, Lesghs, Suans and Jikils) and as many as 20,000 Kipchaks. An earlier army, in the reign of David II, included only 100 Frankish knights but compensated with 5,000 Alans and 15,000 Kipchaks.

THE MONGOLS

Mongol armies were organised on a decimal basis. Marco Polo records the largest unit as being the Tuk of 100,000 men, but this was probably only true of the enormous multi-racial armies of Mongol China. The standard unit was the Touman of 10,000 men, consisting of 10 Minghans of 1,000. Each Minghan (also called a Haraza or, in one early instance, a Guran) was of 10 Jaguns of 100 men, and each Jagun of 10 Arbans of 10 men. The Arban, the basic unit, consisted of a number of Yurts, each of 1-3 men with a family relationship, and was commanded by an unrelated officer called a Baatut (or Bagatur). Two or more Toumans, usually 3, constituted an army and one of the commanders was designated the senior; he was accompanied by a great drum (see note 63 in the dress and equipment section) which could only be sounded at his command, when it was the signal to attack.

Other officers were drawn from among the Darkhat, a special class of freemen, and the Baatuts, Noyans and Nukuts, all noblemen by birth; when the Minghan units were first formally established by Genghis Khan in the early 13th century each was commanded by a Noyan, though similar thousand-strong units recorded in 1193 called Gurans ('Rings'), were commanded by officers called Gurkhans. By the 14th century the commanders of Minghans and Toumans were mostly princes of the Imperial family. In addition there was what can best be described as a central corps of nine staff officers called the Orlok, of whom Subutai and Mukuli are probably the best known.

Military service was due from every able-bodied man between the ages of 14 and 61, though the Great Yasa laws of Genghis Khan say 20 and over. A column of reinforcements recorded in 1235 certainly contained boys of 13-14 years of age, though these may only have been participating in escort duty as part of their training. On campaign each man was accompanied by a minimum of 2 or 3 horses, or on occasion as many as 6 or 7; one version of Marco Polo's travels records each Mongol owning on average 18 horses and mares. Four horses per rider are recorded in the invasion of Khwarizmia in 1219 and 5 for the Ilkhanid attack on Syria in 1299. Friar John de Plano Carpini, who wrote c.1246, records that if possible a horse ridden one day was not ridden again for the next 3 or 4.

Guardsmen and auxiliaries

In addition to the 'line' Toumans there were auxiliaries and the Keshik. The latter was a guard unit that only took the field when the Khan went on campaign. It is first mentioned in 1203 when it consisted of 70 day guards (the Turghaut), 80 night guards (the Kabtaut), 400 elite archers (the Khorchin), and the Baatut or Bagatur, an elite of 1,000 'Warriors' who formed the advance guard in battle. In 1206 the Keshik was increased to Touman strength, with Turghaut of 1,000, Kabtaut of first 800 and then 1,000, Khorchin of 1,000 and an additional 6,000 Baatut, who remained junior to the original Baatut Minghan. Each of these Keshik Minghans rode horses of uniform colour; the Baatut horses were black (possibly for all 7 Minghans). Keshik warriors were higher in rank than commanders of 'line' Minghans, and non-combatants attached to the Keshik were higher in rank than commanders of Jaguns.

Auxiliary troops (the Cherig) included Russians, Baskirs, Volga Bulgars, Alans, Georgians, Armenians, Kurds, Turcomans, Cumans, Uigurs, Qarluqs, Jurchids, Qarakhitai, Kalmuks (Oirats), Tanguts, Khwarizmians, Turks, Bedouin Arabs, Indians and Chinese; Chinese troops first defected to the Mongols in 1214 and were mainly infantry – the first time the Mongols had used large numbers of foot-soldiers. Officers of these various nationalities could even be found as generals in Mongol armies – a Tangut, for instance, commanded the Mongol forces which crushed the Alans in 1239 – but more often Mongol officers commanded auxiliary troops and organised them in Mongol fashion. However, such auxiliary contingents, consisting as they did of peoples the Mongols had conquered, were not totally reliable. Even Carpini records this dissidence, saying that if an opportunity should ever arise and they could be sure that their enemies would not kill them, the auxiliaries would turn on the Mongols themselves and attack them more fiercely than even the enemy would. It is no surprise, therefore, that we sometimes find the Mongols disbanding or distributing their auxiliary troops.

Some idea of the scale on which auxiliaries were employed may be taken from armies operating in China in 1217 and 1225; the former comprised 10,000 Onguts, 20-30,000 Qarakhitai, Jurchids and Chinese, and 50,000 Tanguts, but only 13,000 Mongols, while the latter, although containing a higher proportion of Mongols (80,000 in fact, though some of these were probably Turks), also contained 20,000 Indians, 30,000 Jetes [Turks?] and Cumans, and 50,000 Khwarizmians. Batu's army that invaded Russia in 1236 was similar in proportions, with 70-100,000 'Turks' and other auxiliaries and 50,000 Mongols.

Engineers

Mongol engineers were largely drawn from Arab, Khwarizmian or Chinese auxiliaries and prisoners. Chinese engineers were first employed in 1211 and appeared in large numbers by late 1213, while as many as 10,000 are reputed to have accompanied the army that invaded Khwarizmia in 1219.

They were employed to build siege equipment as and when required. At the siege of Nishapur in 1221 the Mongols' engineers are reputed to have constructed as many as 3,000 Ballistae, 300 catapults, 700 naptha-throwing engines and 4,000 siege-ladders. In addition light engines might be dismantled and carried by camels, yaks and oxen on campaign.

1,000 engineers from Asia Minor employed by Hulagu in 1253 are recorded to have been men specially trained in the use of naptha and grenades. There's also a significant possibility that the Mongols may have used gunpowder, some sources suggesting the use of what may have been a crude mortar in 1232, used to discharge a 'thunder bomb', an iron vessel filled with gunpowder, while Frankish chroniclers speak of the Mongol artillery barrage at the Battle of Mohi in 1241 as being accompanied by 'thunderous noise and flashes of fire'. Later, in the invasions of Japan in 1274 and 1281, 'fire-barrels' are recorded, and in one oft-reproduced illustration from the famous Mongol Invasion Scroll of 1293 what can only be described as some kind of exploding bomb is quite clearly depicted. Perhaps the 'fire-barrels' were primitive cannon, perhaps not, but it is worth noting that Chinese sources certainly record the invention in 1259 of 'fire-lances', which were bamboo tubes from which clusters of pellets could be fired by gunpowder to a range of some 250 yards.

Total strength

When they were first created in the early-13th century there were 95 Minghans, theoretically giving 95,000 men, though of the commanders only

90 names are listed, and one of these is known to have been dead at this date so that there may have actually been less than 90 Minghans at full strength.

The Ilkhanid vizier and historian Raschid al-Din, who wrote c.1306, records that on the death of Genghis Khan in 1227 the army comprised 129,000 men; this consisted of the Junghar (Army of the Left Wing, or East) of 62,000, the Baraunghar (Army of the Right Wing, or West) of 38,000, the Khol (Army of the Centre, the Imperial Ordus) of 1,000 picked men, 4,000 guards each for princes Juchi, Jagatai, and Ogodai (to serve as the nuclei of their own multi-racial armies), and 16,000 guards for other members of the Imperial family. A variant copy of the same source gives a total of 230,000, with Junghar of 52,000, Baraunghar of 47,000, Khol of 101,000, Imperial Guard of 1,000, 4,000 each for the three princes, and 17,000 guards for the remainder of the family. Both sets of figures are slightly suspect – where, for instance, is the Keshik, unless one is to take the Khol in the former and the Imperial Guard in the latter as being mistakes for 10,000?

Even so, only the Mongols themselves are accounted for by these figures. Raschid al-Din also records that in time of war the Mongols could muster as many as 1,400,000 men, while Khan Ogodai (1229-1241) is claimed to have maintained five armies totalling 1,500,000 men, and if they are to be taken seriously such figures must represent levies of vast numbers of subject peoples and auxiliaries, in which case contemporary remarks about the 'legions of the Mongols, who exceeded locusts and ants in number' would seem to be justified.

ILKHANID PERSIA

The Mongol armies of the Ilkhanate of Persia (which was established in 1256) were at first maintained by treasures looted from the preceding administration; by nomadic grazing on the available pasture lands; and by forced levies in cash and sometimes men from the existing populace. However, under Ilkhan Ghazan (1296-1304) and the vizier Raschid al-Din it became apparent that it was impractical, if not impossible, to maintain the army in this way any longer. Therefore a system comparable to the earlier iqta' was established, often even retaining the name iqta' but technically now called Suyurghal or Tuyul depending on whether the grant was hereditary or for the holder's lifetime only; the soldiers had to support themselves from these grants. It has been plausibly suggested that the term iqta' survived in use for the smaller benefices held by the indigenous Turkish and Persian peoples, while the Mongol terms were applied to those lands held by Mongol soldiers.

However, except for an increase in the number of Mongol troops present, military organisation did not change drastically from that which the Seljuks had originally imposed, and Persians, Turks and Turcomans continued to play an important military role. Additional elements of the army were supplied by Kurds, Georgians and Armenians amongst others. Cilician Armenia and the Frankish principality of Antioch both paid tribute to, and were erstwhile allies of, the Mongols from 1246.

One interesting continuation of Seljuk practice that deserves mention was the employment of Frankish mercenaries. The mid-13th-century traveller Simon de Saint-Quentin records that the Mongols were so impressed by the fighting spirit of those Franks they encountered during their conquests that they forbade the princes and kings of vassal states to employ them thereafter, though they employed small numbers themselves – for example Ilkhan Arghun had at least 900 in his employ in 1290, and a company of Frankish crossbowmen was present at the Ilkhanid siege of Herat in 1307.

As with other Mongol states, huge armies are claimed for the Ilkhanate. In 1299 Ghazan is supposed to have mustered 100,000 men for a campaign against Mamluk Syria, and this represented only half his available forces, while Marco Polo reports that in 1261 Hulagu was able to raise 300,000. The Ilkhanate itself lasted only until 1354, though its power declined drastically after the death of the last legitimate Ilkhan in 1335.

TACTICAL METHODS

FRANKS AND MUSLIMS

Strategy

For the Franks, strategy largely involved defending their conquests, by the building and holding of fortresses and, in time of war, the positioning of field armies where they could protect the largest amount of agricultural land and the most towns, fortresses and roads, their primary function being to interfere with any Muslim attempt to take a Frankish fortress. But at the same time these armies were usually only created by drawing from the garrisons of the local fortresses (usually nearly their total strength – just two sick men were left in Faba when its Templar garrison rode to destruction at Cresson in 1187), so the defeat of a field army could mean the almost inevitable loss of several castles.

It was therefore preferable to defeat the enemy by strategy rather than battle, as in Count Roger of Antioch's campaign of 1115, Baldwin IV's campaign of 1182, and the bailli Guy de Lusignan's Jezreel campaign of 1183; Guy, now king, was attempting to pursue this same policy in 1187 before he succumbed to the ill advice of Gerard de Ridefort and led his army to destruction at Hattin. (Hattin is, in fact, a classic example of the dangers of drawing on fortress garrisons to make up a field army. Most of the kingdom's castles and walled towns had been denuded of their defenders for the campaign, and the destruction of the Frankish army resulted in most of the kingdom falling into Muslim hands within the next two months.)

Saracen strategy was therefore obvious – to defeat the Frankish field army, then reduce their thinly defended castles and fortified towns. The disadvantages, however, were that bringing the Franks to battle and reducing their forts could be time-consuming, and if Muslim armies had one major shortcoming it was their inability to remain in the field for prolonged periods. They tended to disperse of their own accord if disaffected (as was often the case) or unable to achieve military success, particularly at the onset of winter, the approach of cold, wet weather usually resulting in the dispersal of Muslim armies. The Franks, therefore, had to try and outlast the Muslims in the field, thus forestalling any chance of military success and by their very presence hastening the dispersal of the Muslim army.

Tactics

Though the tactics of the Franks in a set-piece battle in Outremer were similar to those employed at home in Europe, with the army divided into three or more divisions in line, echelon or column, as described in *'Armies of Feudal Europe'*, climaxing in the delivery of the knights' decisive close-order charge that Anna Comnena says could 'make a hole through the walls of Babylon', such tactics could only be employed successfully against an enemy who would stand and take its full impact.

And alas, in this the majority of Muslim armies of this era – being largely of Turkish composition – did not oblige. Nevertheless under favourable circumstances Frankish knights could manoeuvre the enemy into a situation in which it was impossible to evade the charge (as at Arsuf in 1191), and on occasion even the Turks might decide of their own volition to stand up to it, despite the fact that man for man they were no match for the well-armoured Franks in close combat.

Usually the Turks preferred to make the best possible use of their principal advantages over the Franks – their archery and their mobility – avoiding direct contact with the Frankish cavalry whenever possible. Horse-archers, of course, were the backbone of all Turkish armies, in Syria just as much as in Central Asia, and the Frankish chronicles of this era are full of references to the effects of their archery, describing their showers of arrows which fell 'as though rain was falling from the sky.' 'When the first rank had quite emptied their quivers and shot all their arrows,' writes William of Tyre of the Battle of Dorylaeum, 'the second, in which there were still more horsemen, came on and began to shoot more densely than one could believe. The Turkish squadrons at once flung themselves upon our army, and loosed such a quantity of arrows that you would have thought hail was falling from the air; hardly had the first cloud of them fallen, describing an arc, than it was followed by a second, no less dense.' Fulcher of Chartres, describing the Battle of Marj es-Safar in 1126, wrote that 'no part or limb seemed safe against the shafts, so thickly did they fly.' Such a high rate of fire could be maintained, in fact, that Ambroise, another eyewitness of the Third Crusade, reported of King Richard's advance to Arsuf in 1191 that there was not as much as four feet of ground to be found that was entirely free of spent arrows.[7] One of the Frankish dead at Ager Sanguinus in 1119 had as many as 40 arrows in him, the 12th-century Damascene historian Ibn al-Qalanisi reporting of the same battle that there were 'dead horses bristling like hedgehogs with the arrows sticking out of them,' and more than a century

---

[7] To maintain such withering rates of fire it was obviously necessary to ensure that sufficient ammunition was available. Each Turkish horseman carried at least one and often 2 or 3 quivers, each capable of containing up to 60 arrows; other arrows could be carried in the bowcase, stuffed into boots or belt, and so on. Little information is available regarding replenishing empty quivers on the battlefield, but at Hattin Saladin apparently had 70 camels laden with arrows, as well as 400 loads of spare ammunition for them, and such arrangements probably ensured the availability of an adequate supply of arrows on many other occasions too.

later, at El Mansurah, Jean de Joinville thought himself and his horse fortunate to have been wounded by arrows only 5 and 15 times respectively.

At the same time, however, the effectiveness of Turkish archery should not be overestimated; during the whole 4½ month siege of Tyre in 1111 the Franks lost only 2,000 men according to al-Qalanisi, despite the fact that he reports the Muslim garrison (which was, admittedly, far from exclusively Turkish in composition) to have discharged 20,000 arrows in one day's fighting alone! And it should also be borne in mind that Turkish arrows were relatively light and could strike – and perhaps penetrate – armour, even simple quilted armour, without actually wounding the wearer; at Arsuf, for example, Frankish infantry are recorded by Beha ed-Din marching along unconcernedly with up to 10 arrows stuck in their armour, though the cause for this was often that the arrows were too light and shot at too great a range. Several sources refer to the 'astonishing' range from which Turks sometimes opened fire, and later tests reported by Sir Ralph Payne-Gallwey record Turkish bows being able to fire up to 480 yards – though at anything much over 100 yards its penetrative value was much reduced. The sources imply that at closer range their arrows became far more effective. Anna Comnena, for instance, records that they could pass clean through an unarmoured man.

Inevitably such archery was particularly effective against unarmoured horses, and the Turks were well aware of the important role of horses in Frankish warfare. Writing of Hattin, Abu Shamah (who wrote in the 13th century) observed how 'the Frankish knight, so long as his horse is safe and sound, cannot be felled. Clothed from head to foot with a mail coat that makes him resemble a block of iron, he is not affected by repeated blows, but as soon as the horse is killed the knight is thrown down and captured. Although they numbered in thousands, there were no horses nor mounts in the booty ... It was necessary that his mount fall ... for the knight to lose his saddle.' It was possibly for this reason that on rare occasions we find knights actually dismounting to fight. Bohemond's knights may have been ordered to dismount at Dorylaeum as early as 1097, and certainly the charge of Emperor Conrad's German crusaders before Damascus in 1148 was launched on foot. Ambroise even records an instance in 1191 of a Templar foraging party, surprised by 400 Turkish cavalry, dismounting and fighting back-to-back. Turks too are occasionally to be found dismounting to fight, incidentally, as at Arsuf where the Itinerarium records some 'who had of set purpose dismounted so as to aim their darts and arrows better'.

It was in order to protect the knights' horses until the moment of the charge that Frankish infantry usually preceded their cavalry, defending the knights 'like a wall' as Beha puts it; Imad-ed-Din, who was Saladin's secretary, uses a similar expression, describing Frankish infantry as 'a wall of arms'. At Jaffa in 1192 Richard formed up his infantry with spearmen in the first rank, shields to the front and spear-butts braced against the ground, with two crossbow-armed men behind each of them (one loading, one firing), a veritable 'wall of arms' indeed, one with which on that occasion the Turks declined to close. Louis IX's infantry employed much the same formation whilst holding the beachhead at Damietta in 1249, but in both situations the Franks were undeniably on the defensive. More usually they seem to have formed up in line in relatively close order probably several ranks deep, those armed with bows and crossbows (constituting a large percentage of Frankish infantry) usually to the fore so that they could return the fire of the Turks, who soon learnt a healthy respect for the crossbow in particular. Indeed, the presence of crossbow-armed infantry in Frankish armies may have been the principal reason why Turkish horse-archers often opened fire at such long range that their arrows had little real hope of penetrating armour.

William of Tyre, in his account of Marj es-Safar in 1126, in fact credits Frankish infantry – presumably archers – with the same tactic as the Turks in that they 'turned their attention to wounding the horses of their adversaries and thus rendered the riders easy victims to the Christians [i.e. the knights] who were following.' In the same account he also gives a good description of the role of infantry in close combat, relating how 'they instantly despatched with the sword any wounded or fallen infidel whom they chanced to find and thus prevented all possibility of escape. They lifted up those [of their own cavalry] who had been thrown down and restored them to the fray. They sent the wounded back to the baggage train to receive care.' At the same battle we also have one of the few references to Turkish infantry in action, Fulcher of Chartres describing Damascene infantry trained 'to spring up armed behind the horsemen, who when the enemy drew near descended and fought on foot; for so they hoped to disorder the Franks by attacking them with infantry on the one side and cavalry on the other.'

In addition to their archery the Turks had a second major tactical advantage over the Franks in their mobility, which enabled them to evade the Frankish charge and successfully employ hit-and-run skirmishing tactics. But above all it enabled them to attack the Franks on the march, showering their columns with arrows, suddenly closing and as suddenly falling back, and harassing in every way the army's advance. Attacked thus the Franks had no real option but to press doggedly on, relying on their solidity of array to deter the Turks, keeping together so closely that 'if an apple had been thrown amongst them, it would not have fallen to the ground without it touching a man or a horse.' The infantry, whose iron discipline is demonstrated at its best in such running fights, marched on the outside of the column or on the flank nearest to the enemy, those in the rear (against which most attacks were directed) often having to march backwards in order to beat off the repeated Turkish attacks, the cavalry conforming their own pace to that of the infantry 'that the ranks might not be broken and the enemy given a chance to break in upon the formation'. Often, in fact, the infantry even carried their own dead on camels and packhorses as they marched, so as to conceal the number of casualties from the enemy.

As mentioned, the Turks concentrated on the rearguard when attacking a Frankish column, in the hope that it would be slowed down sufficiently to cause a gap between it and the main body, which could then be exploited (as happened at Mount Cadmos in 1148 and nearly happened at Hattin in 1187). Heavy attacks were also often made on the vanguard in the hope that the whole column might thus be halted. In addition they would often sling their bows behind their shoulders and make short, controlled charges in the hope that, in the words of Abu Shamah, the Franks would be 'carried away by blind fury' and 'would attack us and in this way would give us the opportunity to divide and break their mass'. Concentrated archery could likewise goad Frankish knights into an impetuous counter-attack, as it did at Arsuf in 1191. The Franks, however, learnt in turn to try and control their counter-attacks, the knights only charging out to drive the enemy away to a safe distance if he pressed too close, then rallying and falling back to the main column, a tactic which the author of the Itinerarium likens to beating off a fly 'which, though you may drive it off, will return directly you cease your efforts'! Odo of Deuil, a participant in Louis VII's crusade, gives a good description of the organisation of a Frankish column on the march which includes all these points: 'Because the Turks were quick to flee our men were commanded to endure, until they received an order, the attacks of their enemies; and to withdraw forthwith when recalled ... When they had learned this, they were also taught the order of march so that a person in front would not rush to the rear and the guards on the flanks would not fall into disorder. Moreover those whom nature or fortune have made foot-soldiers ... were drawn up at the rear in order to oppose with their bows the enemy's arrows.' In fact severe penalties awaited any man who broke ranks. Examples of battles fought on the march include Hab (1119), Mount Cadmos (1148), Hattin (1187) and Arsuf (1191). The column formation could also be used to retire off a battlefield in good order, as at al-Babein in 1167.

Because of their military prowess the contingents of the Military Orders usually held the dangerous stations of vanguard and rearguard on the march, being the best disciplined troops available to the Franks; Jacques de Vitry relates how they fought 'not rashly or disorderly but wisely and with all caution[8], being the first to attack and the last to retreat. They were not

---

[8] In fact in reality knights of the Military Orders could be just as willful and headstrong as their secular counterparts, if not more so; witness, for example, the actions of the Templars at Marj Ayyun in 1179 and Cresson in 1187 and of the Hospitallers at Arsuf. But, it should be noted, in all but the last of these instances they were following the orders of their Grand Masters, while the Hospitallers at Arsuf were following the example of their Marshal.

allowed to turn their backs and flee, nor to retreat without orders.' One cartulary of the 13th century states that it was indeed customary for the Orders to hold the vanguard and rearguard positions, and certainly the practice was common enough for the Mamluk Sultan Baibars to march out on one occasion with captured Hospitaller and Templar banners in the van in order to fool the Franks. Examples of the practice to be found in contemporary sources include Templars holding the van at Mount Cadmos and, with the Hospitallers, the rear at Hattin and in the retreat from El Mansurah; Hospitallers the rear and Templars the van at Arsuf and in Galilee in 1204; and Hospitallers and Teutonic Knights the van at Caroublier in 1266. This custom may also be implied in de Vitry's words about the brethren 'being the first to attack and the last to retreat.'

The other principal use to which the Turks put their mobility was in feigning flight, still a characteristic Turkish tactic. The feigned flight could assume one of three different forms: either a steady retreat lasting several days, designed to weary the enemy and draw him away from his bases; as bait for a pre-arranged ambush; or as deliberate provocation in the hope that the enemy would throw caution to the wind and charge in pursuit, thus disrupting his formation. As early as 1096 the Byzantine Emperor Alexius I cautioned the princes leading the First Crusade 'not to pursue the enemy too far if God gave them the victory, lest falling into traps set by the Turkish leaders they should be massacred'. Examples of the feigned flight in practice include Barran (1104), Sennabra (1113), Harim (1164), al-Babein (1167) and Gaza (1239). The Franks too seem to have occasionally employed this ruse, Tancred apparently feigning flight at Artah in 1105, while William of Tyre describes in detail how Baldwin II successfully employed this tactic against the Fatimids at Ascalon in 1125 in conjunction with a concealed ambush, despatching a decoy body of light- armed horsemen to lure the Muslims into his trap.

These 'light-armed horsemen' may have been Turcopoles, sometimes used in a light cavalry role by the Franks. At least, they seem to have often preceded the knights; at Sarmin in 1115, for example, and at Ager Sanguinus in 1119, we find them in advance of the knights, on the former occasion at least fighting as horse-archers, but in both instances they appear to have been pushed onto the knights behind them. Even the Livre au Roi, a legislative compilation of c.1197-1205, seems to imply that they were customarily placed in front of the knights, stating that the Constable's double-strength troop held the first place in battle *after* the Turcopoles, with the Marshal's troop and then the king's behind him. Another occasion on which they are recorded being employed as horse-archers in a skirmishing role takes place during the Third Crusade, when King Richard 'sent his archers forward in the van with the Turcopoles and crossbowmen, to skirmish with the Turks and strive to press them till he could arrive.' Undoubtedly there are other unrecorded occasions too on which the Turcopoles fought as horse-archers, but this aspect should not be overemphasised, the infrequency with which it does occur in the sources tending to suggest that they were not particularly effective in this role; though he does not record how they fought, William of Tyre writes of the Turcopoles at al-Babein in 1167 that they were 'for the most part, useless' – probably as a result of Frankish misuse rather than military incompetence. It is quite probable that instead they often fought alongside the Frankish knights and sergeants. They are also occasionally recorded in a reconnaissance role, as, for example, in the Rule of the Order of the Temple.

Though so far only Turkish tactics have been described, it should not be assumed that all Muslim armies fought in the same way, using horse-archers, skirmishing tactics and the feigned flight. The Arabs of Fatimid Egypt employed none of these, though small numbers of allied or mercenary Turkish horse-archers very occasionally appear in their armies (as at Third Ramla in 1105). Instead they fought with sword, mace and couched lance very much like the Franks, Usamah (himself a Syrian rather than Egyptian Arab) describing in detail how the lance should be held to best effect in the charge, held by the rider 'as tightly as possible with his hand and under his arm, close to his side, and [he] should let his horse run and effect the required thrust.' Their archers were infantry rather than horsemen, supplied mainly by Sudanese ghulams; like the archers of the Franks, these usually preceded the cavalry in battle. Earlier sources record that they were expert marksmen.

Ibn Khaldun, a 14th-century author, states that the Fatimids employed two principal formations in battle, these being the Persian tactic of advancing in line in organised divisions, and the Bedouin or Berber tactic of attacking in small, disorganised groups, and he observes that the Persian method was the more sure of victory in being well-organised and 'as impregnable as a continuous stone wall or a strongly constructed fort'. As already mentioned, archers formed the first rank, with spearmen in the second and cavalry in the third, elite units usually forming the centre, where the army's main standards flew; the density of the formation depended on the strength of the enemy. Sometimes numerical superiority permitted an outflanking movement, and Bedouins are often encountered in this role.

For a set-piece battle the Ayyubids and Mamluks used a very similar formation, but usually without the infantry. They drew up in three divisions, consisting of centre, left and right, still with the elite units and standards in the centre (usually the al-Halqa and/or Royal Mamluks, with the amirs' contingents on the flanks). The Mamluks in addition placed auxiliaries on the extreme wings, usually Bedouins on one wing and Turcomans on the other. In battle it was not uncommon for one wing or both to give way, victors and vanquished dashing from the field in pursuit or rout and leaving the centre to resolve the battle (this occurred at Acre in 1189 and at Homs in 1281, for example). Skirmishers, either Turcomans or the best marksmen, usually preceded the main body of cavalry, Imad describing how at Hattin Saladin 'picked out the advance guard of archers' from each company, while at Arsuf the Frankish sources record light cavalry 'coming down at us in full charge and hurling darts and arrows as fast as they could' while the 'well-ordered phalanxes of the Turks with ensigns fixed on their lances' were drawn up beyond them. The Mamluks usually carried a lance in the charge, apparently having a preference for hand weapons despite the fact that they continued to carry bows in addition and were trained to act as either horse-archers or lancers as need dictated. Infantry still sometimes preceded the cavalry, but under the Mamluks they were extremely uncommon except in sieges and the Mamluks themselves rarely, if ever, fought on foot. (As early as 1192 the Itinerarium records the following alleged debate between some of Saladin's mamluks and Kurdish soldiers: 'The Kurds said, "You mamluks will have to go on foot to seize the king and his people, while we keep watch on horseback to cut off their flight towards the camp." But the mamluks answered, "It is rather your business to go on foot, for we are nobler than you. We are content with that kind of warfare which rightly belongs to us. This foot service is your concern.")

THE BYZANTINES

'When Emperor Manuel took over the Imperial office, he became concerned as to how the Romans [i.e. the Byzantines] might improve their armament for the future. It had previously been customary for them to be armed with round shields and for the most part to carry quivers and decide battles by bows.' Such are the words of the chronicler Cinnamus in the 12th century. Indeed, the bow had always been, and even after Manuel's reforms would continue to be, a principal factor in Byzantine tactics, both in the hands of native troops and – more especially – in the hands of their Asiatic mercenaries. Byzantine appreciation of the bow as a major weapon dated back many centuries, even as far back as the days of the Roman Empire, and constant conflict with armies composed chiefly of swarms of light horse-archers over the following centuries had repeatedly served to confirm its importance in warfare. Horse-archers in particular therefore played an important role in Byzantine tactics now as earlier, and throughout the course of the Crusade era large contingents of horse-archers appear in every Byzantine army that is recorded, principally supplied by auxiliaries of Turkish extraction[9] (Uzes, Seljuks, Pechenegs, Bulgars, Hungarians, Cumans, even Mongols, also Alans and Georgians) but also, until the third quarter of the 12th century, including natives.

Their main role on the battlefield was as skirmishers, in which capacity we often find them utilising their traditional Turkish tactics of harassment, feigned flight and ambush. And like the Turks, the Byzantines too soon came to appreciate the importance of the horse in Frankish tactics, concentrating their fire on the knights' mounts; the Alexiad of Anna Comnena records how in 1083 Alexius I ordered his troops (apparently cavalry, but possibly foot-soldiers) 'to drive hard on the heels of [the Franks] ... but not to fight at close-quarters; they were to shoot great numbers of arrows from a distance and at the horses rather than the riders. Catching up with the Kelts [i.e. the Franks], therefore, they rained down arrows on their mounts and thus completely upset the riders.' Even in the 13th century, at Pelagonia, the Byzantines' Turkish auxiliaries were ordered to shoot down the Frankish horses, a contemporary recording how they 'slaughtered their steeds and won the battle'!

Against Turkish armies such tactics inevitably met with less success, the Turks in turn frequently concentrating their own fire on the horses of their Byzantine adversaries; Nicephoros Bryennius, in his Commentarii, describes how at Manzikert in 1071 one of Alp Arslan's commanders 'ordered his men to surround the Byzantines and discharge a rain of arrows against them from all sides. The Byzantines, seeing their horses struck by arrows, were forced to pursue the Turks ... but they suffered heavily when they fell into ambushes and traps.' And of an earlier campaign Attaliates records how Pecheneg horse-archers 'panicked the horses of their adversaries by the wounds that they inflicted and forced the Byzantines to flee ignominiously.' It was in the hope of reducing the effects of such tactics that Alexius introduced a new formation, the *Parataxis*, unsuccessfully described in the Alexiad as having its ranks 'so organised that the Turks would have to shoot from their right at the Roman left, which was protected by the shield; the Romans, on the contrary, would shoot left-handed at the Turkish exposed right'; perhaps a line angled away from the Turkish formation is intended, but it is unfortunately impossible to be sure. This seems to have been a close-order column such as has already been described being used by the Franks. It is therefore debateable whether the Franks adopted it from the Byzantines or

---

[9] Surprisingly such Turkish auxiliaries were usually extremely reliable – the Pechenegs at Manzikert, for example, remained loyal even in adversity, and we often encounter Cumans in Byzantine service fighting against 'barbarian' Cumans. Needless to say, however, desertions are also recorded.

vice versa, since Anna Comnena describes her father Emperor Alexius advising the Franks 'how to draw up a battle-line, how to lay ambushes' and 'not to pursue far when the enemy ran away in flight'). This formation was called the *Parataxis* by the Greeks, and comprised a hollow square enclosing the army's baggage in its centre with infantry on the outside and cavalry in between. The Alexiad has left us with a good description of such a column, as employed in the Philomelion campaign of 1116, describing how the Byzantines 'marched in a disciplined way, keeping in step to the sound of the flute ... In fact the serried ranks of close-locked shields and marching men gave the impression of immovable mountains; and when they changed direction the whole body moved like one huge beast, animated and directed by one single mind ... The return journey was made slowly and at an ant's pace, so to speak, with the captives, women and children, and all the booty in the centre of the column.' (It is also interesting to note that the Turks' reaction to this formation was the same as if it had been a Frankish column, concentrating their attacks on the rearguard and vanguard and skirmishing along the flanks.)

However, the typical Byzantine battle array remained a series of successive lines, sometimes as many as four but more usually two or perhaps three. The first line was frequently composed of the weaker or least reliable contingents, presumably in the hope that they would successfully disorganise the enemy while at the same time absorbing the impact of his initial charge (particularly important when fighting Franks, whose first charge was recognised by the Byzantines as potentially 'irresistible'). The second line had the task of reinforcing the first if necessary and of frustrating enemy attempts at outflanking, thereby protecting the first line's rear. Skirmishers (i.e. horse-archers) usually preceded the army and/or were positioned on the flanks (detachments sometimes being concealed far out on one or other flank, as at Kalaura in 1078), but they can also be found forming the second, third or even the fourth line; at Durazzo in 1081, for instance, we find the Vardariots (a regiment of Turks) forming the second line, behind the Varangians, the commander of the latter being instructed 'to open his ranks quickly for them (by moving to left and right) whenever they wanted to charge out against the Kelts; and to close ranks again and march in close order when they had withdrawn.' Skirmishers operating in advance of the main army generally withdrew thus when threatened, though usually they took refuge behind lance-armed cavalry rather than infantry; alternatively they sometimes scattered to left and right in the face of an enemy charge, encircling his flanks in the process. The lancers themselves advanced in close order, apparently charging with the lance couched (though it was seemingly only under the Emperor Manuel that Byzantine cavalry first 'excelled the mettle of Frenchmen and Italians' in this form of combat – not that this stopped a 13th-century Frank describing a single Frankish knight as worth 20 Byzantines!).

Otherwise formations and tactics appear to have differed little from those described in *'Armies of the Dark Ages'*, the role of the infantry having changed only in becoming perhaps even more secondary.

THE MONGOLS

The tactics of the Mongols (or 'Tartars' as mediaeval Frankish authors called them) were similar to those of the Turks, having their origin in the same steppe traditions. Like the Turks they relied primarily on their mobility and the use of the bow, many sources testifying to their skill in archery – Frederick II described them as 'incomparable archers', while Marco Polo says that they were 'the best that are known in the world'.

As with the Turks, their mobility demonstrated itself best in the feigned flight. 'When they are pursued and take to flight' says Polo, 'they fight as well and as effectively as when they are face to face with the enemy. When they are fleeing at top speed, they twist round with their bows and shoot their arrows so effectively that they kill the enemy's horses and their riders too. [And] When the enemy thinks that he has routed and crushed them, then he is lost ... [for] as soon as the Tartars decide that they have killed enough of the pursuing horses and horsemen they wheel round and attack.' The Armenian historian Haithon, who wrote c.1307, likewise cautions that 'it is very dangerous to give chase, for as they flee they shoot back over their heads and do much execution upon their pursuers.' The flight was also used as bait for an ambush.

They drew up on the battlefield with units of 100 (i.e. Jaguns) separated from each other by intervals. Each unit drew up in five ranks in close order, Haithon recording how they kept 'very close ranks, so that you would not take them for half their real numbers.' In theory the front two ranks wore armour (and were presumably mounted on armoured horses when available) while the latter three wore no armour. The light cavalry of the rear three ranks advanced through the intervals one rank at a time and poured a hail of arrows and javelins into the enemy while at the same time either one or both Mongol flanks would commence an enveloping manoeuvre. If the light cavalry were repulsed then they would fall back (firing all the while) and the fourth rank, then the fifth, would come forward in turn and carry on where the others had left off; but if they were successful in disorganising the enemy then they would withdraw through the intervals and the heavy cavalry of the first two ranks would lead a frontal assault.[10] By this time, whether the

---

[10] The carnage wrought when two Mongol armies fought against each other using these tactics can be imagined. 'Now you can see arrows flying like pelting rain, for the sky was full of them,' writes Polo, 'and you could see horsemen and horses tumbling dead upon the ground.'

skirmishing tactics had been successful or not, the envelopment of the enemy flanks was usually complete too, and a feigned flight might be used to draw an incautious enemy deeper within the encircling wings (Carpini probably had this in mind when he wrote that the light cavalry fired only three or four arrows, and then feigned flight if their archery was ineffective. Polo, however, speaks of the archers emptying their quivers). Victory was always followed up by a tireless pursuit.

The envelopment movement was often concealed from the enemy by hills, dust clouds, darkness, etc. Carpini records that the enveloping troops usually comprised the Mongols themselves, auxiliary troops generally forming a screen in advance of the centre of their main line of battle. Matthew Paris similarly records the auxiliaries' role in battle, relating how the Mongols compelled them, 'reduced to the lowest condition of slavery, to fight in the foremost ranks against their own neighbours.' However, the more reliable of them (principally the Georgians and Cilician Armenians) are often to be found forming one or both flanks of the main body alongside the Mongols. As well as the screen of auxiliaries the main body was also preceded by Mongol skirmishers, called the Mangudai or 'God-belonging' (which says something for their chances of survival!).

Very occasionally some Mongols might be found fighting on foot, usually if their horses were in poor condition or if they felt that circumstances or the nature of the ground were unsuitable for mounted combat. At Wadi al-Khazindar (Salamiyet) in 1299 some 10,000 Mongols stood behind their horses and poured volleys of arrows into the charging Mamluks, so that when those who had remained mounted counter-charged the Mamluk line of battle was in considerable disorder. Haithon states that the Mongols were slow when on foot.

In addition to their standard Asiatic tactics the Mongols also had a formidable arsenal of assorted tricks and deceptions that could best be classified as psychological warfare. These included tying branches to the tails of their horses and raising great clouds of dust in their wake to deceive the enemy into thinking that Mongol reinforcements were arriving, and even mounting their women – in addition to stuffed dummies – on spare horses to give the impression of a huge reserve force, as they did in Khwarizmia in 1221 (the Mongols customarily maintaining a reserve whenever possible). Another such stratagem was to put stories around which deliberately inflated the actual size of their army; for example Mongke Khan, invading part of the Sung Empire in 1258, spread rumours that he led an army of 100,000 men, when in fact he had only 40,000. Leaving mountains of skulls heaped here and there in the course of their conquests, as a warning to others, also falls into the 'psychological warfare' category.

Franks against Mongols

This is based on the advice of a shrewd observer, Friar John de Plano Carpini, to the rulers of the West, contained in a report written after a long sojourn amongst the Mongols in the mid-13th century.

To start with he stresses the importance of good quality arms and equipment, particularly recommending good strong bows and crossbows, which he says the Mongols particularly feared, the arrows for these to be manufactured Mongol-fashion so that they are sharp enough to pierce their strongest armour. He also especially recommends long-handled axes, plus lances with a hook below the head for dragging the Mongols from their saddles, 'for they fall off very easily'; but he cautions against ignoring dismounted Mongols, since they shoot as accurately and rapidly on foot as on horseback (witness Vochan in 1272 and Salamiyet in 1299).

Armour should consist of double-mail, which arrows from Mongol bows could not easily pierce, plus a helmet and any other available armour. Where possible horses too should be protected against the Mongol arrows. Unarmoured or less-heavily equipped men are advised to follow the Mongol practice of forming the hind ranks and should shoot overhead. But nowhere is Plano Carpini's respect of Mongol military skill more apparent than in his recommendations for organisation, what follows being no more than imitation with units of 1,000, 100 and 10 'organised in the same manner as the Tartar army.'

The battlefield needed to be carefully chosen, preferably a level plain where everything was clearly visible on all sides; if a site could be found where flanks or rear could be protected by a forest or similar all the better. The tactics then given are again emulation of the Mongols. He advises that the army should draw up in several lines, positioned not too far apart, only the first of which should be sent forward to meet the approaching Mongols. If the Mongols feigned flight they were only to be pursued with caution since an ambush would undoubtedly have been prepared beforehand. Another reason for caution was the need to avoid tiring the horses, since Frankish armies did not maintain the large numbers of remounts available to the Mongols. The second line should meanwhile stand by to help the first if needed.

Following advice on constant vigilance, maintenance of the army over a prolonged period, and the advantages of a 'scorched earth' policy (since Mongol armies existed by foraging), Carpini's last recommendation is that the infidelity of the Mongols' auxiliary 'allies' should be exploited, since 'if the opportunity should arise and they could count on our men not to kill them, they would fight against the Tartars, and would do them greater harm even than would those who are their enemies.'

MAJOR BATTLES OF THE PERIOD

MANZIKERT 1071

Taking advantage of a Seljuk attack against Fatimid-held Damascus and Egypt, the Byzantine Emperor Romanus IV prepared an offensive against recently lost Byzantine territories in their rear. He assembled a huge but ill-trained and ill-disciplined army of 200-600,000 men including most of the Western and all of the Eastern Themata, Varangian Guards and the Tagmata, as well as Russians, Uzes, Khazars, Alans, Georgians, Cumans, Pechenegs, Bulgars, Crimean Goths, Armenians and Franks (mainly Normans and Germans). Of the total, however, the largest percentage were engineers, servants and attendants for the vast baggage-train.

Alp Arslan, the Seljuk Sultan, learning of the Byzantine advance into Armenia as he was encamped before Aleppo, ordered an immediate withdrawal from Syria. On reaching Mosul he received news from Seljuk refugees that a detachment of Romanus' army, a large force of Frankish and Turkish mercenaries under Roussel de Bailleul, was laying waste the region round Manzikert and Akhlat, and he now set out northwards to intercept them, sending Soundaq the Turk ahead with a force of about 5,000 cavalry to reinforce Akhlat. Alp Arslan himself was at first accompanied by only his 4,000 personal mamluks since his scattered army had not reassembled, but he issued orders for troops to join him on the march and in addition hired some 10,000 local Kurdish tribesmen.

Romanus, by now forewarned of the Sultan's approach, despatched 20,000 Cuman or Russian heavy cavalry under Joseph Tarchaniotes to assist Roussel's Franks and Turks approaching Akhlat, while the rest of the army took Manzikert. Soon after, on 16 August, Soundaq arrived on the scene and a fierce skirmish ensued between the Seljuks and two bodies of Byzantine troops under Nicephoros Bryennius and Basilakes; weight of numbers eventually forced the Seljuks back but the Byzantines, incautiously pursuing them, suffered heavy losses when they rallied, Basilakes being captured and Bryennius wounded. At about the same time Roussel and Tarchaniotes, also having suffered heavy losses, and receiving news that Alp Arslan himself was now close by, withdrew to Melitene.

On hearing of the defeat of his foremost units Romanus marshalled the main army and marched out for battle, but by this time the Seljuks had melted away and were nowhere to be seen. The army therefore returned to camp and an anxious night was spent under the watchful eyes of the Seljuks, who had set up their own camp three miles away.

Romanus must have been aware by now that Alp Arslan himself had arrived with the main Seljuk army, but he was probably equally aware that this army was numerically inferior to his own – the lowest total given in the sources is 12,000; Ibn al-Athir says 15,000, but the higher figures of 30-40,000 seem more probable. However, Romanus' own army was not as large as it had been at the outset of the campaign, and probably numbered only about 100,000 men of whom many were non-combatants.

Next morning Alp Arslan made an offer of peace, which was contemptuously rejected – since it would be financially impossible for the Empire to raise a similar army again for some time to come Romanus had little choice but to force a decisive solution there and then. In addition it was likely that Alp Arslan's proposal was only intended as a delaying tactic while more troops could be gathered. Therefore, ignoring the advice of his generals, Romanus decided to commit the army to battle on 19 August.

On the day of battle the Byzantines formed up in their customary two lines, with Tagmata in the centre and Thematic troops and Turkish auxiliaries on both flanks of the first line. The reserve line, composed of Archontes, the Hetaeria and German and Norman mercenaries, was put under the command of a certain Andronikos Ducas, a nephew of the previous Emperor and therefore no friend of Romanus; this factor was going to prove decisive. Roussel and Tarchaniotes, meanwhile, had not returned.

The Byzantine advance across the plain of Manzikert towards Alp Arslan's camp met with little resistance except for skirmishes on the extreme flanks, which lacked any kind of security in the open. The bulk of the Seljuk army, however, steadily withdrew before them, drawing them on until late in the day they reached the Sultan's campsite, only to find it abandoned. Romanus, possibly fearing an ambush, therefore resolved to return to his own undefended camp and gave the order to retire, turning the Imperial standard towards the rear. The order, however, was misunderstood and gaps appeared between centre and flanks as units turned this way and that in confusion. Simultaneously, Andronikos Ducas treacherously put about a rumour that Romanus had been killed and, as chaos reigned in the Byzantine ranks, Alp Arslan charged down on them with 10,000 fresh Seljuk cavalry.

A rout ensued, the Byzantines believing themselves betrayed by either their Armenian or Turkish auxiliaries (though the latter in fact remained loyal to the end). The Byzantine right and left wings were swept away, while Andronikos, who might have still saved the day, calmly marched from the field with the desperately needed reserve line. Only the centre under Romanus stood and fought on, until the Emperor was recognised amidst his Varangian Guards and captured by a Seljuk mamluk. After suffering an unknown number of casualties the remainder of the army then broke, pursuit of its scattered units continuing through the night.

The subsequent Seljuk conquest of the Anatolian heartland of the Empire had two important results: it led ultimately to the foundation of a new Seljuk state, aptly called the Sultanate of Rum – literally the Sultanate of Roman Lands; and, even more importantly, it was responsible for the Crusade movement, for in Western European eyes the Byzantines had, in Sir Steven Runciman's words, 'forfeited on the battlefield their title as protectors of Christendom. Manzikert justified the intervention of the West.'

KALAURA 1078

In command of an Imperial army, the future Byzantine Emperor Alexius I Comnenus faced the rebel Dux of Dyrrachium, Nicephoros Bryennius, at Kalaura in Thrace.

When Bryennius drew up his army he placed a detachment of Pecheneg light cavalry about a quarter of a mile away on his left flank with orders to attack Alexius' forces in the rear and generally harass them while the main army advanced shield to shield. Alexius likewise threw out a detached flank unit, concealing it in ravines on his left with orders to fall on the rebel rear as soon as Bryennius had advanced past their position. The bulk of his army, which was inferior to that of Bryennius, consisted of the newly raised Immortals and Chomatenoi and a few Frankish and Seljuk mercenaries.

His attack on the rebel rear and right flank met with only initial success and was soon repulsed, while in the centre the Frankish mercenaries deserted to Bryennius and the Immortals began to give way. Almost simultaneously the Seljuks and Chomatenoi on Alexius' right flank were routed by the Pecheneg detachment. Fortunately, however, Alexius himself managed to capture Bryennius' spare horse, managing to rally many of his troops by spreading a rumour that Bryennius himself had been taken.

Even so, the battle was still very much in Bryennius' favour – despite the fact that the Pechenegs, having satisfied themselves with loot taken in part at least from Bryennius' own camp, had now lost interest in the fighting and were heading for home.

At this point Alexius was joined by a fresh body of Seljuk reinforcements, and with a detachment of these and a rallied portion of his own army he counter-attacked, then feigned flight and drew the overconfident rebels back to where two other bodies of Seljuks had been placed in ambush. Disorganised in pursuit and attacked from both sides the rebel army was routed, Bryennius himself being captured by the Seljuks.

DURAZZO 1081

A Byzantine army of 70,000 men under the Emperor Alexius I attempted to relieve the coastal city of Dyrrachium (Durazzo), under siege by an Italo-Norman army of 15-18,000 men, including Italians, Saracens, Greeks and Balkan Slavs, under Robert Guiscard and his son Bohemond of Taranto. The Byzantine force included household troops, some Frankish mercenaries, Thessalian cavalry, Serbs under King Constantine Bodin, Macedonian Slavs, Vardariots and Varangians. Alexius divided his army in two, half to stand before the Norman camp and half to take a route through the coastal marshes and attack from the rear.

The Normans, seeing only the half to their front, abandoned their camp and formed up for battle, their right flank protected by the sea and their left by high ground. Alexius then arranged his forces in three lines, with the Varangian Guard and other Varangian units (some of them English) forming the vanguard, the Vardariot horse-archers behind them, and then the main body under Alexius.

The first Norman attack was launched by Italian cavalry under Amaury of Bari. These were repulsed by the Varangians, who in their enthusiasm then marched too far from the main body and were cut off by Bohemond's left wing wheeling against them. His crossbowmen and knights, the latter 800 strong, all but wiped them out, many of the survivors being burnt in the small church of St Michael where they had taken refuge.

The main Norman body then charged and smashed the Byzantine line. In the centre the Vardariots broke and fled and the Serbs deserted without joining battle. The remainder of the Byzantines were then put to flight and their camp captured. Wounded and alone, Alexius only just escaped the close Norman pursuit. A sortie from the city was also repulsed.

As few as 30 of the 1,300 Norman knights were killed, though Amaury's Italian division suffered considerable losses. The Byzantines lost 5-6,000, mostly Varangians. Dyrrachium surrendered to Robert four months later, in February 1082, after a three-day street fight following the admission of the Normans into the city by a Venetian traitor.

LEVUNIUM 1091

A combined force of Byzantines under Alexius I and 40,000 Cumans under Tugorkhan and Bonyak faced a superior Pecheneg army.

Despite distrust between the allies, the Pechenegs were routed by the Cuman and Byzantine cavalry and forced back against their own wagon laager which effectively blocked their line of retreat. Unable to escape, many were massacred together with their women and children within the laager. Large numbers of prisoners were taken, but these were slaughtered almost to a man during the night by their Byzantine guards through fear that either they might break loose or that the Cumans might release them. The Cumans, likewise distrusting the Byzantines, took to their heels under cover of darkness.

DORYLAEUM 1097

After the capture of Nicaea during the First Crusade the Franks divided their forces into two columns, the first of which was attacked soon after by a superior Seljuk force allegedly 150-350,000 strong under Sultan Kilij Arslan I, including Cappadocian and Danishmanid contingents under their amirs.

The Frankish commander, Prince Bohemond of Taranto, at first ordered his knights to dismount and assist the foot-soldiers and non-combatants in pitching camp, but before the task was completed it proved necessary for the knights to remount and ride out against the Turks, leaving the infantry to complete the preparation of the camp-site. However, the archery and mobility of the Turks, attacking from all sides, soon forced the Frankish cavalry to fall back beneath a hail of arrows, until knights, camp, foot-soldiers and pilgrims became one confused, tangled mass in which some knights were killed by the spears of their own infantry. But in fact crowding together thus actually saved them, for in such a tightly packed formation the Seljuks found it impossible to destroy them and could only attack indecisively.

Eventually, after about three hours of fighting, as Bohemond was beginning to despair of his situation, the second crusader column under Count Raymond de Saint-Gilles began to arrive on the field, surprising Kilij Arslan who had been under the impression that he had surrounded the entire Frankish army. As the Seljuks hesitated and faltered in their attack a further detachment from the relief division, under the Papal Legate Adhemar le Puy, appeared in their rear, and at this they panicked and fled, abandoning their own camp to the Franks.

The crusaders had suffered about 4,000 casualties, and the Turks allegedly as many as 30,000. The losses of the former were somewhat higher in horses than in men, most of whom were amongst the foot soldiers and non-combatants.

ANTIOCH 1098

The crusaders under Prince Bohemond, having just captured Antioch but being numerically unable to defend the walls, decided to march out into the open to face 12-28,000 (or according to some sources 150-400,000) Seljuks and Arabs, including 28 senior Turkish amirs, under Kerbogha of Mosul, who had arrived too late to relieve the Seljuk garrison (10,000 of whom had been massacred by the crusaders after the fall of the city).

The Franks left the city by a single gate in a column of four divisions, each of infantry and cavalry (the latter perhaps totalling only 1,050 men), the fourth composed mostly of dismounted knights acting as a reserve under Bohemond himself; other sources record the Franks to have been organised into between 6 and 13 divisions. Their plan was to secure their left flank on high ground about two miles from the city walls before advancing against the Turks, who were massed on their right flank. Kerbogha, watching them deploy, seems to have deliberately allowed their whole army to emerge from Antioch rather than launch a premature attack, presumably to ensure that his victory over them would be as complete as possible. However, he did despatch one body of 1,500 or 15,000 Turks to cut across the head of the Frankish column and get behind their line of battle before the leading division succeeded in securing the army's flank; these did considerable damage before, seeing the withdrawal of the main Seljuk army in the face of an attack in echelon by the Frankish divisions, and suffering at the hands of a detachment from the Frankish reserve, they broke and fled.

A sharp melee followed the advance of the Frankish divisions, with heavy losses being sustained by both sides, until the Turks, suffering as they were from dissension amongst their commanders (who resented Kerbogha), disillusioned by the desertion of a large contingent of Turcoman auxiliaries, and finding themselves unable to outflank their adversaries, began a retreat which steadily deteriorated into a rout.

The Frankish pursuit was only slightly hindered when the Seljuks fired the dry grass to cover their withdrawal, the crusader horses apparently trampling out the flames as they advanced. The Franks pursued the routed Turks as far as the Iron Bridge across the River Orontes, slaying great numbers of them, and in addition many more Turks were later killed by local Armenians and Syrian Christians. Kerbogha himself escaped to Mosul, his power and reputation ruined.

A sortie by the remnants of the Seljuk garrison of Antioch, still holed up in the citadel, was contained by an infantry holding force of 200 men under Count Raymond de Saint-Gilles. Seeing the defeat of Kerbogha, the commander of the garrison surrendered the citadel to Bohemond after the battle.

ASCALON 1099

A Fatimid counter-attack by 20,000 infantry and cavalry under the vizier al-Afdal, including Syrian Turkish auxiliaries, was defeated by 1,200-5,000 Frankish cavalry and 9-15,000 infantry under Godfrey de Bouillon. The Franks' nine divisions appear to have been formed up in line, with Raymond de Saint-Gilles on the right flank, Robert of Flanders, Robert of Normandy and Tancred in the centre, and Godfrey on the left; their infantry archers were stationed in the front rank, where they engaged the Fatimids' contingent of 3,000 Sudanese archers.

The battle was of very brief duration, the Egyptians having been caught completely unprepared. An attempt by Bedouin cavalry to encircle the Franks' left flank was beaten back and the Franks launched their charge into the bulk of the Egyptian army, closing with them so fast that the Sudanese archers succeeded in getting off only one volley before being driven back onto their cavalry, who fled almost immediately.

A fair number of Egyptians managed to reach the safety of Ascalon, others running into the sea and swimming out to their fleet moored offshore. In fact the regular cavalry escaped virtually intact, though the infantry and the militia levies and other irregulars lost some 10,000 men killed, drowned or crushed in the rout.

The Franks captured the Fatimid camp, including the standard and personal tent of al-Afdal. They gathered all the booty they could manage and burnt what they could not carry away.

FIRST BATTLE OF RAMLA 1101

A Fatimid army of allegedly 11,000 cavalry and 21,000 infantry under Sa'ad ad Daulah, marching on Jerusalem from Ascalon, was intercepted at Ramla by a Frankish force of 260 knights and 900 infantry under King Baldwin. The Franks drew up in five or six divisions, possibly in echelon, with Baldwin commanding a reserve. The Fatimid line outflanked them on both wings.

The ensuing battle was a confused affair. The first two Frankish cavalry divisions to make contact (against the Fatimid left) were repulsed and almost annihilated by the Muslims, but Baldwin's reserve then charged in and restored the line, Baldwin himself possibly killing Sa'ad ad-Daulah at this point. The Fatimid centre broke soon after. A body of 500 cavalry on their left wing, however, had outflanked Baldwin's line and fallen on the Frankish infantry assembled to the rear, badly mauling them before moving on against Jaffa. (These were defeated by Baldwin the next day as they returned from their sortie.)

Despite the confusion it was the Fatimid army that fled the field after only an hour's combat, and a promising Frankish pursuit was only ended by nightfall. The Muslims lost allegedly 5,000 men, the Franks 70-80 knights (probably the 2 routed divisions) and 'a much larger number of foot-soldiers'.

RAMLA AND JAFFA 1102

When news of a relatively small Fatimid raiding force of 700-1,000 men approaching Ramla was received by Baldwin in Jerusalem he gathered 200 knights and set out to attack them, his force including a number of the leaders of the Crusade of 1101 such as Stephen of Blois, Stephen of Burgundy and Conrad, the Constable of Emperor Henry IV. However, Baldwin had been misinformed of the strength of the Fatimid army, which, though it is improbable that it comprised the 20,000 Arab cavalry and 10,000 Sudanese infantry that contemporaries claim, was vastly superior to his own force. Even when he learnt of this Baldwin persisted in his attack, and in the battle that followed his small army, with no infantry support, was surrounded and virtually wiped out. Baldwin himself and five companions, keeping close together, attempted to hack their way out but only one man actually escaped with the king. A few others sought refuge in Ramla but were smoked out after two days and in a fierce fight most of these were killed, including Stephen of Blois and Stephen of Burgundy. Conrad was amongst those taken captive.

Escaping to Jaffa, Baldwin was joined by reinforcements of 170 knights and mounted sergeants from Jerusalem and Galilee plus a large force of English and German pilgrims. Shortly afterwards he marched out against the Fatimids for a second time, but now with a considerably larger army. The Fatimids again encircled the Franks, falling on the infantry each time the knights charged and thereby obliging the cavalry to fall back to defend them. However, the infantry held together and their showers of arrows coupled with the knights' repeated charges eventually broke the Muslims.

The Franks were too few in number to mount a pursuit, but they captured the Fatimids' camp and their herds of asses and camels. The Muslims lost about 3,000 men.

HARRAN 1104

To distract a Turkish attack against Edessa by Suqman ibn-Ortoq of Mardin and Jakarmish of Mosul, the armies of Edessa and Antioch, under Count Baldwin II of Le Bourg and Prince Bohemond, invested the

Muslim city of Harran. However, before they could occupy the town the Turkish army (having abandoned its brief siege of Edessa) arrived on the scene, dividing into two bodies of which one revictualled Harran while the other advanced to occupy the besieging army, drawing it away from the town by a feigned flight.

The Franks, 3,000 cavalry and more than 7,000 infantry including many Armenians, drew up with Baldwin on the left and Bohemond concealed behind a hill about a mile distant on the right, the plan being for the Edessans to tire the Turks, and possibly even to feign flight and draw them into an ambush. Unfortunately the Turks had a very similar plan and when they feigned an attack against the Frankish left and turned in flight the Edessans threw caution and their plan to the wind and charged off in pursuit.

Once they were across the River Balikh the main Turkish army (some 10,000 fresh cavalry) emerged from ambush, the Edessans breaking in rout at the first onset. Meanwhile Bohemond and the Antiochenes had advanced from hiding and repulsed the Turks opposing them, but they were too late to save the Edessans, instead quitting the field in panic and being overtaken and routed in turn.

Frankish casualties were very heavy, possibly as many as the 10-12,000 men claimed by Ibn al-Athir and other Muslim sources (these figures probably including non-combatants). Many Franks drowned attempting to re-cross the Balikh, a large number of horses were also lost, and certainly very few of the Franks actually escaped to Edessa. In addition Count Baldwin was taken captive by Jakarmish's men, and other Christian leaders were captured by Suqman.

THIRD BATTLE OF RAMLA 1105

A Fatimid army, making yet another attempt to reconquer Palestine, this time under al-Afdal's son Sena al-Mulk, again found itself opposed at Ramla by King Baldwin with an army of 500 knights, an unknown number of mounted sergeants, and no more than 2,000 infantry. The Fatimids numbered 5-15,000 Arab cavalry and Sudanese infantry, plus a contingent of 1,000-1,300 bow-armed Turkish cavalry from Damascus.

The battle took place near the Fatimid camp about four miles from Ramla. The Damascene horse-archers led the Fatimid attack, showering the Franks' five divisions with arrows before wheeling and falling on their flank. But Baldwin, commanding the reserve, successfully repulsed the Turks then advanced to the support of the other divisions.

Though they put up a stiff resistance for some time the Fatimid army, weakened by the departure of its left wing on a raid against Haifa, at length broke and fled, the sources recording how the Sudanese infantry, unable to outrun the Frankish pursuit, 'were slaughtered in the fields'. They lost 1,200-4,000 men, both cavalry and infantry, and their camp was captured. The Franks claimed to have lost only 60 men, though Muslim sources say losses on both sides were about equal.

SENNABRA 1113

Drawn in pursuit of a foraging party of 500 Turks, a Frankish army of 2,000 infantry and an unknown number of cavalry under King Baldwin was ambushed by 2-7,000 more Turks under Toghtekin and Mawdud, atabeg of Mosul, and severely defeated. The battle was spontaneous, neither side having time to draw up in any formal array, and hand-to-hand combat began without any preliminary skirmishing. The Franks were broken in the third Muslim charge.

The Franks lost 30 knights and 1,200 infantry (Ibn al-Qalanisi says 2,000 men) and though Baldwin himself escaped he lost his standard in the rout. The Frankish camp and baggage were also captured. It was only the arrival of the troops of Antioch and Tripoli that enabled the king to extricate the remnants of his army. The Turks appear to have lost about 400 men.

SARMIN (TELL DANITH) 1115

A Seljuk army under Sultan Bursuq of Hamadan was surprised by a Frankish army under Roger of Antioch whilst making camp in hilly wooded country. A large part of Bursuq's force was away foraging, while others were scattered in preparing the army's campsite.

The Franks emerged from ambush and attacked in echelon in three divisions, the left flank leading. This division routed the main body of Seljuks, which had withdrawn to a hill behind their camp, while the centre seized the camp itself. The Frankish right was attacked by a single body of 300 Turks under the amir of Sinjar who drove the screen of Turcopole Light cavalry back onto the knights and caused some confusion before being surrounded by the Frankish reserve and all but wiped out.

Bursuq managed to rally just a few hundred men, but after a desperate fight he fled the field.

AGER SANGUINUS (THE FIELD OF BLOOD) 1119

Roger of Antioch, without awaiting the reinforcements he had requested from Baldwin II and Count Pons of Tripoli, set out against Ilghazi of Mardin with a force of 700 knights and 3-4,000 infantry, which included Turcopoles, Armenians and native Syrian infantry (Ibn al-Qalanisi reports that the Antiochenes totalled 20,000 men!). Encamping without due caution he was trapped in a valley with steep, thickly wooded sides by Ilghazi's numerically superior army, which descended by hidden paths and had surrounded the Frankish camp by dawn. The Turks, including many Kurds but largely composed of Turcomans, numbered at least 7,000 men, some sources claiming 40-60,000.

Roger told off one division to guard his rear then drew up his remaining forces in four or five divisions, each of cavalry and infantry. On the right two or three of these had some success before the Frankish line was disorganised by the division of Robert de St Lo, on the left, breaking in rout and carrying away part of Roger's own division with it. In the ensuing confusion, made worse by a dust storm blowing into the faces of the Franks, the Turks successfully closed in round the Frankish flanks and rear cutting off all escape, and a massacre ensued. The battle was over inside an hour.

100 knights managed to escape before the encirclement was complete, and a few of the rearguard under Renaud Mazoir also got away (though the latter – except for Renaud – were captured and executed only a few hours later), but of the remainder only 70 knights and 500 infantry were taken alive. Most were tortured to death in the streets and gardens of Aleppo, though 40 of the richer knights appear to have been spared for ransom. Usamah records that less than 20 men ever returned safely to Antioch. The same figure of 20 is also reported in another source as the total number of Turkish casualties.

HAB 1119

A Frankish column of 700 knights and some 2-3,000 infantry under King Baldwin II and Count Pons of Tripoli was attacked on the march by allegedly 20,000 Turks under Ilghazi of Mardin and Toghtekin of Damascus, who succeeded in separating and routing the three cavalry divisions of the vanguard and then attacking the infantry in the main column, inflicting heavy losses.

On the left flank the Antiochene knights under Robert of Zerdana succeeded in routing the Damascenes and pursued them from the field, failing to return, but on the right the Tripolitanians were driven back onto the main body. Baldwin managed to rally his reserve and by reinforcing the weakest points in the column and delivering a series of controlled charges with his fresh troops he forced some of the Turks to flee and the rest to withdraw in good order.

The engagement was indecisive, both sides claiming a victory. The Franks had lost 100 knights and 700 infantry on the field of battle plus an additional unknown number of Antiochene knights, these being defeated as they returned by the retiring Turks; Ilghazi executed 30 knights he had captured, including Robert of Zerdana, and these were fairly certainly all Antiochenes. The Turks, on the other hand, are said by Frankish authorities to have lost 2-4,000 dead, plus additional losses in wounded and prisoners.

ESKI ZAGRA 1122

After their defeat at Levunium in 1091 the Pechenegs remained quiet until 1121, when they again crossed the Danube into Byzantine territory. The Emperor John II Comnenus managed to hold the passes against them through the winter and in the spring of 1122 he invited a large number of Pecheneg chieftains to various cities as guests. When these arrived they were arrested, and a Byzantine army under John himself, containing large numbers of Flemish and French mercenary knights and 540 Varangian Guardsmen, immediately marched against the remainder of them, encamped in a vast wagon laager into which they withdrew after initial Byzantine successes.

The Pechenegs could still muster a considerable force, outnumbering the Varangian contingent by perhaps 60 to 1. They formed up before their laager and repulsed first the Byzantine units and then the Flemish and French mercenaries. After this the Varangians attacked. It seems that this time, when the Pechenegs tried to part their wagons – presumably to let the cavalry out (see section on Asiatic tactics in *'Armies of the Dark Ages'*) – they could not be moved, and because of this or for some other reason the Pechenegs seem to have panicked and fled, many being killed and their commander being captured in the pursuit. (Possibly this was a feigned flight which got out of hand, since the Pecheneg commander was a half-blind old man who may have had difficulty controlling such a manoeuvre through his subordinates, all but six of whom had fled when the wagons were found to be stuck.)

The wagon-laager was then stormed and breached by the Varangians and the rallied mercenary and Byzantine units, and the Pechenegs were slaughtered en masse. This battle seems to have virtually exterminated the Pechenegs, the survivors being settled as military colonists in Byzantine lands; thereafter the Cumans annexed their territory. The Byzantines henceforward celebrated the victory annually as 'Pecheneg Day' until at least the end of the 12th century.

IBELIN (YIBNEH) 1123

Encouraged by the capture of King Baldwin II by Balak of Khanzit, an army of 16,000 Fatimids invaded the Kingdom of Jerusalem. They were intercepted at Ibelin by a Frankish army of 7-8,000 men under the Constable, Eustace Garnier, and – despite their numerical superiority – they broke and fled almost before the Frankish charge had even made contact, abandoning their camp to the Franks. 6-7,000 Fatimids were apparently killed, presumably mostly during the Frankish pursuit, and the camp yielded up 400 camels, 500 asses, three 'very rich banners' that Fulcher of Chartres describes as *'Standarz'*, and much other loot besides.

'AZAZ 1125

Invading the Principality of Antioch at the head of a confederacy of northern Syrian amirs, il-Bursuqi of Mosul laid siege to the Frankish fortress of Zerdana. Hearing, however, of the approach of a relief force of 1,100 cavalry and 2,000 infantry under King Baldwin II he raised the siege and retired northwards towards 'Azaz, where Baldwin's force caught up with him. The Franks drew up in 13 divisions, each of cavalry and infantry.

Relying on their superior numbers (possibly totalling 15,000 horsemen) the Syrians seem to have voluntarily closed for hand-to-hand combat early in the battle. But the superiority of the Franks' armour and physique told heavily against them and after a protracted and bloody melee the Turks were scattered in rout, the Franks collecting an immense amount of booty from the battlefield.

Frankish sources claim that the Turks lost 2,000 men including 15 amirs, but that their own casualties amounted to only 20-24 men. In addition both sides lost large numbers of horses.

MARJ ES-SAFAR 1126·

Marching against Damascus a Frankish army under Baldwin II was confronted by the Damascenes under the Atabeg Toghtekin about 20 miles from the city. The Damascenes included 2,000 Turcomans and perhaps 1,000 'askaris as well as 'an immense number' of infantry. The Franks drew up in 12 divisions of cavalry and infantry.

At first the Turcomans put the Franks to flight, the horse-archers taking a heavy toll and Toghtekin's 'askaris even pushing through to the royal camp. But after being pursued for four miles the Franks rallied and as evening drew in launched a concerted attack, the Frankish archers shooting down many of the Damascene horses and

Baldwin's knights riding down their disorganised cavalry, who panicked when Toghtekin was unhorsed. The victorious Franks went on to pursue the routed Muslims to within sight of Damascus, the Damascene infantry being cut to pieces in the pursuit. The Muslims lost at least 2,000 men.

The Franks claimed to have lost only 24 knights and 80 infantry themselves, though they also record that the infantry suffered badly in the initial rout. Certainly the Frankish casualties were heavy enough to oblige Baldwin to abandon his projected attack on Damascus. Instead the army gathered a considerable amount of booty from the battlefield and withdrew to Jerusalem.

MOUNT CADMOS 1148

Early in 1148 during the Second Crusade a French army under King Louis VII was ambushed on Mount Cadmos by the Seljuks. The vanguard (composed largely of royal mercenaries and a contingent of Templars), disregarding its instructions to halt and encamp before the mountain, outstripped the rest of the army so that a wide gap opened up between them. The main body, losing sight of the vanguard, piled up in confusion at the foot of the mountain as its foremost units hesitated, upon which the Seljuks – who had been lying in ambush awaiting just such an opportunity – fell upon the infantry and baggage in the middle of their column.

Louis and the 40 knights of the rearguard, hearing the sounds of battle, advanced rapidly to the scene of the ambush, while a messenger was despatched to retrieve the vanguard. The latter, however, was obstructed in trying to return by large numbers of non-combatants in rout from the main body.

The charge of Louis and the rearguard succeeded in distracting the Seljuks' attention from the remainder of the non-combatants, but in the confused melee which followed all 40 knights were cut down and Louis, himself unhorsed, was forced to fight his way to safety alone and on foot.

It was only the oncoming of night that brought an end to the Seljuk attack, upon which Louis and the survivors rallied on the baggage train. There he was at last reinforced by the uncommitted vanguard, but darkness prevented the mounting of a counter-attack.

FONS MURATUS 1149

Learning of the siege of the fortress of Inab by the 6,000-strong combined armies of Aleppo and Damascus, under Nur ed-Din and Asad ad-Din Shirkuh, Raymond of Antioch set out with a relief force. However, he had failed to await a full muster and although accompanied by a few Assassin allies his total force numbered only 4,000 cavalry and 1,000 infantry.

Misinformed of the strength of the Frankish force, Nur ed-Din retired on its approach. Raymond then weakened his army further by putting reinforcements into Inab, and Nur ed-Din – watching his movements from a distance – now became aware of the Franks' inferior strength. Therefore when Raymond encamped in a hollow in open country near to the Spring of Murad the Turks surrounded his camp overnight.

Raymond realised his plight in the morning and led a charge against the encircling Turks, but this was defeated by the incline of the slope and the wind blowing dust in their eyes from the summit. They were subsequently virtually wiped out. Shirkuh himself slew Raymond, and Nur ed-Din sent his silver-decorated skull as a trophy to the Abbasid Caliph at Baghdad.[11]

HARIM (HARENC) 1164

On hearing that Nur ed-Din had laid siege to the Antiochene fortress of Harim a Frankish relief force set out under Bohemond III of Antioch, Raymond III of Tripoli and Joscelyn III, titular Count of Edessa. In addition it included Byzantine troops under Constantine Coloman, the Byzantine Dux of Cilicia, an Armenian contingent under Thoros II, a band of French crusaders under Hugh de Lusignan, and a contingent of Templars and/or Hospitallers. Altogether the army totalled 13,000 cavalry and infantry, Bohemond's own contingent including 600 knights.

Nur ed-Din, particularly alarmed by the presence of Byzantine troops in the approaching army, decided to raise the siege rather than risk a battle, but prepared a contingency plan to destroy the Franks should they pursue him – which, ignoring the advice of Thoros and others, Bohemond was foolish enough to do. As the Frankish cavalry chased after the retiring army Nur's left wing rallied and turned back to fall on

---

[11] Since none of their own frontiers bordered on those of the Frankish states the Abbasids were passive throughout the Crusades; though Caliph Muqtafi (1135-1160) is alleged to have sent an army of 20,000 men to fight against the Franks I know of no evidence of it seeing action.

the unprotected infantry, so that when the disorganised cavalry were in turn attacked they no longer had infantry support. Nur's cavalry then trapped them in 'a confined and swampy place' and broke them in the first charge.

A large number of Franks were killed (including all the military brethren) and most of the remainder were forced to surrender, the prisoners including all the leaders except Thoros, who had pursued with more caution than his allies and succeeded in escaping with his own contingent.

THE DAY OF AL-BABEIN 1167

During the Syrian invasion of Egypt, a Frankish army under King Amalric I, fighting in this instance as allies of the Fatimid Egyptians, managed to cross the Nile despite the proximity of Syrian forces under Asad ad-Din Shirkuh, and as a result the Syrians, discovering the crossing too late to oppose it, withdrew into Upper Egypt. Amalric pursued them as far as al-Babein, 'The Two Gates', on the edge of the desert ten miles south of Minya, where Shirkuh decided to give battle.

Shirkuh's plan was to convince the Franks that his main strength was in the centre, and to this end he placed his baggage in the centre of the line but covered it with only a small force of cavalry under Saladin. Shirkuh himself commanded the right wing, composed of elite cavalry, intending to fall on the Frankish rear when they charged his centre, where Saladin was to feign flight to draw them away from the field. His forces numbered 9,000 heavy cavalry, 3,000 horse-archers and 10-11,000 Arabs who appear to have been infantry. (Muslim sources record only 1-2,000 horsemen.)

To face them Amalric, whose forces had been depleted by detachments during the pursuit, could muster 374 Frankish knights, an unknown number of sergeants and Turcopoles, and a large contingent of unreliable Egyptians; Bar Hebraeus records that his army totalled 10,000 men. For the attack he placed his knights in the vanguard and the Egyptian contingents in the rear.

The battle went entirely according to plan. When Amalric charged Saladin turned in flight, and as the Franks followed in pursuit Shirkuh fell on the Egyptians. When Amalric managed to rally his scattered knights and return to the main part of the field he found that the majority of the Turcopoles and Fatimids had been routed, but although the Franks had to abandon their baggage train they managed to rally a considerable number of men and, forming a column, retired from the field in good order.

They had, however, lost 100 knights and an undoubtedly larger number of Egyptians and others, and strategically it was a Syrian victory, even though the Syrians themselves are said to have lost 1,500 men. The Muslims called the battle 'The Day' or 'The Event' of al-Babein.

Soon after, hearing of an attack on Frankish Syria by Nur ed-Din, the Franks withdrew from Egypt.

MYRIOKEPHALON 1176

In an attempt to crush the Seljuks of Rum, the Byzantine Emperor Manuel I gathered a huge but largely mercenary army, containing in particular considerable numbers of Uzes and Franks, and marched on their capital, Iconium, intending to capture both the city and the sultan, Kilij Arslan II.

Their march was orderly but slow, the large number of non-combatants attending the baggage train dictating the army's speed. In addition they were dogged by bands of 5-10,000 Turcomans, who Kilij Arslan had instructed to adopt a scorched earth policy as they withdrew before the Byzantines. On reaching the abandoned fortress of Myriokephalon an embassy was received from the sultan proposing peace, which Manuel contemptuously refused – probably for the same reasons as Romanus had refused Alp Arslan's offer before Manzikert a century earlier. Kilij Arslan then occupied the Tzibritze Pass, at the head of which Myriokephalon stood.

Next day, ignoring the advice of his officers, Manuel led his army into the pass, where the Seljuks – at least 50,000 strong – could apparently be clearly seen in their positions on the mountain slopes.

They gave way before the Byzantine vanguard and allowed the bulk of the army to enter the narrow defile unmolested, where the Byzantines were packed so close that they could scarcely move. As soon as the long convoy of Byzantine baggage carts was halfway into the pass the Seljuks charged down from both sides.

The wagons, harassed by Seljuk infantry (who had set some of them on fire), were unable to turn in the narrow pass and completely blocked the road, fully preventing any retreat by the bulk of the army, and the Turks closed in on the disorganised Byzantines. A confusing battle ensued in which a fierce sandstorm blinded the combatants so that both sides killed many of their own men, but as the storm subsided towards evening it became apparent that although the Byzantine vanguard had successfully forced its way to the other end of the pass it was the Seljuks who had the advantage.

On the plain before the pass Manuel managed to rally with many of his senior officers, and here the main part of the surviving Byzantine army encamped for the night, in such a precarious situation that Manuel even considered abandoning the army and secretly slipping away. However, Seljuk casualties had been heavy too, and despite the severe losses of the Byzantines Kilij Arslan now sent an envoy offering peace in exchange for an agreement by Manuel to dismantle the fortresses of Dorylaeum and Sublaeum and a payment to the sultan of horses, rich cloth and 200,000 gold and silver pieces, terms which Manuel now willingly accepted. It was only on the withdrawal of the Byzantine vanguard from the far end of the Tzibritze Pass that it became apparent to them just how heavy Turkish casualties must have been – the heads and genitals of the corpses littering the pass had even been mutilated or removed by the Seljuks overnight so that it was impossible to distinguish Muslim from Christian or therefore calculate Kilij Arslan 's losses.

Despite the peace treaty the Byzantines were harassed as they withdrew by Turcoman tribesmen, over whom the sultan had little or no control, and not until they reached Chonae did the pursuit end. Safe within his own territory, Manuel refused to dismantle the fortifications of Dorylaeum, and Kilij Arslan felt obliged to retaliate by despatching a force of 24,000 cavalry to raid the Maeander valley. These did considerable damage and sacked several towns before Manuel's forces caught and destroyed them at the crossings of Hyelion and Leimmocheir.

There were further sporadic skirmishes and counter-attacks against Turcoman raiders between Phrygia and Bithynia that were more or less successful by turns, but the campaign of 1176 was really at an end. It left both Byzantine Anatolia and the Empire's military resources seriously weakened.

MONTGISARD 1177

While invading Frankish Syria an Egyptian army under Saladin was surprised and defeated by the Franks under Baldwin IV. After blockading Baldwin in Ascalon the Egyptians, originally over 26,000 strong according to William of Tyre (8,000 Toassin and 18,000 Qaraghulams, all cavalry, plus infantry mounted on camels and mules), had scattered to loot and pillage, confident that there were no further enemy forces between them and Jerusalem. But Baldwin succeeded in gathering 375-500 knights (including 80 Templars from Gaza) and somewhat under 3,000 infantry and, evading the small

Egyptian holding force, surprised Saladin's main army as it was negotiating a ravine near the fortress of Montgisard.

Many of the Egyptian units were foraging, others were encamped, and the Frankish attack caught the main body almost completely by surprise. They had time only to draw up a very loose battle array, their units milling about in total disorder and even attempting to revise their formation in the face of the Frankish charge. Inevitably under such circumstances some units broke and fled even before the Franks made contact with them, and those that stood were practically annihilated. Saladin's own escape was covered by his personal guard of 1,000 mamluks.

So complete was the Frankish victory that the Egyptians abandoned their booty, baggage and prisoners. In addition to their heavy losses in the battle the Egyptians suffered further casualties as a result of Bedouin harassment during their withdrawal. Frankish losses were also high, the Master of the Hospital recording 1,100 dead and at least 750 wounded.

MARJ 'AYYUN 1179

On receiving news that Saladin had invaded the district of Banyas and Sidon a Frankish army under King Baldwin IV and Count Raymond of Tripoli set out to intercept him. Reaching high ground overlooking the Marj 'Ayyun they could see the tents of Saladin's main encampment at Banyas in the distance and resolved to descend to the plain without further delay, though such was their haste that many of their infantry, already exhausted by the long march, were unable to keep up as the army hurried down the steep slope.

Once on the plain there was a delay of 'several' hours (in which most of the infantry were presumably able to catch up) before Saladin's advance guard of skirmishers, returning from raids further to the west, were intercepted and defeated, losing many dead. Encouraged by their success many of the Frankish cavalry charged off in pursuit under the Master of the Temple and Count Raymond, only to be confronted by Saladin and the main body of the Muslim army, on which the fleeing skirmishers now rallied. The Franks had no time to reform in orderly array before the Muslims were on them, but though disorganised they managed to hold out for a while before Saladin's superior numbers overwhelmed and broke them, driving them back in rout upon Baldwin's main body, where the infantry were still collecting booty and resting after the initial defeat of the skirmishers.

Many more Franks were killed or captured in the pursuit, though some including the king himself managed to escape to the fortress of

Beaufort. Others, who hid overnight amongst the rocks and caves, were hunted down and taken prisoner the next morning. The Master of the Temple, who was blamed for the disaster, was amongst those taken captive.

CRESSON 1187

Following a raid on a Muslim caravan by Reynald de Châtillon, Lord of Kerak, during a period of truce Saladin resolved to invade the Kingdom of Jerusalem.

In preparation for this, Kukburi of Harran and two other amirs were despatched to make a reconnaissance in force (6-7,000 strong) into Palestine. As a result of open enmity between King Guy and Count Raymond of Tripoli, permission to cross his Galilean possessions was granted by the Count on condition that the Muslims would cross and return in a single day and should not pillage.

Probably Kukburi's reconnaissance would have passed without incident but for the fact that the Masters of the Hospital and Temple, sent by King Guy to patch up a reconciliation with Raymond, learnt of it en route to Tiberias. The Templar Master, Gerard de Ridefort, immediately summoned his Marshal and 80 more brethren (from the Templar garrisons of Qaqun and Faba) and mustered in total a force of 140 knights and 3-400 infantry with which he and Roger des Moulins, Master of the Hospital, set out to intercept the Muslims.

They caught up with Kukburi at the Spring of Cresson (the Spring of Saffuriya according to Muslim sources) as his men were watering their horses during the return journey, and though numbers were utterly against them Gerard de Ridefort goaded the knights into charging, without even waiting for their infantry to catch up. Inevitably they were all but massacred. Roger des Moulins and the Marshal of the Temple were amongst those killed, though Gerard himself managed to escape with two other brethren. Of the rest, 40 secular knights were captured and the other 97 Templars and Hospitallers all killed.

THE HORNS OF HATTIN 1187

As a result of the disaster at Cresson Raymond of Tripoli felt obliged to put aside his quarrel with King Guy in the face of the common enemy and peace was made between them. The Frankish forces then mustered at Acre to dispute Saladin's forthcoming invasion. Various sources record this muster as between 20,000 and 60,000 men, the most convincing figures, for troop-type proportions rather than for quantities, being those of the Historia Regni Hierosolymitani, where the following breakdown is given: 1,000 knights, 1,200 mercenary knights and 7,000 mercenary infantry, 4,000 Turcopoles, and 25,000 infantry. No mounted sergeants are mentioned, though they are possibly meant by the mounted Poulains recorded in the anonymous Libellus de Expugnatione Terrae Sanctae; the same source records 'innumerable Turcopoles', but however many there may actually have been they appear to have had no effect on the subsequent fighting. By comparison Saladin's army contained 12,000 mamluks from Egypt, Damascus, Aleppo, Mosul, Mardin and elsewhere, in addition to a large number of volunteers. Judging from contemporary accounts partisan to both sides the Muslim army was clearly the larger, one source recording as many as 80,000 men, another the impossible figure of 700,000! The lowest total recorded in Frankish sources is 25,000.

On 1 July Saladin encamped at Kafar Sebt, six miles south-west of Count Raymond's fortress of Tiberias, a position which commanded the main road to both Tiberias and Sennabra. Half his army remained there while the other half attacked and sacked the town and environs of Tiberias the next day; the fortress itself, however, held out under the command of Raymond's wife, the Countess Eschiva, who sent an urgent appeal for aid to King Guy.

The message probably reached the king at Saffuriya, where his army had now encamped, the same evening. Raymond, whose castle and wife were those threatened, wisely advised against going to the relief of Tiberias; he pointed out that their own position at Saffuriya was a good one, amply provided as it was with water and pasturage, and should not be abandoned at any cost, particularly when their presence alone could severely restrict Saladin's movements. But Guy foolishly took contrary advice from the Master of the Temple, Gerard de Ridefort (who probably still seethed about his defeat at Cresson, for which he undoubtedly held Raymond solely responsible), and on the morning of 3 July the Franks broke camp at Saffuriya and prepared for their advance across the waterless Plain of Toran. They abandoned the Sennabra road in favour of a more northerly route, probably in part at least because of the threat of the Muslim positions on Kafar Sebt and also because it would lead them to the springs of the Wadi Hamman.

Saladin, probably forewarned of their changed route by deserters or by traitors within Raymond's contingent, now shifted his position from Kafar Sebt to the hills of Hattin, which commanded the northerly road the Franks were now taking. There he was joined by the majority of the troops who had been besieging Tiberias, a small force having been detached to continue with the siege, while skirmishers commenced to harass the Frankish column.

All morning the Franks marched on, constantly under attack by the Muslim skirmishers. Raymond's vanguard lost many knights, and so hard-pressed was the rearguard of Templars, Hospitallers and Turcopoles that it had been dangerously slowed down and ran the serious risk of being separated entirely from the centre of the column, commanded by King Guy. Being made aware of this danger by messengers from Gerard de Ridefort and Balian d'Ibelin, Guy ordered the army to halt and encamp for the night, even though they had covered barely five miles and it was still early afternoon. Raymond, who appears to have been the only sane commander in the whole Frankish host, urged that it was imperative they should push on and reach a nearby spring, but with the rearguard demoralised and the infantry exhausted his advice was pointless; he is alleged to have then prophesied, 'The war is over; we are dead men; the kingdom is finished!' By now the Muslims had also blocked the pass to this spring, however, and though there was clearly some heavy fighting near the village of Marescallia attempts to dislodge the Muslims seem to have been unsuccessful. Left with no other option, Raymond advised the king to encamp at Marescallia itself, with only half the distance to Tiberias covered and Saladin still holding the wells.

During the night Saladin's army closed in. When morning came the Franks made one final attempt to reach the spring near Hattin but again found their way blocked by the Muslims; battle was joined at about nine o'clock, the main Muslim army advancing towards them with the centre held back and the wings thrown forward, preceding their charge with a cloud of arrows.

The Frankish infantry, exhausted and desperate for water, failed to hold formation and refused to stand; they made a disconcerted drive towards the Sea of Galilee, which they could see below them, but finding their path blocked they herded onto a low hill, probably one of the pair known as the Horns of Hattin, and despite entreaties from King Guy would not join the battle, pleading that their thirst prevented them. They took no further part in the battle until the Muslims fell on them and killed many, taking the rest prisoner.

The rear and main battles, unsupported by their infantry, were now hard-pressed, particularly the Military Orders and the Turcopoles, apparently still in the rearguard position; Raymond and the vanguard of about 200 knights, meanwhile, had been separated from the bulk of the army when called upon by Guy to deliver the first charge at about noon, when Taqi ad-Din had opened his ranks to avoid the impact and so let them through, though inflicting heavy casualties on them as they passed (Raymond himself receiving three wounds and one of his sons being captured). Seeing how hopeless the situation was and that he could not get back to the army, Raymond rode from the field and withdrew to Tyre. It was probably at this stage that Prince Reynald of Sidon and Balian d'Ibelin escaped from the reayguard, as did a small number of Templars.

It was also at about this stage, after the escape of Raymond, that the Muslims took advantage of a wind at their backs to fire the dry scrub. The smoke, blown towards the exhausted Frankish knights, must have tortured throats that had not touched water for 24 hours or more, and possibly even choked some to death. The remaining knights then fell back towards one of the Horns of Hattin, the Muslims revolving round them 'as a globe turns on its axis'. But the Muslim attacks were repeatedly repulsed, despite the death of the Bishop of Acre and the capture of the 'True Cross' (see Figure 29) by Taqi ad-Din himself, and the knights made a number of counter-attacks that came within an ace of success. Their numbers steadily dwindled, however, and the last 150 retired to the summit of the hill, where King Guy's red tent had been set up.

The Muslim attacks persisted until finally the king's tent was overthrown, on which the last few knights, exhausted, dismounted and threw themselves on the ground. The Muslims immediately surrounded them and took them captive, together with the king, his brother the Constable Amalric, Reynald de Châtillon, Gerard de Ridefort, Joscelyn de Courtenay, Humphrey de Toron and many others.

The extent of the disaster is well put over by Ibn al-Athir, who wrote 'When one saw how many were dead one could not believe that there were any prisoners; and when one saw the prisoners one could not believe that there were any dead.' Beha ed-Din claims that 30,000 were captured in all, and a further 30,000 killed. Another source records that 1,000 knights were killed or captured; the prisoners were probably all secular knights, since the 200-260 Templars and Hospitallers taken alive (Bar Hebraeus records only 80) were executed. Gerard was spared, but Reynald de Châtillon was executed for his crimes, possibly by Saladin 's own hand.

The next day Tiberias surrendered, realising that no help would now be coming, Countess Eschiva being allowed to depart with honour by Saladin.

THE GREAT BATTLE OF ACRE 1189

Cramped by the close proximity of Saladin's field army whilst besieging Acre, King Guy was encouraged by the arrival of reinforcements to launch an attack against the Muslim camp. The Franks drew up in four divisions, each of cavalry and infantry with archers and crossbowmen to the fore. His left flank rested on the sea, his right on the River Belus.

When the Frankish cavalry charged both the Muslim flanks gave way, the right wing under Taqi ad-Din possibly feigning flight to draw the Templars of the Frankish left from the field in pursuit. Saladin reinforced his own left from his centre, which, thus weakened, subsequently broke when the Frankish centre charged. Some Franks pushed on right up to the Muslim camp before Saladin, reaching high ground and successfully rallying the centre and left, launched a counter-attack. The Franks, by now dispersed in search of plunder, broke in panic and were driven back to their own camp with heavy losses.

Guy lost 7-10,000 men, 4,000 of whom fell on the right flank, including many Templar brethren; Gerard de Ridefort, Master of the Temple, was again captured and this time Saladin had him executed. Muslim losses totalled 1,500 including 150 Royal Mamluks and two senior amirs. In addition the Diyar Bekr contingent, which had formed part of Taqi's right wing and fled during the initial rout, failed to return after the battle, only next being heard from when they had reached Galilee!

The magnitude of the Frankish defeat might have been greater if Guy had not had the foresight to anticipate a sortie against his own camp by the garrison of Acre and told off a holding force to contain it.

ACRE 1190

Hearing that Saladin's right flank, commanded by his nephew Taqi ad-Din, had been weakened by the despatch of several detachments to watch the approach of the remnants of Frederick Barbarossa's German crusade, a large number of Frankish soldiers decided to march out from their entrenchments round Acre and fall unexpectedly on the Muslim army, against the will of their leaders.

They caught the Muslims completely unawares, and by the time the latter had armed and mounted the Franks had already smashed through the weakened right wing and penetrated as far as the camp. They then began to loot and pillage and became disorganised so that Taqi, rallying those of his troops that were nearest, successfully launched a counter-attack. The Franks stood at first but were routed when a fresh division, the Mosul 'askar, followed by Saladin with most of the Muslim centre, joined the battle. As in the great battle of the previous year they were then chased back to their own camp.

The battle lasted little more than a couple of hours, by the end of which the Franks had lost some 4,000 men. Muslim sources claim that the Franks lost 7-8,000, themselves losing only ten, both figures obviously highly improbable. Few prisoners were taken and most of them were executed.

ARSUF 1191

Marching along the coast road towards Arsuf during the Third Crusade, an army of crusaders and Syrian Franks under King Richard I of England was attacked by a large Muslim force under Saladin, possibly outnumbering the Franks by 3:1.

Anticipating the attack, Richard had taken meticulous care in arranging his line of march that morning, organising the army in five battalions composed in all of 12 divisions of knights, flanked on the landward side by a tightly-packed wall of infantry and on the seaward side by the baggage train and more infantry. The vanguard was held by Templars and the rearguard by Hospitallers and 'choice knights divided into squadrons, its members ... so close together that an apple could not be thrown to the ground without touching the men or their horses'.

Saladin had been harassing the Frankish column for several days but had failed to disrupt its formation or draw the knights away from the protection of the main column. Now, at a point where the Forest of Arsuf came down to within three miles of the coast, he launched an all-out attack on the Hospitallers of the rearguard.

For some time the Franks struggled on under a constant hail of arrows, with pressure steadily increasing on the hard-pressed rearguard until the Hospitallers, twice having been refused permission to counter-attack, finally disobeyed and charged out against the Muslims, just before Richard gave a general order to do so, their premature charge giving many of the Muslims a chance to fall back and avoid the full impact of the Frankish charge which might have otherwise smashed them. For a few minutes the rearguard was thrown into confusion as the Muslims rallied until Richard brought up reinforcements from the centre and drove them back, Muslim counter-attacks on both the Hospitallers and the Normans and English guarding the royal standard likewise being repulsed. The knights then rallied on the standard and reformed their ranks, and the army continued its march to Arsuf.

Muslim casualties amounted to 7,000 dead, including 32 amirs, while the Franks' losses were under 700, including only one nobleman of distinction. However, the apparent victory was indecisive; the

Muslims attacked again later the same day as the Franks were pitching their tents outside Arsuf, but they were again repulsed and driven back to the forest.

JAFFA 1192

King Richard, commanding a small force of only 2,000 infantry, including 400 crossbowmen but for the most part Pisan and Genoese sailors (Beha ed-Din says that there were only 300-1,000 infantry in all), and 55-80 knights of whom only 9-17 (including the king) were mounted, drew up as an infantry phalanx in two lines, the first of spearmen and the second of archers and crossbowmen. The spearmen set their shields before them to form a wall behind which the archers could shelter, and fixed their spear butts in the ground so that the heads were levelled against the chests of any horses that dared to approach. Before the whole force a rough barricade of tent pegs had been set up to disorganise the enemy charge.

The Muslim army under Saladin, composed of Kurds and mamluks, was reluctant to close with this formation but attempted to charge against it in seven successive waves, their attacks lasting until mid-afternoon when, after a single concerted volley by the Frankish crossbowmen, they were driven away by a general advance of the spearmen, led by Richard himself with his few mounted knights, leaving 700 of their attackers and 1,500 horses dead. Richard lost only two men in addition to a number of wounded.

An attempt by the Muslims to seize Jaffa in the rear of the Franks was foiled by Richard's timely return with a small number of knights. The town was then re-garrisoned by him with the Pisan and Genoese seamen who had abandoned the defences when the Muslims attacked.

ADRIANOPLE 1205

Whilst besieging Adrianople the Romanian Franks under the Latin Emperor Baldwin I and Doge Dandolo of Venice were attacked by a Bulgarian army under Joannitsa, including Greeks as well as 14,000 Cuman auxiliaries.

Having learnt from bitter experience that it was inadvisable to pursue retreating Cumans the Franks decided to assume a defensive formation and let the Bulgarians attack rather than take the offensive themselves. However, when the Cumans harassed their camp the morning after they had made these plans the Franks forsook their caution and pursued them piecemeal, upon which the Cumans turned and routed them, capturing Baldwin in the process.

The rout was halted by a relief force that had been left to continue the siege of Adrianople, and when the Bulgarian pursuit saw this second army they halted. The two sides faced each other thus until nightfall, the Cumans persistently harassing the Franks with arrow-fire all that time. The Franks finally withdrew under cover of darkness, having lost 120-300 knights and a large number of sergeants and infantry, abandoning their camp to the Bulgarians. Baldwin died or was murdered in captivity.

ANTIOCH-IN-PISIDIA 1211

Accompanied by Frankish mercenaries supplied by the Latin Emperor Henry, as well as Phrygian troops under the deposed Byzantine Emperor Alexius III and his nephew Manuel Mavrozomes, the Seljuks under Sultan Kai Khosrou I of Rum marched against Emperor Theodore I of Nicaea. In the summer they took Attaleia, then advanced towards Nicaea and laid siege to Antioch-in-Pisidia.

The 2,000-strong Nicaean army, also including a contingent of Frankish mercenaries (800 men, chiefly Italians), confronted them near the city. The whole Nicaean army carried crosses on their shields in imitation of the army of Constantine the Great at the Battle of Milvian Bridge in 312.

In the ensuing battle the Italians forming the Nicaean vanguard were overwhelmed by the Seljuks and practically wiped out. Kai Khosrou then led an attack against Theodore himself and personally unhorsed him, the Emperor only saving himself by hacking at the forelegs of the Sultan's mare, bringing down both horse and rider upon which Kai Khosrou was instantly decapitated by a Nicaean soldier. Despite this the battle appears to have been indecisive, authorities variously claiming the rout of the Nicaeans or of the Seljuks, though it seems more probable that it was the leaderless Turks who broke and fled. Alexius and Manuel Mavrozomes were captured during the pursuit. At the same time, however, Theodore's losses can only be described as crippling.

DAMIETTA 1219

As a result of dissension in the Frankish camp during the siege of Damietta, the leaders of the Fifth Crusade acquiesced to the demands of their army and marched out against the encampment of the encircling Muslim field-army.

The Muslims, drawing up, feigned flight with their centre and drew the inexperienced and foolhardy Frankish infantry in pursuit. At the same time Bedouin auxiliaries fell on the Frankish camp-followers, obliging the King, John de Brienne, to fall back to their defence, and when the Roman infantry of Cardinal Pelagius saw this they thought that the knights were running away and themselves turned and fled. The panic spread and the entire army broke in rout, only a rearguard action by King John, the Military Orders and some French and English knights preventing a major disaster.

The Franks appear to have lost 200-400 knights (including 33-50 Templars, 32 Hospitallers and 30 Teutonic Knights) and 1-2,000, or possibly as many as 5,000, infantry.

BAHR ASHMUN 1221

Advancing from Damietta towards Cairo under King John and the infamous Cardinal Pelagius, a Frankish army numbering 1,200-5,000 knights, 4,000 archers (including 2,500 mercenaries, possibly all Turcopoles), mounted sergeants and 20-40,000 infantry was pinned down by Egyptian and Syrian forces under Sultan al-Kamil and al-Malik al-Ashraf of the Jazira. The Muslim army included some 7-40,000 cavalry.

After being blockaded within their fortified encampment for a month, their lines of communication cut by an Egyptian fleet on the Nile in their rear, the Franks finally resolved to fall back on Damietta. They set out at night, but the Teutonic Knights were stupid enough to advertise the fact by setting fire to the abandoned tents. To impede their withdrawal, the Muslims opened sluice gates along the banks of the Nile and by morning, as the Franks floundered through the waterlogged fields and ditches, the Muslims had intercepted and surrounded them. The Franks managed to hold out for a day, repulsing the mamluks and Sudanese infantry sent against them (and inflicting about 1,000 casualties on the latter), but further retreat was impossible. The army surrendered on moderate terms 3 days later.

AKHLAT (ERZINJAN) 1230

While expanding into the Seljuk domains of Rum, Jalal ad-Din, Shah of Khwarizmia, besieged and captured Akhlat from al-Ashraf Musa of Damascus, brother of the Ayyubid Sultan of Egypt. This was a politically unwise move since it prompted an alliance between the previously implacable adversaries al-Ashraf and Sultan Kai Kobad of Rum against the Khwarizmians.

Jalal ad-Din advanced to Khartpert in the hope of catching and defeating the allies individually, but falling ill he was unable to prevent the juncture of their forces at Sivas. Al-Ashraf led 5,000 elite cavalry, and Kai Kobad 20,000 men including naptha-throwers and crossbow-armed infantry.

In the meantime Jalal's forces had been reduced by detachments and he was consequently soundly defeated at Erzinjan, from where he withdrew to Akhlat and then to Azerbaijan. The Seljuk-Syrian allies did not pursue. Instead they made peace with Jalal, appreciating Khwarizmia's value as a buffer state between them and the Mongols.

CASAL IMBERT 1232

This battle took place during a civil war between the Imperialist faction of Frederick II, under the Imperial Legate Richard Filangieri, and the Ibelin party of Jean d'Ibelin, the 'Old Lord of Beirut', supported by King Henry I of Cyprus.

Encamped at Casal Imbert with only a very small force, King Henry, accompanied by Anseau de Brie and the Old Lord's sons Baldwin, Hugh and Guy and nephew Jean (author of the 'Assises'), was defeated by the 'Lombards' (i.e. the Imperialists). When darkness fell the Lombards had set sail from Tyre with 22 galleys and surprised the Ibelins. Encamped badly (Jean d'Ibelin's sentries, for example, had been posted on the wrong side of the camp) the king's party were caught totally unprepared (the chronicler Philip of Novara speaks of 'some on foot, others on horse without saddles, some armed with hauberks and otherwise naked, others wholly unarmed'), but they managed to hold the camp until daylight; King Henry himself, 'almost entirely naked', was mounted on a horse by his bodyguard and escaped to Acre with a small retinue.

At dawn Lombard reinforcements were landed from the Tyrean galleys and the Ibelin camp was finally taken, the Lombards capturing 24 Ibelin knights, nearly every horse left in the camp, and most of the arms and equipment stored there. The surviving Ibelins rallied on a nearby hill, where a relief force from Acre under the Old Lord found them soon after. The Lombards, seeing the relief force approaching, transferred as much loot as possible to the ships and began a precipitate withdrawal to Tyre by land and sea, archers and crossbowmen holding off those Ibelins who tried to fall on the rearguard of their land-bound force as it withdrew through the Pass of Poulain.

AGRIDI 1232

Following up his success at Casal Imbert six weeks earlier, Filangieri had invaded Cyprus with the intention of completely reducing the island, which was already largely in the hands of the Imperialist faction.

Intending to relieve the besieged fortress of Dieu d'Amour, besieged by Filangieri, the Old Lord of Beirut left 50-60 dismounted sergeants to hold the village of Agridi then proceeded along a narrow pass towards the fort in four divisions, in the hope that the Lombards would come down and join battle.

His vanguard was commanded by his sons Hugh and Balian with Anseau de Brie; the second division by Baldwin; the third by John of Caesarea; and the fourth by King Henry and the Old Lord himself with his other sons and nephew Jean. Their force was short of horses and probably in all totalled only about 230 horsemen, as opposed to about 2,000 Imperialist cavalry, the latter including Cypriote Turcopoles and Tripolitanian and Cilician mercenaries.

The Lombards, seeing this inferior force, descended from their strong position higher up the pass and attacked in three divisions, with Filangieri commanding the rearguard. The impetus of the Lombard vanguard's charge carried it 'clear beyond' the Ibelins, upon which it fled the field. The second division, however, fought a fierce battle with the first two Ibelin divisions until Count Berard, its commander, was unhorsed by Anseau de Brie and killed by the Ibelin infantry who had come up from Agridi, as were many other Lombard horsemen. More than 60 of their knights were killed, and 40 more captured, while of the Ibelins only one knight was killed, and he in error by an Ibelin infantryman.

Filangieri, meanwhile, with the bulk of the 2,000 Imperialist cavalry, had been prevented from coming to Count Berard's aid by Balian d'Ibelin who, with a handful of knights (five, of whom one was the chronicler Philip of Novara), had distracted and disorganised his division by constant harassment in the confined space of the pass until the Imperial Legate was forced to flee.

The Lombards' vanguard division, which had failed to return to the battle, was later trapped in a fosse before Gastria and its commander and about 100 more knights were captured there. Dieu d'Amour was meanwhile relieved.

DARBSAQ 1237

Whilst besieging the Muslim fortress of Darbsaq a Frankish army under William de Montferrat, the Templar Preceptor of Antioch, was surprised and defeated by a Muslim relief force despatched from Aleppo. William had been warned of the enemy's approach by Christian prisoners in Darbsaq but had failed to act on the information, as a result of which his army was cut to pieces and he himself killed.

More than 100 other Templar brethren died as well as 300 crossbowmen in their employ and a number of secular knights. The Muslims themselves allegedly (but highly improbably) lost 3,000 men.

GAZA 1239

A detachment from King Tibald of Navarre's crusade set out to attack an Egyptian force in the vicinity of Gaza reported to number only about 1,000 men. The Frankish force probably numbered something between 1,500 and 2,000 men, including 500 cavalry, under Count Henry of Bar.

Unfortunately, however, the Egyptians were considerably superior in numbers and their slingers and crossbowmen encircled the Frankish army as it paused for a meal amongst the sandhills and dunes near Gaza. At length realising their mistake several of the native Syrian Franks withdrew, but Count Henry refused to abandon his infantry in the face of the enemy.

The ensuing battle was short and bloody. The Frankish crossbowmen at first seemed likely to succeed in driving the Egyptian missile-men from the dunes but ran out of ammunition. The knights then charged into a narrow valley between two dunes where they could shelter from the devastating barrage the Egyptians were laying down, scattering the infantry who attempted to hold it against them. Almost simultaneously, however, the Egyptian cavalry arrived and, feigning flight, drew the knights back into the open where, unable to manoeuvre their heavily laden mounts in the deep sand, they were picked off by the Egyptian archers and cut to pieces by the cavalry.

The sources differ regarding the number of casualties, but it would seem that 1,000-1,800 men were killed and at least 80 knights and 250 others captured; another report gives one count, 15 knights and 500 others taken captive. Count Henry was amongst the slain. The main body of King Tibald's army subsequently withdrew to Acre.

KUZA DAGH 1243

Invading the Rumi province of Armenia, a Mongol force under Baichu, including Georgian and Armenian auxiliaries, attacked Erzerum and razed it to the ground after a brief siege. They then withdrew to winter on the plain of Mughan, but in response to belligerent threats from the Seljuk sultan of Rum, Kai Khosrou II, they marched out again, this time towards the Seljuk positions in the pass of Kuzadagh near Erzinjan.

Baichu, wary of the large numbers of auxiliaries in his army, disbanded a number of Georgian and Armenian units as untrustworthy and distributed the rest amongst his Mongol troops to prevent desertion or treachery. On the day of battle his command is reported to have been 10-30,000 strong, probably his own Touman of 10,000 and 20,000 auxiliaries. Kai Khosrou's army was clearly larger, some sources claiming 100-160,000 men. It included Bedouins, Georgians, Syrians from Aleppo, 2,000 or more Frankish mercenaries (chiefly Cypriotes) and probably a contingent of Trapezuntine Byzantines. The battle itself was indecisive. The main part of Baichu's Armenian and Georgian auxiliaries defeated the Seljuks' right flank, where a number of amirs were killed, though the Seljuk left successfully drove back the Mongols. Nightfall ended hostilities and both sides encamped on the field, but during the night the Seljuk forces evaporated, and when Baichu launched a sudden attack against the Seljuk camp at first light the next morning it was found to be deserted. It seems that Kai Khosrou, dubious of the loyalty of many of his amirs (who wished to surrender), had slipped away through fear of treachery, and his army seems to have followed suit; alternatively it may have been his army which slipped away first!

On discovering the Seljuks' flight the Mongols suspected that it was a ruse intended to draw them into an ambush. Their pursuit was therefore delayed by a full day, but even then many Seljuks were overtaken and killed. Kai Khosrou himself escaped to Ankara. Thereafter the Sultan of Rum became a vassal of the Mongols, paying an annual tribute of 12 million Hyperperes, 5,000 sheep, 500 camels and 500 pieces of silk.

LA FORBIE (GAZA) 1244

Allied to al-Mansur of Homs and an-Nasir of Kerak, a Frankish army under Philip de Montfort and Count Walter de Brienne of Jaffa marched against as-Salih Ayyub, Sultan of Egypt. In addition to 6,000 Franks, including infantry, Cypriote knights, contingents from the Military Orders (Hospital, Temple, Teutonic Knights and St Lazarus) and Turcopole cavalry, their combined army included 4-5,000 or more Syrian and Bedouin cavalry.

At La Forbie, near Gaza, an Egyptian army under the amir Baibars consisting of 5,000 elite troops and 10,000 mercenary Khwarizmian cavalry opposed them. Al-Mansur advised that the allied army should fortify their camp and act on the defensive since the Khwarizmians were unhappy attacking strong positions and would probably desert, thereby forcing the withdrawal of the remainder of the inferior Egyptian force. Count Walter, however, insisted that they should advance and engage the Egyptians immediately, and unfortunately his counsel prevailed.

Confronted by the Khwarizmians, most of the Syrians of the allied centre took to flight when counter-attacked; only the 2,000-strong Homs contingent did not flee outright, fighting their way off the field in good order despite suffering perhaps as many as 1,720 casualties. The departure of the Syrians, followed post-haste by the Bedouins posted on the left flank, left their Frankish allies on the right hopelessly outnumbered. These the Khwarizmians now attacked in flank while the Egyptians pressed in on their front (alternatively the Egyptians may have fled, leaving the Khwarizmians to encircle the Franks).

After several hours of hard fighting the Franks were routed. Ernoul says that barely a quarter of the army escaped, but they may have lost as many as 5,000 dead. Certainly 325 Hospitallers, 312 Templars and perhaps 297 Teutonic Knights were killed, only 12-65 brethren (5-26 Hospitallers, 4-36 Templars and 3 Teutonic Knights) managing to escape, the Master of the Temple being amongst the dead. The Lazar contingent (possibly about 40 men, certainly no more) and the Cypriote contingent of 300 men were wiped out. In addition the Egyptians took 800 prisoners, including Count Walter and the Master of the Hospital (both of whom died in captivity) and perhaps 100 other brethren of the Military Orders. Not without reason has this battle been described as 'a second Hattin'.

EL MANSURAH 1250

After capturing Damietta during the Seventh Crusade, an army of 20-40,000 crusaders under King Louis IX of France marched on Cairo. Although largely French in composition, including 1,800-2,500 knights and 5,000 archers, the army also included 400 Achaian knights, 200 English knights under Earl William of Salisbury, and about 700-1,000 Hospitaller, Templar, Cypriote and Syrian Frankish knights.

Their advance was held up for nearly two months by the Egyptians' defence of a canal just north of El Mansurah, the Bahr as-Saghir, but eventually a local Copt revealed a ford to them four miles to the east near the village of Salamun. Two days later the cavalry of the Frankish army crossed the canal by this ford, the plan being for them to then ride back along the canal to cover the crossing of the infantry over a makeshift wooden bridge. However, the vanguard under Louis' brother Robert d'Artois, composed of some 1,500 knights including 290 Templars, failed to follow these instructions and once across rode straight for the Egyptian camp. The Muslims were caught completely by surprise and driven from their camp and into El Mansurah with heavy losses, their commander Fakr ad-Din being killed in the confusion. But despite this initial success, when the Franks followed the fleeing Egyptians into the town they were routed by two mamluk regiments (the Bahriyyah and Jamdariyyah) commanded by the amir Baibars, and shot down by archers positioned on the rooftops, perhaps as many as 1,000-1,500 Frankish horsemen being killed including Robert d'Artois, the Earl of Salisbury, most of the 200 Englishmen and 285 Templars.

The main body of Frankish cavalry under King Louis, with the element of surprise now lost, managed to secure a bridgehead only after a hard fight, the Egyptians only being finally driven back when the crossbow-armed Frankish infantry began to cross by their hastily completed causeway towards nightfall. By this time at least a third of the knights were dead and many more were without horses, and although they succeeded in holding the bridgehead against a fierce night-attack the Franks no longer had the strength to advance further. Three days later another Egyptian attack was repulsed after heavy fighting in which the contingents of the Military Orders were almost annihilated.

After another eight weeks, with disease rampant throughout the Frankish camp, the presence of an Egyptian flotilla on the canal in their rear prevented further supplies getting through from Damietta and finally forced Louis to withdraw. Racked by disease and hunger the Franks were surrounded and destroyed as they withdrew after a running battle with the Egyptians. When they finally surrendered the sick and weak (perhaps totalling 7,000) were massacred by their captors. Of the other 20,000 or so survivors Louis eventually managed to negotiate the release of 12,000 by the surrender of Damietta and the payment of a huge ransom of one million gold bezants.

Although Louis remained active in Outremer for a further four years his army never again exceeded about 1,400 men and the disaster of El Mansurah effectively ended the Seventh Crusade.

PELAGONIA 1259

In 1259 Michael II of Epirus formed an alliance with Achaia and Sicily against the Nicaean Empire, principally to dispute Nicaea's possessions in the Balkans. Against this array a Nicaean army was mustered under the Emperor's half-brother John Palaeologus, composed of 1,500 Hungarians, 300 Germans, 600, 1,000 or 5,000 Serbs, 500-1,500 Turks, 4,000 Cumans and Alans and an unknown number of Bulgars (all these contingents being cavalry), as well as Slavs and Anatolian Greeks, probably totalling in all 20-25,000 men. John's principal reliance was placed in the various contingents of horse-archers, who prior to the battle persistently harassed the Epirotes and their allies and permitted them no rest day or night.

The Epirotes themselves numbered some 8,000 cavalry and 18,000 infantry. Of their allies the Achaians, under Prince William Villehardouin, mustered an equal number of cavalry and 12,000 infantry, and the Sicilians 400 first-class heavy cavalry, probably on barded horses, and perhaps 2,600 Saracen archers (this would explain the discrepancy in the figures of 400 and 3,000 Sicilians quoted by Akropolites and Pachymeres respectively). The Epirotes also included an unknown number of Vlachs (Wallachians) under Michael's son John. The total allied forces therefore mustered in excess of 50,000 men.

However, their advantage in numbers was negated by distrust and dissension amongst the various contingents – William, for instance, was almost certainly acting entirely in his own interests and, with his better-quality troops, probably intended to impose his will on Michael after the defeat of the Nicaeans. Michael certainly suspected the loyalty of the Achaians and during the night before the battle large numbers of Epirotes slipped away. That same night a squabble with the haughty Achaians alienated the Vlachs, and this led to their leader, John, secretly sending messengers to the Nicaean camp as a result of which it was agreed that he and his troops would withdraw from the line at the commencement of battle.

So on the morning of the battle the Achaians seem to have found themselves left to face the Nicaeans alone, since during the night Michael II himself appears to have deserted, the remainder of his force presumably following suit at first light. (It is possible that he did in fact remain, but was inactive during the battle because part of his son's agreement with the Nicaeans was that Michael and the Epirotes should not be attacked.)

Prince William at first considered executing a hasty withdrawal, but failed to do so. Instead the Franks drew up in formation and charged. The Nicaean counter-attack was spearheaded by their 300 German mercenaries, who were deliberately sacrificed to absorb the impact of the initial Frankish charge.

Becoming inextricably mixed with the Achaian cavalry they began to suffer heavy losses, despite a simultaneous attack in William's rear by the Vlachs. John Palaeologus then ordered his Turkish, Cuman and Hungarian horse-archers to fire into the whole entangled mass of cavalry, with complete disregard for the lives of the German mercenaries therein. Their volleys were directed principally at the Franks' unarmoured horses, so that the Achaian (and German?) knights fell in large numbers beneath this barrage as their horses were mowed down. The remainder then broke and fled.

Few actually escaped. The battlefield was littered with the corpses of 'thousands' of Franks, and those who lived were mostly captured by the Nicaeans' Turkish light cavalry. The 400 Sicilian cavalry who, one suspects, probably declined to get involved in the one-sided battle since they appear to have suffered no losses, surrendered to one of the Nicaean generals. Prince William himself was taken captive while hiding in a haystack, and 30 of his nobles were also captured. In fact the nobility of Achaia were practically annihilated in this one battle.

'AIN JALUT 1260

An Ilkhanid army of 10,000 cavalry under Kitbugha, chiefly Mongol-officered Turks but including Georgian and Cilician Armenian troops, was defeated by a superior force of about 12,000 Mamluks that included Khwarizmians and Bedouin auxiliaries supplied by the Ayyubids of Kerak.

The Mamluks sent forward an advance guard of Egyptian troops specially chosen for their unreliability and poor morale; these were commanded by the amir Baibars, now commander-in-chief of the Mamluk army. As anticipated, they broke and ran in the face of the Mongols' arrow storm and first charge, drawing Kitbugha into a pre-planned ambush in the hills where the bulk of the Mamluk army under Sultan Qutuz awaited them, filling the valley from side to side. These withstood the Mongol charge and successfully enveloped their flanks. The fleeing Egyptians of the first line now also rallied and returned to the fray.

Despite their inferiority in numbers the Mongols nearly succeeded in breaking through, the battle remaining in the balance until midday when they were routed in a final counter-attack. They rallied once near Beisan, but broke after another fierce fight. Those that could fled, but they suffered severe losses in the pursuit, which took the Mamluks 300 miles to the very banks of the Euphrates. Kitbugha himself was either killed in battle or captured after his horse had been shot under him and promptly executed, his head being used for an impromptu game of polo! Not long after this victory Baibars had Qutuz murdered and himself proclaimed Sultan.

JAULAN 1261

A large Templar force under the Marshal, comprising most of the kingdom's brethren (the contingent of the main convent being joined by the garrisons of Safed, Beaufort and Château Pèlerin), plus lay knights under Jean d'Ibelin and the Marshal of the Kingdom, mounted a raid against a large Turcoman encampment near Tiberias. The Turcomans, however, got wind of their advance and soundly repulsed them, presumably in an ambush. In addition to those killed 16 Templars were captured, plus Jean d'Ibelin and several other counts and lay knights, the Templars in addition losing 'all their harness'; the prisoners were ransomed for 20,000 bezants. The Templar Marshal was blamed for the defeat and temporarily lost his habit and was removed from office.

MAKRYPLAGI 1264

A Byzantine army, including Tzakones, Slavs and Turkish cavalry, was defeated while campaigning against the Achaian Franks.

The Byzantines' 6,000 Turkish auxiliaries, disgruntled because their pay was six months in arrears, decided to offer their services to the Franks, who readily accepted. The Franks then advanced towards Kalamata, but on the rising crest of the pass of Makryplagi their vanguard was ambushed by the Byzantine forces. The Franks were twice repulsed as fresh Byzantine units successively emerged from ambush, but on their third attempt they successfully stormed the ridge when the Turkish auxiliaries simultaneously appeared in the rear of the Byzantines and routed them. Seeing this those Byzantine units still concealed in hiding panicked and abandoned their positions.

The Byzantine commanders, the Grand Domestic Philes and Makrenos, were captured together with 354 nobles and officers and 5,030 other ranks. Philes died in captivity, while Makrenos was blinded by the Byzantines after his release, following accusations of collaboration with the Franks.

CAROUBLIER 1266

Following Mamluk raids through Galilee, King Hugh III of Cyprus (bailli of Jerusalem) launched a chevauchée towards Tiberias, mustering the contingents of the Military Orders and the mercenary French regiment from Acre. His force probably numbered about 400 cavalry plus a larger number of infantry and included Cypriotes. However, the vanguard of Hospitallers, Teutonic Knights and some lay knights, becoming careless, got separated from the main army whilst searching for loot and was ambushed by the Muslim garrison of Safed. 500 Frankish cavalry and infantry were killed, plus the Grand Commander of the Hospital and 45 Hospitaller brethren, while many of those who escaped were massacred in a night attack on their camp by local Bedouins.

ALBISTAN 1277

To thwart a projected invasion of Syria by the Ilkhanids, Baibars entered the Jihan and intercepted the Ilkhanid army, which was composed of the Mongol garrison of Rum – 11 divisions under Tukuz (each of 1,000 or more men, including 3,000 Georgians) – and probably a similar number of Rumi Turks under the Pervana (Keeper of the Seals) Suleiman. The Ilkhan Abaqa had, in fact, been forewarned of the Mamluk attack by King Leo III of Cilicia, but the Pervana, who was hatching an ambitious plot of his own, deliberately suppressed the information and lulled the Mongols into a false sense of security so that when the Mamluk army appeared it caught the Mongols unprepared.

The two armies met at Albistan. The advantage was with Baibars from the outset since his army numbered in excess of 30,000 men, but the Mongols gained some headway before the Mamluks put them to flight; probably the terrain was not suitable for the Mongols' mode of warfare, and John Bagot Glubb says that they in fact fought on foot because of the mountainous terrain. Whatever the reason, the Mongols were routed with appalling losses; 6,770 Mongols and 2,000 Georgians were killed, including Tukuz, and the Seljuks probably suffered about the same number of casualties. In addition Baibars executed all those Mongols who were taken prisoner, though he spared the Seljuks.

Soon after, hearing of the approach of a much larger Mongol army under Abaqa himself, Baibars withdrew to Syria. Abaqa then had the treacherous Pervana Suleiman arrested and put on trial; he was found guilty not only of deserting the army in the face of the enemy but of actually arranging for the Mamluk invasion, and was promptly executed as a traitor.

HOMS 1281

Two Mongol armies invaded Syria under Ilkhan Abaqa and his brother Mangu Timur. While the former proceeded to subdue the Mamluk frontier fortresses along the Euphrates, Mangu was joined by Georgian and Cilician Armenian troops under their kings Dimitri and Leo III, Rumi Seljuks, and a small number of Hospitallers from al-Marqab, and proceeded down the Orontes valley with his army 30-80,000 strong. The Georgians and Armenians constituted about one-third of this total (perhaps 30,000 men). Outside Homs they encountered the Mamluk army under Sultan Qalaun.

The Mamluks, numbering 50-60,000, formed up with al-Halqa, Royal Mamluks and Egyptians in the centre, Bedouins and Ayyubids from Hamah and Kerak on the right and Syrians and Turcomans on the left, while Mangu drew up with the Mongols forming the centre and left and the bulk of the allied contingents – Cilicians, Georgians and Hospitallers – constituting the right flank.

Despite heavy losses the Christians of the Mongol right routed their Turcoman opponents and the 12,000 men of the Mamluk left flank early in the battle and pursued them from the field right up to their camp before the gates of Homs, where they killed many more. Many of the survivors then fled on towards Egypt, while the victors looted the abandoned camp. The Mongol centre with which they had now lost touch meanwhile continued to press the Mamluks, until a Mamluk officer, pretending to desert, succeeded in penetrating the Mongol ranks and wounded and unhorsed Mangu. Simultaneously a band of 300 Bedouin auxiliaries attacked the Mongol left flank and proceeded to plunder the baggage train.

Unnerved and fearing encirclement Mangu ordered a withdrawal, and the Mamluks launched a final charge to clear the field. When the isolated Armenians and Georgians learnt of this they immediately turned back to rejoin the main army, passing so close to Qalaun's command post – where the Sultan had a guard of only 1,000 men – that he had to conceal his standards and silence his drums for fear of discovery. But once they had passed he fell upon their rear and harassed their withdrawal so that they suffered heavy losses as they fought their way out, especially since they also bumped into the Mamluk right flank as it returned from its successful pursuit of Mangu. In fact Mongol losses suffered during the pursuit were apparently heavier than during the battle, but Mamluk losses had also been heavy.

ACRE 1291

Encouraged by riots within the city, a Mamluk army of 60,000 cavalry, 100-160,000 infantry and 92 siege-engines commenced the siege of Acre on 5 April. The Frankish garrison, under the absent King Henry II's brother Amalric, consisted of only 7-900 knights and 14-18,000 infantry composed of the Military Orders, Syrian and Cypriote Franks, the mercenary French regiment under Jean de Grailly, an English contingent under a Swiss mercenary officer named Otto de Grandison, Pisans, Venetians and the Commune of Acre. Reinforcements of 200 knights and 500 infantry under King Henry himself arrived from Cyprus on 4 May.

On 15 May, six weeks after the commencement of the siege, the city's outer wall fell, undermined and breached in several places by the Muslim engines, and though the brethren of the Military Orders were at first successful in driving out the Mamluks, by evening the Franks had been forced to withdraw behind the inner walls. Just three days later the inner wall was also breached in the vicinity of the Accursed Tower and the Mamluks fought their way into the city in the face of stiff opposition from the Military Orders in particular, the Templar Grand Master and the Marshal of the Hospital being amongst those killed in the chaotic street-fighting which ensued. But the Mamluks' penetration to the inner city marked the end of organised resistance.

King Henry, Amalric and some others, including Jean de Grailly and Otto de Grandison, escaped by ship to Cyprus, but most of the defenders and a huge number of citizens died in the streets or were captured and sold into slavery. The surviving Templars and other refugees continued to hold out from their fortress by the sea under the command of their Marshal, but on 28 May, ten days after the fall of the city, their defences were breached as a result of undermining and incessant bombardment. 2,000 Mamluks then stormed the breach, only to bring the crumbling walls down on Muslim and Christian alike.

The Franks abandoned Tyre the day after the fall of Acre, and Beirut and Sidon fell to the Mamluks in July. With just two exceptions no vestige of the mainland crusader states remained by the end of the summer, the exceptions being the lordship of Jebail, which survived until 1298, and the offshore Templar fortress of Ruad at Tortosa, which fell in 1303.

WADI AL-KHAZINDAR (SALAMIYET) 1299

The conversion of the Ilkhanid Mongols to Islam in 1295 did little or nothing to lessen their enmity towards the Mamluks, and in 1299 the Ilkhan Ghazan Mahmud launched yet another Mongol invasion of Syria. This time they were intercepted by the Mamluk army at Wadi al-Khazindar. The Mongol army, which included Georgians and 5,000 Cilicians, is recorded as 100,000 strong but was in fact much smaller, possibly fewer in number than the Mamluks' 20-40,000.

The Mamluks were led by Sultan Mohammed, but since he was only a child a senior amir, Salar, took command on the battlefield. He formed up the Mamluk forces with 5,000 Bedouin auxiliaries on their right flank, taking command of the centre himself while another senior amir, Bektash, commanded the left. The Mongols decided to remain on the defensive and were ordered to stand fast until Ghazan himself led the charge.

For some reason the Mamluks decided to rely on their swords and maces and put their lances (and bows?) aside. Their advance was preceded by 500 mounted engineers equipped with 'naptha tubes', but these seem to have had no effect and consequently the cavalry charged. Bektash successfully broke the Mongol right and pursued it from the field, but on the opposite flank the Mamluks met fierce resistance, the Mongols having dismounted 10,000 of their men who now stood behind their horses and poured volleys of arrows into the charging

Mamluks. The Bedouins and Syrian contingents seem to have suffered particularly severely, losing large numbers of horses, and were forced to fall back.

Though still hard-pressed by Salar, Ghazan chose this moment to launch his counter-attack. The elite Mamluk Burjiyyah regiment broke in the first charge, and after a brief engagement a second charge routed the rest of the Mamluks. The Mongol pursuit took some as far as Gaza and Jerusalem, while in addition 12,000 Lebanese Druzes seriously harassed the Mamluks as they withdrew. Mongol casualties appear to have totalled some 14,000 men.

Damascus fell to Ghazan early in 1300, and for a while there seemed a possibility that Christendom stood a chance of regaining Syria by an alliance with the Ilkhan who, Muslim though he was, would have welcomed Christian allies. Nothing was done however, and the opportunity evaporated after the Mongols' defeat by the Mamluks at Shaqhab in 1303. In 1308 his successor Oljeitu actually reached Jerusalem itself and rumour had it that he would have handed the city over in exchange for a Christian alliance. But no such alliance was offered, and the death in 1304 of the pro-Christian Ilkhan Ghazan really ended forever the chance of a Mongol-backed crusader kingdom.

DRESS AND EQUIPMENT

1 & 2. PILGRIMS

The distinguishing feature of all crusaders was the cross, worn 'on the shoulders of their mantles or cassocks or tunics' once they had declared their intention to go on a crusade.

Although the shoulder or right breast seem to have been the most common places to wear the cross it is also recorded worn between the shoulders (apparently signifying the pilgrim to be returning from crusade). It normally consisted of a cruciform piece of cloth sewn onto everyday clothes. Traditionally it was red in colour but, although this was generally the case, by the Third Crusade of 1189-1192 certain colours had begun to adopt national identities – red for the French, green for the Flemish, white for the English and yellow for the Germans. To a certain extent these distinctions lasted into the 13th century when, for example, Simon de Montfort's army at Lewes in 1264 wore 'the white cross of the crusader', while the French who fought against Manfred of Sicily in 1266 wore red crosses (the enterprise having been declared a crusade). By the very end of this period, however, the red cross had become a national insignia of not the French but the English, while the white cross (often on a blue background) was nationally adopted by the French rather than the English. Undoubtedly crosses of any colour could be found in any army at any time, depending on what material was to hand at the moment of 'taking the cross'; many nobility, for instance, wore crosses of such substance as woven gold.

These figures are typical of the' non-combatants' who accompanied the early crusades in vast numbers. Both date to c.1170 and wear everyday clothes. They carry the characteristic staff and wallet or scrip-bag, the latter suspended from a shoulder-strap. Although some carried a bow or spear most were unarmed or only poorly equipped with farm implements, and it is a heart-felt plea from more than one contemporary chronicler that more such pilgrims of the early crusade armies might have been equipped 'with the sword instead of the wallet and the bow instead of the staff.'

3. FRANKISH KNIGHT c.1097

The development of armour in the crusader states followed exactly the same course as in Europe. Since this has already been discussed in *'Armies of Feudal Europe'* it is not intended to cover the subject in detail again and the following six figures should be taken only as a representative selection.

It is generally accepted, quite rightly, that knights of the First Crusade and, to a lesser extent, the Second Crusade would have been little different from the Norman knights depicted in the Bayeux Tapestry, and this conclusion is borne out by this figure who, though he dates to the mid-12th century, represents a knight of the First Crusade. He carries a kite-shield, wears a conical helmet (with or without nasal) and a knee-length, ¾-sleeved hauberk, and is armed with lance and sword.

He carries the crusader device on helmet and gonfalon and could also have had it painted on his shield. An English knight of the First Crusade is described as having crosses on his helmet, shield, saddle and horse accoutrements, and certainly during the earlier crusades knights carried the cross device chiefly on shield and/or helmet. Shields were otherwise painted in bright colours and patterns rather than heraldic devices, many probably resembling Bayeux Tapestry types; Albert of Aix, describing crusaders at Antioch in 1097, speaks of 'shields of gold, green, red and other colours'.

At what stage crusaders who stayed on in the Holy Land gave up wearing the cross is an unanswerable question. Apparently some never did, though it seems probable that the majority of settlers did so soon after fulfilling their pilgrim's vows.

4. FRANKISH KNIGHT c.1150

This figure is very little different from the last, though in accordance with prevailing fashion his tunic, as well as his hauberk, is somewhat longer. The hauberk now has wrist-length sleeves, which became standard in the course of the 12th century. The cross is again in evidence on his helmet. Lighter forms of armour such as this would have remained in use amongst sergeants for much of this era.

5. FRANKISH KNIGHT c.1189

This figure is based on the seal of the most famous crusader of them all, King Richard I of England, known to posterity as Richard Coeur de Lion – Richard the Lion-Heart. The seal was probably executed immediately prior to his departure for the Third Crusade. The sleeves of the hauberk now have mail mittens attached, and in addition separate mail defences (called hosen or chausses) are worn to protect the legs. Chausses had been in use since the mid-11th century but only came into widespread use about a century later; certainly they were standard equipment for wealthier knights by this date, and the author of the Itinerarium Regis Ricardi notes with alarm how Richard went into battle at Jaffa without his.

His helmet is hemispherical rather than conical; a flat-topped variety could also be worn, and 5a, from Richard's second seal of a few years later, shows another type of helmet with a face-guard, just beginning to appear at about this date; note also the early crest. Another early occurrence of a crest is in an incident at the siege of Tyre in 1187, where a knight is recorded with a pair of stag's antlers fixed to his helmet. The shield displays Richard's heraldic device, two rampant lions facing each other, which also appeared on the back of his saddle. Heraldry evolved in about the mid-12th century and, in Outremer, may have been encouraged by the Saracens' use of personal devices.

6. FRANKISH KNIGHT c.1250

By 1230 the helmet type depicted in 5a had evolved into the barrel-helm (the casque or heaume) depicted here, padded on the inside and with eye-slits and

breathing holes pierced in the mask. A quilted head-defence, the arming cap, was usually worn under the coif from c.1200 onwards.

Other differences from the last figure are the addition of surcoat and cuisses. The former was most probably adopted in imitation of Saracen dress, possibly as early as c.1127 when a knight is recorded by Usamah ibn-Munqidh to have worn a long, sleeved green and yellow silk coat over his armour. Its use was probably far more widespread in Outremer than in Europe, where it was not widely worn until the early-13th century. It was usually sleeveless and at first plain in colour, but after the introduction of heraldry it often displayed the wearer's heraldic device. In this particular instance the surcoat, as well as the lance pennon, displays crosses. The upstanding cross at each shoulder may indicate he is wearing some form of reinforced leather cuirie or iron breastplate under the surcoat.

Cuisses were quilted tubes worn over the thighs as additional protection. They first appear c.1220 and are common thereafter.

7. FRANKISH KNIGHT c.1275

Taken from the seal of John de Montfort, lord of Tyre and Toran (1270-1283), this figure shows little change from figure 6 except that he substitutes a banner for the latter's pennon. Like 6 he carries a flat-topped shield (this type first appeared c.1140 and was the predominant shield-type by the 13th century, its size generally decreasing somewhat as time went by).

More interesting is the cloth covering for his horse, the housing. In Europe this only first appeared c.1185 but it may have appeared in **Outremer** at a somewhat earlier date under Muslim influence (see figure 93), some Frankish horses possibly wearing housings at Hattin in 1187. Quite probably some housings consisted of several layers or were quilted, in which case they would have been quite capable of stopping Turkish flight-arrows except at close range. The housing was also useful for displaying the rider's heraldic device, for which purpose it was already being used before the end of the 12th century.

8. FRANKISH KNIGHT c.1290

This figure, based on mss. illustrated in Acre between 1280 and 1291, shows how knights were equipped during the kingdom's closing years. The barrel-helm has been replaced by a type called a 'sugar-loaf' after its shape (though the heaume also remained in use) and he carries a cross-emblazoned shield. Colours of cross and field on crusader shields in the Acre mss. indicate that practically any colour combination was possible, irrespective of heraldic rules, including red on black, brown on red, red on mauve, blue on yellow, etc. The cross itself also appeared in diverse forms and shapes.

Attached to his chausses are iron poleyns (knee-guards), which could also be attached to the quilted cuisse. Other pieces of plate-armour in use by this time but uncommon until the 14th century were couters (elbow-guards which, like poleyns, probably first appeared c.1225) and schynbalds (greaves, protecting either the front or both front and back of the lower leg). There were also shoulder pieces called ailettes which first appeared c.1270, but these were of leather rather than metal; their defensive value remains questionable.

9. FRANKISH MOUNTED SERGEANT

In addition to knights there were also armoured horsemen of lesser status available to the Frankish host, referred to variously in the sources by the terms milites gregarii, milites plebei, equites levis armaturae, serjans à cheval

and servientes loricati among others; all refer to mounted men of less than knightly status including sergeants (servientes), the non-knightly elements of noblemen's retinues and probably the wealthier burghers of the towns. They are not always easy to find in the sources, which often list only the number of knights present, 'excepting,' as Fulcher of Chartres admits in one passage, 'those who were not counted as knights although they were mounted.'

They were less heavily equipped than the knights (hence 'levis armaturae'), wearing lighter or old-fashioned armour but carrying the same armament of lance and sword. This mid-13th-century figure from Matthew Paris' drawings of crusade battles is probably fairly typical.

In strict feudal terminology the sergeant was, by the late 12th century, the holder of a grant of land called a sergeanty (in Europe usually half the size of a knight's fee), but contemporary chroniclers more often tended to use the word 'sergeant' and its variants as blanket-terms for all non-knightly soldiers, often not even distinguishing between mounted men and infantry. Turcopoles too are sometimes described as sergeants.

10, 11, 12 & 13. FRANKISH INFANTRYMEN

Infantry in the crusader states ranged from pilgrims armed with no more than a spear or bow (see figures 1 and 2), through to well-armed and armoured mercenaries and feudal retainers, the latter elements comprising the largest percentage of foot-soldiers in most armies, armed chiefly with spear, bow or crossbow though some may have been equipped with both spear and bow. The Anonymi Gesta Francorum records crossbows in use as early as the First Crusade, as does Anna Comnena, and certainly by the middle to late-12th century the crossbow was the weapon par excellence of the Frankish infantryman.

Figures 10 and 11 are based on descriptions of the 12th century. Beha ed-Din, writing of Frankish infantry at Arsuf in 1191, describes how they were 'clothed in a kind of thick felt, and mail corselets as ample as they were strong, which protected them against arrows. I have seen men with up to ten arrows stuck in their bodies marching no less easily for that.' Ambroise, describing the same battle, likewise records that the infantry were 'armed quite well according to the custom of foot-soldiers, [with] head protected by an iron cover, [and] a hauberk and a linen tunic padded many times and difficult to penetrate, ingeniously worked with a needle and consequently

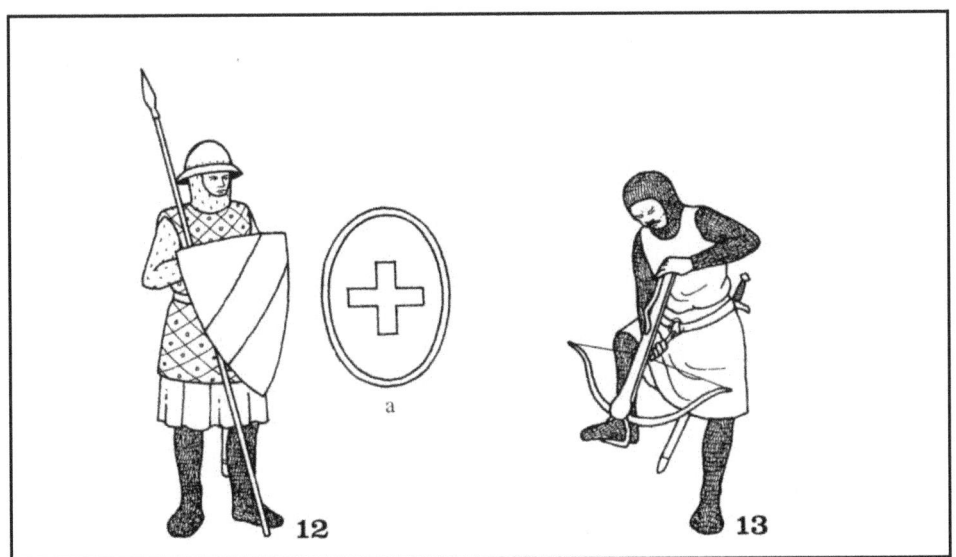

called in the vernacular a pourpoint.' Such quilted corselets, though known in Europe for several centuries, only came into widespread use during the Crusades through contact with the Muslims, amongst whom quilted armour was a standard form of body-defence (see note 35-38); the Muslims called it al-qutun, literally 'cotton', a term which the Franks soon corrupted to aketon (see figures 26-28 in *'Armies of Feudal Europe'*). 'Gambeson' was an alternative term that first appeared c.1160, possibly differing from the aketon in having sleeves. Basically all such armour consisted of a leather, linen or woollen tunic padded with wool, cotton and old rags and quilted either vertically or diagonally,

Figure 12, based on illustrations in an Acre ms. of c.1280, gives a general idea of the appearance of such armour, in this instance two such corselets being worn one over the other (possibly aketon over gambeson). Figure 13, similarly dating to the late 13th century, substitutes mail corselet and surcoat. Both wear mail chausses in addition.

Unlike spearmen, crossbowmen and archers apparently carried no shields. Although most shields were like those of figures 10 and 12 it should be noted that some of the mss. illuminated in Acre as late as 1290-1291 show circular shields in use amongst Frankish infantry, one ms. of 1287 even depicting oval shields such as 12a.

The clothes of Franks in Outremer were of cotton, wool, linen and silk. Colours were generally bright, principally red, green and yellow, and also black, those of the upper classes often being richly embroidered in gold and coloured thread. The Franks were generally clean-shaven by the mid-12th century, one contemporary pilgrim noting that of all the peoples of Outremer they 'are the only ones ... who shave the beard'. For other infantrymen of this era see *'Armies of Feudal Europe'*. In addition, in crusading armies many knights were frequently reduced to the role of infantry by the loss of their horses.

14. TURCOPOLE

Turcopoles were Syrian mercenaries employed in considerable numbers by the Military Orders as well as by the king and Frankish nobility.

Despite the statements of R.C. Smail in his *'Crusading Warfare'* that 'there seems little justification in assuming, on the basis of the scanty information usually quoted, that all Turcopoles were both horsemen and archers' and, of horse-archery, 'that there is no reason to suppose that many natives of Syria were adept in its use', it seems fairly certain that the Turcopoles were all horsemen and that although not all were necessarily armed with a bow by far the majority were. Those at Sarmin in 1115 were certainly archers, and Usamah ibn-Munqidh actually calls the Turcopoles 'the archers of the Franks'; in addition a chronicler of the Third Crusade, describing an engagement with Byzantine troops on Cyprus, wrote 'like a swift Turcopole did the Emperor ride ... and shot two arrows at the king.'

Further evidence that they were mounted may be inferred from the wording of Muslim treaties, such as those of 1267, 1269 and 1283, all of which equate 'a knight for a knight, a Turcopole for a Turcopole, a merchant for a merchant, a foot-soldier for a foot-soldier'. Saladin, dictating terms for the surrender of Jaffa in 1192, likewise equated knight for horseman, foot-soldier for foot-soldier and Turcopole for light-armed soldier; in all these instances the very specific 'foot-soldier for foot-soldier 'clearly excludes the Turcopoles, by which we may take it they were mounted. William of Tyre states quite categorically that they were 'light-armed horsemen '.

At first they were probably composed mainly of mixed-race natives, Syrians

14   15   16

and Turkish converts, but later they included a great many Poulain sergeants who were probably equipped to fight Saracen-fashion, Dr. J. Riley-Smith suggesting that by the 13th century the term Turcopole 'referred to the function rather than the race of the holder'.

In addition to the bow the Turcopoles would have carried a light lance and/or javelins plus a sword and possibly a mace. Whether they were armoured or not is a moot point. As already seen, William of Tyre and Saladin both described them as 'light -armed', but that is also the standard contemporary description of Saracens, many of whom wore light or not-so-light armour. The fact that Turcopoles were often mustered alongside the knights would tend to suggest that they wore light armour of some description, even if only quilted al-qutuns, and it is interesting to note that when Guy de Lusignan first established fiefs in Cyprus in 1192 those of Turcopoles owed the service of a man with mail armour (as well as two horses).

It seems probable that those employed by the Military Orders would have carried some kind of recognition device, probably a cross (of the appropriate colour) on shield and/or tunic. (Confrère brethren and mercenaries of the Orders probably carried similar devices; we hear, for instance, of shields with a 'chief gules' and a 'cross argent', indicating allegiance to the Hospitallers.)

15. MARONITE OR SYRIAN CHRISTIAN

This shows the probable appearance of Maronites and the few Syrian soldiers in Frankish armies. The native Christians wore the same basic dress as Muslims (Burchard of Mount Sion says they were distinguished by 'a woollen girdle') and were in fact forbidden by legislation to wear Frankish-style clothes. They also differed from the Franks in growing long beards of which they were extremely proud (Jacques de Vitry relating how they 'cherish them with great care, and specially glory in them').

The composite bow was the principal weapon of the Maronites, and de Vitry records that the few warlike Syrians also 'use bows and arrows, but are unarmoured and ready for running away' (though this may be a reference to the tactics of Turcopoles).

Some Maronite chieftains at least fought on horseback and wore armour, and various sources attest the taking of considerable amounts of arms and armour from the Muslims, which was undoubtedly reused after capture. Many armoured Maronites would therefore have been indistinguishable from Saracens, and it was fairly certainly for the purpose of recognition that one Maronite chieftain is recorded as having the sign of the cross on his armour. Some Frankish equipment was undoubtedly also in use.

16, 17 & 18. CILICIAN ARMENIANS

The Armenian principalities relied chiefly on bands of paid retainers (largely natives but including Turks, Persians and Franks) and militia infantry. In equipment and organisation Frankish influence soon came to predominate (particularly under Leo II, 1198-1221) and feudalism was introduced from neighbouring Antioch, the titles Cunstable and Baron being adopted in place of the old Sparapet and Nakharar. In addition there were some Armenian knights even in Edessa and Antioch, of whom figure 17 is probably fairly representative.

Figures 16 and 17, based on Cilician ms. illuminations and one of the Acre mss. of c.1280, are fairly typical of Cilician Armenian horsemen, composed of the nobility and their retainers. Both wear mail corselets, that of figure 16 being of a distinctly Byzantine design. Frankish equipment probably predominated by the 13th century, some late 13th century and early 14th-century Cilician mss. showing warriors indistinguishable from Frankish knights (though simple helmets of the types worn here appear to have been worn in preference to the Frankish heaume), but it seems likely that a mixture of Byzantine, Muslim and Frankish gear was in widespread use throughout most of this era; figure 16 certainly betrays evidence of all three styles. Shields were either circular or kite-shaped, the latter apparently adopted prior to the Crusades, probably under Byzantine influence.

Figure 18, like 17 based on Frankish mss. of c.1280-1290, wears typical oriental garb. The cap is of a type worn by both Jews and Armenians in the sources and was apparently a common form of headwear, even amongst Franks. Many Armenians wore turbans, and all wore beards. Commonest infantry weapons were bow and spear.

17 18 19

19, 20 & 21. BRETHREN OF THE MILITARY ORDERS IN HABITS

Figure 19 wears the black hooded mantle, the cappa clausa, of the Hospital, with a white cross sewn on; the cross, adopted at some time before 1153, was probably quite small, Riley-Smith stating it to be only three or four inches deep. The characteristic eight-pointed cross of the Hospitallers (19a) seems to have been introduced during the first quarter of the 13th century but didn't completely replace the cross formée and apparently wasn't worn with military dress. A black skullcap officially completed the habit, though white turbans were often worn in Outremer. A broad-brimmed hat (like that of Figure 2) could also be worn.

Figure 20 wears the habit of white woollen tunic, mantle and skullcap granted to the Poor Knights of Christ – the Templars – in 1128; prior to this date they dressed like secular knights, wearing donated cast-offs. The red cross was worn by all brethren from 1147 onwards. Other items of official issue dress included linen shirts, tunic, breeches and sheepskin jerkin. In addition, however, some brethren of both Temple and Hospital wore more worldly garments such as bright silks and gold or silver embroidered clothes and turbans.

Figure 21 is based on the tomb effigy of Conrad of Thuringia, Hochmeister of the Teutonic Knights 1239-1241. Like the Templars – and despite their opposition – they wore a white habit, their right to wear this being secured for them by the Holy Roman Emperor Frederick II (King of Jerusalem 1225-1228). The cross was black. Sergeants later wore a grey habit with a 3-armed Tau cross like a capital 'T' (also called a crux commissa), and it seems probable that this dress was also worn in 13th-century Outremer. Beards were obligatory in all three Orders.

The following are brief details of the other Military Orders active in Outremer:

Order	History	Habit	Device
Knights of the Hospital of St Lazarus.	A leper Order. Established early-12th century. Probably turned military c.1123.	Black(?)	Green cross from 16th century.
Knights of St Thomas of Canterbury at Acre (St Thomas Acon).	An English Order. Established 1191. Probably turned military c.1220.	White	Red cross with white scallop shell at centre.
Knights of Our Lady of Montjoie (Knights of Trufac after 1187).	A Spanish Order. Papal confirmation 1180. Withdrew from Outremer after Hattin in 1187 and returned to Spain. Absorbed by another Spanish Order, the Knights of Calatrava, in 1221.	White	Parti-coloured red and white cross.

Readers may also be interested to know that in a crusading treatise of 1305 it was proposed that all the existing Military Orders should be amalgamated; had this been done the new Order's habit was to have been black with a red cross.

22, 23 & 24. KNIGHTS TEMPLAR

An avid admirer of the Templars, St Bernard de Clairvaux proudly wrote in the 12th century that they were ill-kempt and unwashed, with their beards

22

a

23

wild and their hair cropped short, 'reeking of dust, soiled by their armour and the heat'; the Victorian adage about cleanliness being next to Godliness clearly had no place here!

Figure 22 is taken from a map of Jerusalem dating to c.1170. He wears a long, white surcoat and carries a white shield with a red cross painted on it. A cross-embroidered surcoat, apparently adopted by the Templars relatively early in their history (some authorities mention cloaks), replaced the cassock on active service; this was white except for confrère brethren and sergeants, the latter of whom wore surcoats of black, or brown or some other plain colour. In fact a second figure in the same source wears a dark green but otherwise identical surcoat to that worn here and, despite no cross being apparent on his shield, he may well represent a sergeant. In all cases the cross was red.

Figure 23 comes from frescoes of a similar date in the Templar chapel of Cressac-Saint-Genis in **Charente, Angoulême**, depicting Templars fighting Saracens. He appears to wear either a long-sleeved surcoat or some form of cassock over his armour, though others wear more typical sleeveless surcoats. The mixture of dress and the absence of beards where chins are visible, together with the personal heraldry apparent on some shields (as here), tends to suggest that these frescoes may depict a mixture of knights, sergeants and confrère brethren. However it should be noted that it is not known for certain how early Templar shields were decorated, though it is probable (since some means of identification would have been necessary from the very earliest days) that they carried crosses from the very beginning. However, extant

versions of the Order's Rule which probably predate 1147 state that no decoration may be added to brethren's shields or lances, but probably this refers only to personal heraldry. 23a depicts a Templar shield as it appears in the best-known Templar seals, though probably shields such as those carried by figures 8 and 22 were more common; the diagonal arms are probably strengthening bars.

However, figure 24, based on an illustration of Templars in Matthew Paris' mid-13th-century Chronica Majora, carries an alternative type of shield, painted black and white like the Order's banner, Bauceant (see 27a and b).

Regulation arms consisted of lance, sword, dagger, mace and shield. In addition all armour – comprising hauberk, chausses, helmet and later foot and shoulder pieces – was official issue. One interesting point regarding armour is that amongst the Military Orders mail mittens with separate fingers were apparently forbidden as being a luxury!

25 & 26. KNIGHTS HOSPITALLER

Figure 25 represents the likely appearance of a 12th-century Hospitaller knight. The voluminous enveloping mantle, worn over their armour on active service, must have impeded the wearer considerably in battle, and in 1248 a Papal Bull finally authorised the adoption of a 'wide' cross-embroidered black surcoat (as worn by 26) as 'a remedy for the fact that when you are wearing the cappa clausa over your armour, which hampers both your hands and your arms, it makes it easier for your enemies to attack you and harder for you to defend yourselves'. The surcoats of brother knights were changed to red in 1259, still with the Order's white cross sewn upon them, the wearing of red surcoats being extended to brother sergeants from 1278. Hospitaller Donats wore the uniform of brother knights.

As with the Templars, it is not known in what way early Hospitaller shields were decorated though probably most carried a cross. The Hospitallers apparently only universally adopted a red shield with a white cross under the Grand Master Nicholas de Lorgne (1277-1285). Unlike the Templars there is also a fair chance that at least some late-12th and 13th-century Hospitallers, probably the senior officers, bore their own coats-of-arms on their shields (or so one must assume from 13th-century Hospitaller legislation repeatedly – and apparently unsuccessfully – forbidding the decoration of arms and equipment). By the middle to late-14th century Grand Masters often quartered their personal arms with the arms of the Order.

27. STANDARDS Of THE MILITARY ORDERS

27a and b represent two variants of the Templars' black and white banner Bauceant as it appears in Matthew Paris' Chronica Majora. Its name, usually corrupted to Beau Seant or Beauseant, derives from the Low Latin for a

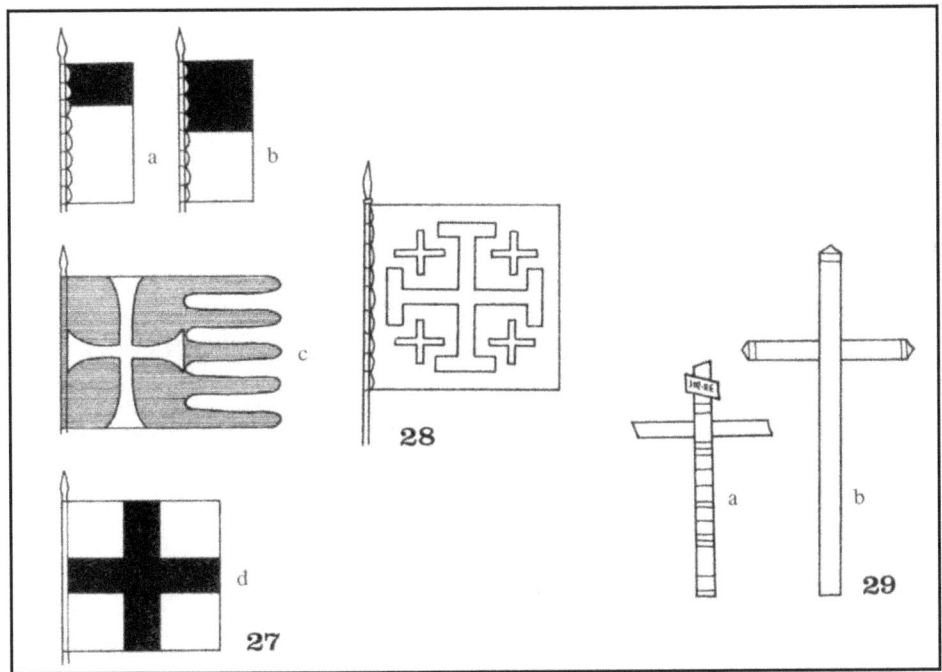

piebald horse, and Jacques de Vitry describes how it signified 'that they are fair and kindly towards their friends, but black and terrible to their enemies'. In use at least as early as 1128 (though at that date probably a gonfalon rather than a banner), it was apparently not actually carried by the Order's standard-bearer, the Gonfanonier; on the march it was borne instead by one of his esquires, and in battle it was borne by a Turcopole (the Gonfanonier himself taking command of the esquires). In battle it could have a guard of ten knights, and its loss by a brother meant expulsion from the Order. In addition the Templars had a secondary banner or gonfalon of a red cross on a white field, and each commandery had its own banner plus a reserve one to be unfurled if the first was lost.

27c, the standard of the Hospitallers, consisted of a white cross on a red field; this particular example is again taken from the Chronica Majora, though Paris' Historia Anglorum shows a variant with a plain cross. This standard was in use by 1182 at the latest and probably earlier, and like the Templars' Bauceant was the responsibility of the Order's Gonfanonier but was carried by an esquire.

The banner of the Teutonic Knights, 27d, was simply a black cross on a white field. In the Order's early days the pattern of the cross may have been formée rather than plain, but certainly the latter form soon came to predominate. The shields of brethren displayed the same black cross on a white field.

28 THE ROYAL BANNER

This depicts the banner of the Kingdom of Jerusalem. Contrary to the heraldic rules of tincture that condemn the use of 'metal' on 'metal' it consists of yellow or gold crosses (a cross potent between four Latin crosslets) on a white or silver field. Earlier 12th-century examples often show the large cross with small balls rather than bars at the ends of its arms. This banner may have been adopted as early as Baldwin I's reign (1100-1118), his own being described as white in contemporary sources though no device is mentioned. One modern authority says that the flag remained plain white until Amalric I's reign (1163-74), when the gold crosses were added. In battle the royal banner was carried by the Marshal of the Kingdom.

Throughout this era most Christian armies in Outremer carried in addition other cross-embroidered flags as well as the noblemen's heraldic gonfalons and banners.

29 THE TRUE CROSS

This was a holy relic often used by the Franks as a battle standard after 1099, such as at the First and Third Battles of Ramla (1101 and 1105), the Battle of Sarmin (1115), Hab (1119), Yibneh (1123), Bosra (1147), Ascalon (1153), Montgisard (1177), and Hattin (1187) where it was finally lost to the Saracens. It was always carried by a cleric, often the Patriarch of Jerusalem himself but otherwise an archbishop, bishop or abbot. Its bearer at Hattin, the Bishop of Acre, wore the armour of a knight.

29a is based on an illustration in the Chronica Majora depicting the capture of the Cross at Hattin; Imad ad-Din, who was present at the battle, describes it as cased in gold and adorned with pearls and precious stones, Fulcher of Chartres likewise recording it to have been 'partly covered by gold and silver'. 29b is an alternative rendering of the Cross as it appears in a History of Outremer ms. executed in Rome in 1295.

Other similar 'standards' were also in existence, Roger of Antioch, for example, having a large jewelled cross with him at Ager Sanguinus in 1119.

30 FATIMID INFANTRYMAN c.1100

Muslim infantry were generally unarmoured. This figure, from an 11th or 12th-century Egyptian ms., is armed with sword and thrusting spear, the latter either a tirad or a mitrad, apparently the standard terms for infantry spears. Others might substitute javelins, called harbah in Arabic, while in his memoirs Usamah mentions infantry several times as carrying only shield, sword and dagger (the last called by various names such as dashan, nimga, sikh and sikhina). Other infantry, of course, would have been archers, though under the Fatimids these were chiefly Armenian and Sudanese slave-soldiers (see figure 33).

The shield is taken from reliefs on the Babal-Nasr (the Gate of Victory) in Cairo, executed in 1087. It is of a type called turs by the Arabs, described by Murda al-Tartusi in his 12th-century Tabsirah (a military manual written for Saladin) as 'a round shield which covers most of the holder', capable of protecting him from most sides and therefore clearly convex in shape. It could apparently be of 'considerable circumference' and is usually depicted with a reinforced rim and a boss or several bosses (see 33 – where the shield is taken from the 1187 gate of Qal'at al-Gindi in Syria – 44 and 54). Al-Tartusi describes shield surfaces of untanned, varnished or painted hide, polished or bare wood, and horse, ass, camel or giraffe skins (one wonders whether zebra was used too). He records in addition shields of cane sewn together with cotton and says that 'some choose shields of iron'. The daraqa, a circular shield smaller than the turs, was always of hide.

His short, tight-sleeved coat and tunic are the standard costume of a Muslim warrior, allowing far more freedom of movement than the wide-sleeved, flowing dress worn by civilians. Round the upper arm are the usual tiraz bands worn by Muslims, usually strips of brocade or cloth of a contrasting colour richly embroidered in gold and coloured thread, often with quotations from the Koran, but sometimes plain. Ibn Khaldun later records that they might have the Sultan's or an amir's name embroidered on them. L.A. Mayer, in his 'Mamluk Costume', explains that real tiraz 'in the sense of an honorific formula' were granted only to iqta'dars, either by the Sultan or an amir; all other tiraz were 'technically decorative fakes'.

31. FATIMID INFANTRYMAN c.1150

This figure and the next come from a ms. fragment from Fustat that depicts Muslims and Christians in battle before a fortress. It probably dates to c.1150 but may be somewhat earlier, so the Muslim warriors depicted are fairly certainly Fatimids.

This figure is barefoot, armed only with shield and fringed spear, and wears an unusual pair of what are apparently baggy breeches, perhaps the skirt of his tunic pulled up through a belt. The kite-shield was called tariqa by the Muslims, a term which, it has been suggested (curiously), evolved from the name of the small circular European shield, the targe; this seems improbable. The tariqa was possibly even adopted prior to the Crusades (there are kite-shields carved on the Bab al-Nasr) but certainly during the Crusades tariqas would have become available in far larger numbers, shields – together with other Frankish equipment – being recorded to have been reused by the Muslims after capture; al-Qalanisi, referring to the equipment of Nur ed-Din's troops in 1157, specifically speaks of 'Frankish' tariqas. The tariqa appears to

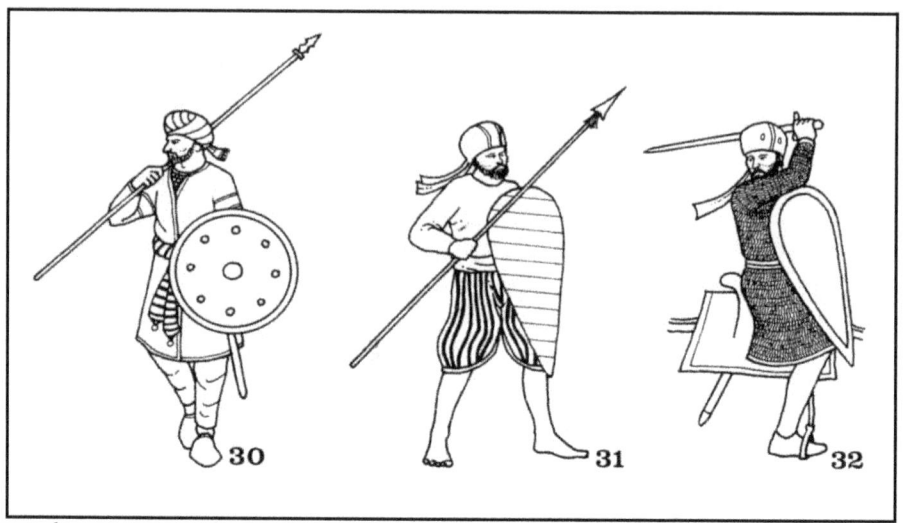

have become popular as far east as Persia (see figures 50 and 87) but dropped out of use in Syria during the Bahriyyah Mamluk era, though al-Maqrizi still records a unit of young Mamluks equipped with tariqas.

Ibn al-Athir actually records archers in Saladin's army with tariqas, and al-Tartusi's Tabsirah describes the tariqa in detail. He records it as 'the shield used by the Franks and Byzantines, which is shaped like an onion and painted in all sorts of colours, designs and artistic patterns. It is a long shield of a shape acceptable to both the horseman and the foot-soldier; it begins round [at the top], but narrows down little by little and at the bottom ends in a sharp point like the tip of a spear'. A variant of the tariqa was the januwiya, described as like a tariqa but with a flattened base so that infantry in a defensive formation could stand their shields before them. A second Muslim infantryman in the source appears to wear the same 'breeches' but is bareheaded and wears short, black ankle-boots. Neither wear tiraz bands.

32. FATIMID CAVALRYMAN c.1150

The Saracen coat-of-mail seems to have gone under a variety of names, such as dir', zard, yelba, lamat al-harb, zardiyyat sabila and zardiyyat musbala to mention but a few, these referring variously to shorter or longer corselets. Some are described as 'dragging', while sabila and musbala mean 'fountain-like', both of which tend to suggest that they might reach well below the knee, possibly even down to the ground. This would be unusual, however, since generally Muslim armour remained considerably lighter than that of the Franks; the Itinerarium Regis Ricardi, for instance, describing armoured as well as unarmoured Muslims at Arsuf in 1191, says that they were 'not weighed down with heavy armour like our knights'. This is more true of the Turks than the Arabs, however, and even then there were exceptions (see figure 58); from the sources it is apparent that native Arab cavalry, as opposed to Bedouins or Turks, were usually armoured, and Mayer concludes in his *'Mamluk Costume'* that mail was the commonest form of Muslim armour.

This man appears to wear a turban rather than a helmet. It has been argued that the turbans worn here are in fact no more than caps or coverings concealing helmets, but since 31 wears an almost identical turban this seems unlikely (though still not impossible). Undeniably helmets were sometimes concealed beneath turbans, but it should also be noted that in the 13th century Jean de Joinville wrote of Muslim turbans that they were capable of 'warding the heavy blow of a sword'. The original ms. depicts this man's turban as dull red with black markings. They were most commonly white but could also be blue, black, brown or any other colour.

Though the original depicts him with only a sword a lance would normally be carried too, but it is important to note that as he is an Arab he would not carry a bow. Usamah, a Syrian Arab, does not record the bow in use by horsemen anywhere and he certainly never used one himself; his battle anecdotes are almost exclusively of sword and lance thrusts, and the Arabs clearly relied on their proficiency with these weapons rather than the bow, though some may also have employed javelins.

Cavalry lances generally went under the names rumh, mizraq and hattiyya, apparently all very similar weapons probably differing only in length, weight and blade shape; the heavy rumh occurs most often. Another type, the quntariya (cf. the Byzantine kontaria), was widely used by the Franks as well and was a long weapon, only just short of 12 feet. The Berber kabarbara, recorded by al-Tartusi, was also of considerable length, with a shaft of some 11½-12½ feet and a (socketed?) blade of another 2-2½ feet. Usamah records that c.1120 the Arabs of Hamah adopted an even longer lance, lengthened 'by

33   34   35

attaching one lance to another' and reaching a length of 18-20 dhira' – 27-30 feet! This must surely be an exaggeration, despite the fact that ordinary lances could certainly reach 15 feet. However, it is interesting to note his description of such a compound lance in use, 'trailing on the ground like a rope, the warrior unable to raise it', which certainly indicates that it was of unusual (not to say ridiculous) length; one imagines the experiment was short-lived. Lances were usually of cane or wood, Imad ad-Din writing of 'brown lances' at Hattin.

33. SUDANESE ARCHER

Sudanese infantry, predominantly archers, were an important element of Egyptian armies during the earlier part of this period, featuring prominently in the Fatimid era (as many as 30,000 being employed by 1169) and less prominently under Saladin and the Ayyubids. Sudanese troops do not seem to have been employed at all under the Mamluks, and after the fall of the Ayyubids it was to be several centuries before they again appeared in large numbers in an Egyptian army in any role other than as grooms or horse-boys.

Surprisingly – since so few Europeans could have ever seen a black man at this date – Sudanese soldiers in Muslim employ excited little or no comment from most Crusade chroniclers, from which we may surmise that they were largely, to all appearances, identical to the average Arab in all but skin colouring, though at least one later source records that they scarred their faces.

The uniforms of Sudanese guardsmen appear to have been of richly decorated brocade or damask, but it should be noted that, contrary to the impression created by most modern-day historians, far from all such soldiers were guardsmen.

Fulcher of Chartres, who refers to the Sudanese as Aethiopes, notes their black skin and implies in at least one passage that they fought with bow or spear. Albert of Aix adds that they carried maces (undoubtedly the 'flails or scourges of iron' noted by both Gibbon and Oman) and records that at the battle of Ascalon in 1099 the Sudanese archers knelt on one knee to fire, 'according to their custom'.

The Itinerarium, written by an eyewitness, also mentions the Sudanese, referring to those at Arsuf (1191) as the Nigreduli, 'a race of demons very black in colour'. The ensuing passage is unclear, but Ambroise (the Old French, and possibly more reliable, version of this chronicle) renders the same passage as 'Following these came a black race – Noirets is their common name, or Saracens of the berruie [uncultivated land] – loathsome and as black as soot in colour, swift and agile footmen armed with bows and with light shields'.

34. SUDANESE SPEARMAN

Though most Sudanese in Fatimid and Ayyubid employ were archers some were instead armed with a spear, and it is as one such that I have interpreted this figure from the St Denis windows (see note 35 below). The spear could be used as a thrusting or throwing weapon, Baldwin I being badly wounded in 1103 by the thrown spear of a Sudanese infantryman.

It is apparent from his simple dress that he is not a guardsman and he carries only a spear and a circular turs. The latter has a reinforced rim and an acutely spiked boss like that of figure 36. A sword would have also been carried, and Black swordsmen appear in a list of Fatimid regiments recorded c.1047-1054.

Usamah's anecdotes include references to Black horsemen too, and some modern authorities – such as Lane-Poole – have even interpreted Saladin's Qaraghulam cavalry as Blacks (Qaraghulam translating literally as 'Black slave'); more probably, however, the term Qaraghulam merely denoted non-White, non-Turkish mamluks, no doubt including some Blacks.

35, 36, 37 & 38. MUSLIM CAVALRYMEN c.1150

These figures are from a series of ten painted windows once in the monastery church of St Denis in Paris. These windows, of mid-12th-century date, the commissioning of which has been accredited to Louis VII's chief minister Abbot Suger, were destroyed during the French Revolution but are known from sketches executed by Bernard de Montfaucon in 1729 (in *'Les Monuments de la Monarchie Françoise'*) in which, alas, the originals were not copied altogether clearly.

The equipment portrayed was probably based on the reports of eyewitnesses who had participated with Louis in the Second Crusade, though the episodes

depicted actually all took place during the First Crusade. Judging from their arms and armour the figures themselves are probably Syrian Arabs or even Egyptians.

Figures 35, 36 and 37 all appear to wear quilted al-qutuns (see note 10), strengthened with scales in the latter two instances, though possibly figure 36 may be a very poor representation of a lamellar djawshan (see 48); certainly the Charlemagne window of c.1210 in Chartres Cathedral, wherein certain details were inspired by if not copied directly from the original St Denis windows, shows Muslims wearing corselets that are undoubtedly lamellar, so it is possible that some of the St Denis figures likewise wore lamellar armour. Other figures in Montfaucon's sketches quite clearly wear mail corselets, sometimes with coifs, while a few, of which figure 38 is the clearest, wear scale.

Helmets are all either conical – probably the type called baida (egg) because of its shape – or hemi-spherical, or of spangenhelm construction, sometimes apparently with cloth, leather or mail aventails. Shields are circular and come in various sizes, often with acutely spiked bosses like that of 36. Arms consist chiefly of sword and lance, the latter of no outstanding length (undoubtedly restricted by the confines of the illustration area); although a few horse-archers are also apparent bows are, rather curiously, heavily outnumbered by lances, and none of Montfaucon's sketches show bowcases or quivers.

These particular figures are taken respectively from scenes depicting the battles of Nicaea (1097), Ascalon (1099), Dorylaeum (1097) and Antioch (1098).

39, 40, 41 & 42. TURKISH CAVALRYMEN

Contemporary Christian chroniclers generally used the term 'Turk' to describe

Seljuks, Turcomans and Syrians or armies comprised mainly thereof – Saladin's armies, for example, are described as Turkish even though they also contained many Bedouins, Arabs, Kurds, Sudanese and others. Of these four figures two are Syrians (41, from the Jazira, a region of Northern Syria round Mosul, Raqqa and Diyar Bekr, and 42, from Raqqa) and two are Seljuks (39, from a Persian ceramic, and 40, from Azerbaijan; these are typical of Seljuk warriors in general, figures identical to 39 appearing on Seljuk painted bowls as early as the 11th century).

All four wear longish topcoats with a right-over-left flap (the muqallab) at the front, plus embroidered hems, cuffs and collar; round the upper arms are the usual tiraz bands. Tall, loose boots, baggy trousers and, in the case of 39, a small cap with a turban wrapped round it, complete the costume; 39a shows the same type of turban but without the embroidered, trailing headband. Turbans proper such as that of **figure** 40 (who dates to c.1200) were also being worn at least as early as the late 11th century. Figure 41 wears instead a fur-trimmed hat which bears a striking resemblance to the mitre-caps of 18th-century European grenadiers and was characterised by a metal plate above the forehead. This stiff, triangular type of hat, called by the name sharbush, was of Turkish origin and seems to have been worn only by amirs and chieftains as an indication of rank, even Saladin being recorded to have worn one (concealing a mail cap beneath). It was worn under both the Ayyubid and Bahriyyah dynasties but was later abolished by the Circassian Mamluks. It appears in illustrations only from the late-12th century but had probably been in use somewhat earlier, the illustrations themselves being principally of Rumi, Jaziran, Iraqi and Azerbaijani origin.

As can be seen here and in other illustrations the Seljuk and Syrian Turks generally (though by no means exclusively – see 49 and 50) wore their hair very long in three tails, one at each side of the head and one at the back. Moustaches were usually long (Alp Arslan could allegedly tie the ends of his

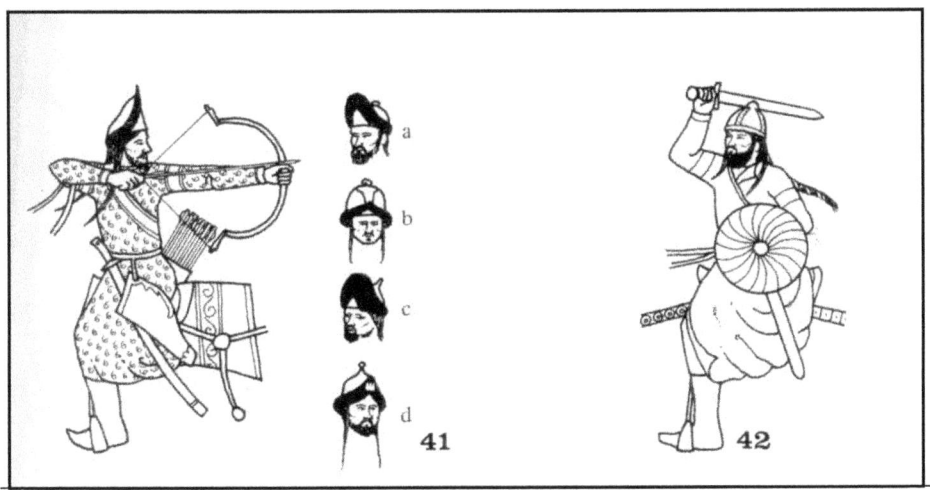

behind his head), while beards could be full, short or very wispy, sometimes comprising no more than a 'shadow' on either side of the jaw and a small tuft under the lower lip.

As for arms, the Itinerarium Regis Ricardi, describing Saladin's largely Syrian army at Arsuf in 1191, records that 'the Turks are ... almost weaponless, carrying only a bow, a mace furnished with sharp teeth, a sword, a lance of reed with an iron tip, and a lightly hung knife'. Some Turks carried in addition a small axe suspended from the saddle. The short but powerful composite bow was their principal weapon. The arrows were light, limiting their penetration somewhat so that although they could pierce armour they often did not, and when they did might inflict only a shallow wound or no wound at all. The bow was often slung behind the left shoulder during close combat.

The bowcase, which could double as a quiver, hung on the left, while the quiver was suspended from the belt at the right; these are occasionally depicted the other way round. Quivers could contain up to 60 arrows. In addition spare bows and extra quivers were often carried, sometimes as many as three of each, so it was quite feasible for well over 100 arrows to be carried. The light lance could be used for thrusting or throwing, but javelins might also be carried. Small shields held by a single, central grip were in general use, that of figure 40 being of a rather unusual design; the rose painted at the centre may possibly be an 'heraldic' device.

Swords could be curved like that of 47, long like that of 40, or short and straight. From its length and shape that of 42 is quite definitely an Indian weapon, Indian swords still being held in high esteem throughout the Muslim world during this era, just as they had been since as early as the 7th century. Whether this was because Indian swords were particularly good or because Egyptian-Syrian swords were particularly bad is not altogether clear. Certainly al-Tartusi reckoned Egyptian blades as inferior not only to Indian swords but also to Andalusian, Maghribi and Chinese swords too. Whatever the reason, Indian blades, either of the traditional type shown here or of more 'modern' design were imported into the Muslim world in great numbers, often then being re-hilted and decorated according to local taste and prevailing fashion. Captured Frankish swords also feature and underwent similar adaptation. Other equipment imported from India included lances and corselets (type unspecified but probably scale and/or lamellar).

Turkish clothes were often of brocade or silk and were very bright, usually involving geometric patterns or floral or arabesque motifs on a bright base colour.

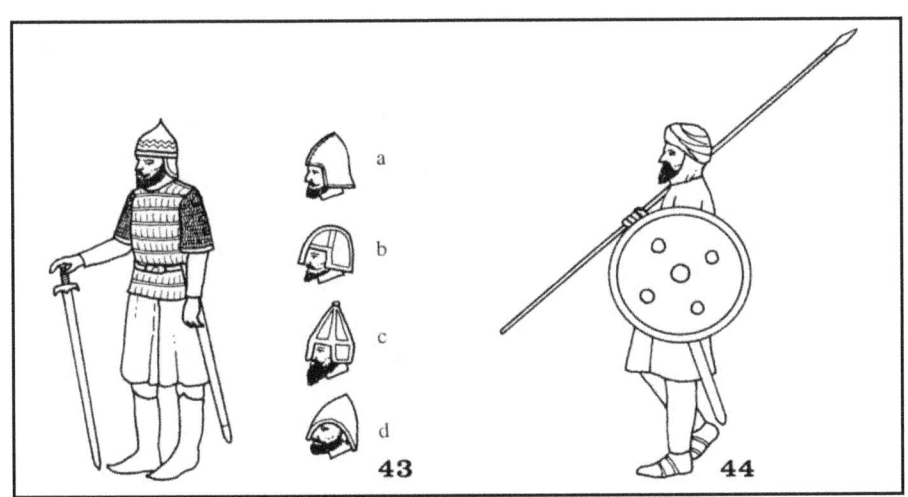

43   44

43. SYRIAN CAVALRYMAN c.1220

This Ayyubid warrior from Mosul wears quilted hip-length armour with mail sleeves, undoubtedly a kuzaghand, and a helmet with nape-guard. Other figures in the same source wear lamellar and mail corselets.

The kuzaghand (Persian kazhaghand, called in Western sources a gazeganz, from which the term jazerant almost certainly evolved) was basically an early type of brigandine, sometimes apparently worn in conjunction with a mail corselet. Al-Tartusi implies that it was invented by Easterners – Syrians or Iraqis; he describes it as a mail corselet covered in cloth and silk, quilted, and with an outer surface of embroidered material or brocade. Al-Maqrizi records Fatimid kuzaghands covered with brocade and silver stars, probably rivets. Usamah has left us with a detailed description of one owned by his father, which consisted of two coats-of-mail, a long 'Frankish' one with a shorter one, apparently waist-length, over it, lined on the inside and covered on the outside with felt, the whole being padded with felt, rabbit hair and silk and, presumably, quilted. From Ibn al-Athir we also know that the kuzaghand had a collar, apparently upstanding, while later sources tend to indicate that it could have sleeves – as here – though more often it did not. Kuzaghands recorded in use by a contingent of Syrian Arabs at Homs in 1280 were covered with red satin and brocade, Qalqashandi recording in the 14th century that coverings were usually of red or yellow brocade. By the 14th century, however, Saracen brigandines were manufactured in the European style, the armour element consisting of iron or steel laminae riveted together; the resulting brigandine was called by the name qarqal and was the most common type of later Mamluk body-armour.

Helmets with solid iron napeguards appear to have been fairly common during this period. Qalqashandi records two types of helmet in addition to the baida mentioned under 35; both were called mighfar, one with a mail aventail (the mighfar al-zard), the other (apparently older) type with a solid neckguard; 43a probably depicts a variant of the latter from a mid-14th-century edition of Joinville's Memoirs. Imad ad-Din too refers to helmets with neckguards. 43b, c and d show alternative helmets with nasals as well as napeguards from two versions of William of Tyre's History of Outremer executed in Acre c.1280; again writing of his father's armour as worn in the 12th century Usamah mentions a 'Muslim helmet' with a nasal. 'Visors' are also occasionally mentioned, but probably aventails or coifs – perhaps like that of 58 – are meant. Baidas at least were often painted and some helmets were even gilded (as, for example, was Saladin's).

44. SYRIAN INFANTRYMAN

In Syria, Iraq and the Jazira infantry always took second place to the mounted military elite of the amirs and 'askaris. They were provided largely by city militias such as the Ahdath and other irregular volunteers, and appear most frequently either in battles in the immediate vicinity of their home towns or in sieges. Certainly the infantry of some Syrian cities, particularly Aleppo, were especially noted for their abilities as siege-engineers; these came in 3 categories – the Hajjarin (artillery crews), Naqqabin (miners) and Khurasani (crews for the rams and penthouses).

This figure, from the same source as the last, is probably fairly typical of Syrian militiamen, composed chiefly of poorly armed and armoured levies from the indigenous Arab population. Though most were Arabs the militias of some cities in Northern Syria and the Jazira (such as Aleppo and Mosul) would also have included Kurds and Turks as well as peoples of older native stock, while elsewhere Greek- speaking elements also survived.

Being largely Arabs most would have been armed with spear or sword, but javelins, bows and sometimes even crossbows also feature prominently in the sources.

45. SARACEN CROSSBOWMAN

During the Crusades the crossbow soon earned a healthy respect from the Muslims for its accuracy and deadliness and they quickly adopted the weapon themselves (though it may have been in use in parts of Persia as early as the 9th century).

In fact the Saracen crossbow (often called the qaws Farangi, or Frankish bow) was a superior weapon to that of the Franks, using a composite bow as opposed to the simple self-bow used by the latter. Al-Tartusi, speaking of crossbows, describes four different categories – the qaws al-rigl (or 'leg-bow', a name comparable to the 'one-foot crossbow' of Europe) which was smallest, probably with a stirrup; the somewhat larger 'aqqar, probably comparable to the 'two-foot crossbow'; the garh, the largest, mounted on a stand for use in

siege-work; and the husban or 'grass-hopper', apparently a crossbow with a barrel for shooting short, thick bolts, slingstones, or small naptha grenades. He also describes the method of loading using a two-clawed hook, attached to a toughened ox-hide belt, to pull back the string.

The Franks in turn adopted the composite crossbow from the Saracens, realising its superiority, and for some time Levantine crossbows and their manufacturers were in high demand in Europe; King John of England's crossbow-maker, for instance, was Peter 'the Saracen', and King Louis IX's was John 'the Armenian'.

This figure is based on an illustration in Matthew Paris' Chronica Majora depicting the Ayyubid garrison of Kerak in 1241. He wears mail and a helmet of a type that frequently appears in contemporary illustrations of Muslims, principally in Spanish sources. In the original he is shown wearing an arming cap under the helmet. The crossbow itself has been substituted from a 13th-century Egyptian military manual. The stirrup is of interest since it appears to be of leather or rope rather than iron.

46. AYYUBID HEAVY CAVALRYMAN

Illustrations in Matthew Paris' chronicles and some other 13th-century sources tend to depict Muslim warriors in equipment that makes them almost if not totally indistinguishable from the Frankish knights they are fighting, and the tendency in the past has usually been to dismiss these as the products of artists ignorant of the appearance of 'real' Saracen armour. However, one need only look at a few of the contemporary chronicles to see that this is not an altogether justifiable conclusion. It is a well-recorded fact that much Frankish equipment was reused by Muslims after capture, including shields, lances, swords, helmets and corselets (see 31, 42 and 43) – we read, for example, of Arab horsemen at Ramla in 1101 who 'took up the shields, lances and shining helmets of the slain and proudly adorned themselves', and one Ayyubid warrior at Acre in 1191 similarly put on the armour of a Frankish knight he had killed; certainly figure 32 above needs only to substitute a helmet for his turban to become a 'Frankish' knight. The St Denis windows too show some Muslims in armour that resembles very closely that of the crusaders they fight.

At the same time Matthew Paris' illustrations also depict Muslims in more distinctive forms of armour, of which this particular figure, based on his drawings of the battles of Arsuf and Bahr Ashmun, is one. He wears a stiff, sleeveless scale corselet (probably based on a leather foundation) over a short coat-of-mail with a coif, and apparently also wears quilted cuisses. Whether or not such equipment was ever actually worn by Egyptian or Syrian Muslims is open to debate, but it was certainly worn by the Muslims of Andalusian Spain, as explained under figures 75 and 76 in *'Armies of Feudal Europe'*.

One point that should be noted, however, is that according to L.A. Mayer the flat-topped variety of kite-shield depicted here was never actually adopted by the Saracens (though again captured shields would have almost certainly been used). 46a and b show two more typical shields of the turs variety from other illustrations by Paris.

47. AYYUBID MAMLUK c.1240
Since he carries a Turkish sabre rather than the usual sword this figure may very well represent one of the new wave of Khwarizmian or Kipchak mamluks to be found in Ayyubid employ in the 1230s and 1240s. In addition steppe influence is apparent in his hat with upturned brim; this was the saraquj, typical of Mongol dress (see 84) and adopted by the Ayyubids and early Mamluks via such mercenaries. The saraquj was usually white. In the source the tunics and coats (the latter called 'Tartar coats' – see 55 and 56) of such figures are all of rich brocade, principally blue, green or pink in colour.

The sabre came into more widespread use in the late 13th or early 14th century under Mongol influence though curved swords are occasionally depicted or recorded in use as early as the 11th century, probably introduced from Central Asia via slave-soldiers purchased in the East. Note the spurs fixed to his boots. Usamah mentions khuff boots with spurs but pictorial sources tend to indicate that spurs were uncommon amongst Muslims during this era except in Andalusia and 13th-century Mamluk Egypt.

48. SELJUK HEAVY CAVALRYMAN
Although the majority of Turkish cavalry seem to have been unarmoured horse-archers, 'heavy' cavalry were also to be found in their armies, these

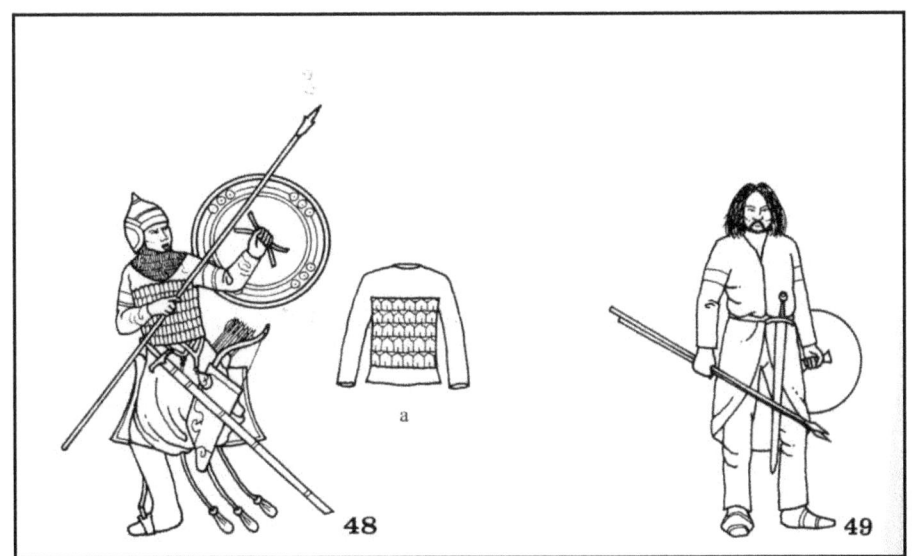

48   49

being generally supplied by the retinues and mamluks of the amirs and other chieftains. The chronicler Bar Hebraeus makes much of Alp Arslan, the victor of Manzikert, putting on his armour before the battle, adding that 'all the Turks did likewise'.

This late 12th or early 13th-century Seljuk from Azerbaijan wears armour that is of typically Eastern design, comprising a mail hood, Persian-style helmet with neckguard and a waist-length djawshan that reaches only to the chest. 'Djawshan' seems to have described a lamellar corselet of any length and al-Tartusi says it was of Persian origin. The lamellae were chiefly of iron, horn or treated leather and could be gilded, varnished or painted (Sultan Khai Khosrou I is recorded wearing red armour in 1210), though Seljuk armour was apparently often blackened. That worn here may very well be attached to the tunic itself in the same way as is 48a (with alternate rows of lamellae painted different colours), from a store of arms and armour depicted in an early 13th-century source. It is possibly an armour of similar length that is recorded being worn by an Abbasid amir in one of Usamah 's anecdotes; describing the Battle of Qinnasrin in 1137 he mentions how a Frankish horseman's lance pierced this amir through the chest and came out at his back, despite his gilded djawshan.

This man's equipment includes lance, shield, and sword as well as a bow, though Bar Hebraeus states that Alp Arslan cast aside his bow and arrows and fought with spear and shield when he donned his armour. The length of the sword should be noted, such long weapons frequently appearing in Syrian and Persian sources of the 12th and 13th centuries. The helmet could be plumed.

By the late 13th century and probably somewhat earlier most Seljuk heavy cavalry would have closely resembled figures 58 and 89.

49 & 50. SELJUK INFANTRYMEN

Despite the predominance of cavalry in their armies Seljuk infantry were, seemingly, not uncommon, for example featuring prominently at Myriokephalon in 1176, while Anna Comnena records as many as 80,000 'fully-armed infantry' opposing the First Crusade at Heraclea in 1097. They were usually unarmoured and most were either javelinmen or archers, some carrying short spears too. By the mid-12th century at the latest crossbows were also in use, becoming an important infantry arm by the 13th century; Rumi crossbowmen recorded at the Battle of Akhlat in 1230 were protected by large cowhide shields, presumably wielded by shield-bearers.

49 is from an early 13th-century Persian painted bowl which shows a number of similar figures as well as horsemen like 39. Clothes are depicted mainly dark blue, light blue, turquoise, brown and tan; alternative sources depict red,

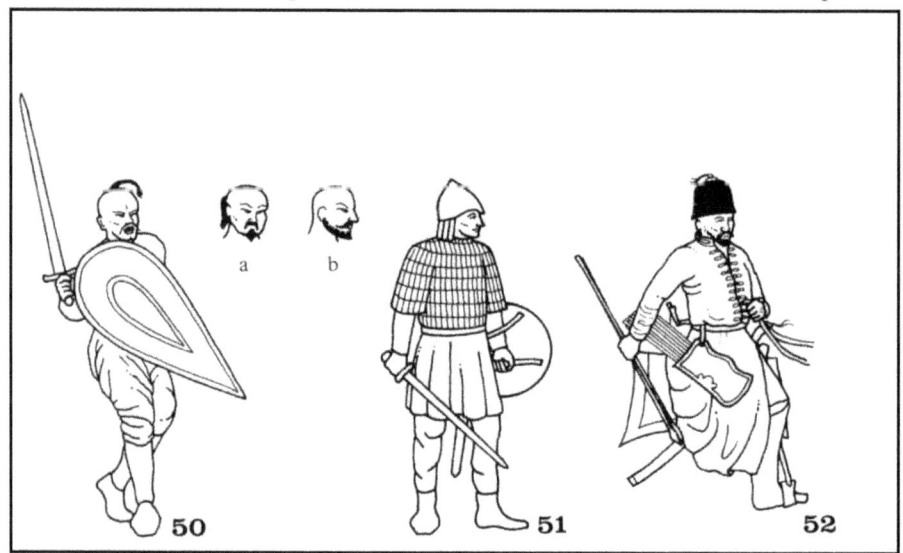

green, black and most other colours also being worn. On the bowl some infantrymen have their trousers cross-gartered.

Figure 50, from Azerbaijan (the same source as figures 40 and 48), is interesting in showing that the Seljuks too used the kite-shield (some infantry figures on the painted bowl mentioned above also substitute kite-shields for circular ones), and also in its depiction of the more 'characteristic' Turkish hairstyle which during this era seems to appear only in Eastern frontier regions and amongst the 'uncivilised' Turcoman nomads. 50a and b are alternatives from a Persian source of c.1225.

51. RUMI 'FIRENK' HEAVY CAVALRYMAN

This 12th-century figure in short lamellar corselet bears a remarkably close resemblance to contemporary Byzantines (see, for example, 66 and 67). This is probably because he is himself a Byzantine, possibly a member of one of the indigenous Greek Christian units, uniformed and armed in Byzantine fashion and with their own commanders, raised and maintained by the Seljuk Sultans of Rum and later known as Kafir-Sipahiler and Martolos by the Ottomans. Some were brigaded alongside Frankish mercenaries and the general term 'Firenk' or Franks was often applied to them collectively. For lamellar armour in use amongst Muslims see note 48 above.

52. TURCOMAN TRIBESMAN

Turcomans (who still exist today under the name Turkmens) supplied the bulk of Seljuk armies, as well as providing large numbers of auxiliaries to the late Fatimids, Ayyubids, Mamluks and Ottomans. Some even served with the Almohades in Spain and North Africa, where they were still called by their earlier name of Ghuzz. Though they fielded some infantry armed with spear, sword and bow they relied on their light horse-archers in battle.

This figure is based on the 14th-century drawings of Ustad Mehmed Siyah Qalem; 13th-century illustrations indicate that there had been no change of dress in the interim. His topcoat shows the alternative upright fastening rather than the oblique muqallab flap generally worn by Turks. Ustad Mehmed shows tunics chiefly in shades of blue, black, brown and red. The black fur or felt cap is fairly standard. However, Ibn Bibi describes 13th-century Karamanli Turcomans in Anatolia wearing red caps and black coats and boots.

Basic equipment appears to have consisted of bow, sabre and two or three light javelins. In addition bags of loot were normally much in evidence.

Turcoman women also regularly fought alongside their men folk, Marvazi comparing the Amazons to such female Turcoman warriors in the 12th century. Much later (in the 15th century) one tribe is said to have raised as many as 30,000 female warriors.

53 & 54. BEDOUIN TRIBESMEN

The Bedawis or Bedouins were principally noted as brigands during this era and were as likely to be found robbing their fellow-Muslims as they were to be fighting the Franks, 'it being well-known,' as Joinville records, 'that the use and custom of the Bedouins is always to fall upon the weaker side.' Nevertheless Bedouins appeared as auxiliaries in most Muslim armies (and also some Frankish ones), serving mainly as cavalry though infantry are also recorded on occasion. In Frankish employ they usually supplied scouts and spies.

These two figures date respectively to c.1237 (Hariri's Maqamat) and c.1306 (Raschid al-Din's World History) and tally closely with the description of Bedouin dress left to us by Joinville in his Memoirs of the Seventh Crusade. He records their characteristic camel-wool tunic, the long, wide-sleeved gubba, as covering the whole body down to the ground, while the turban was wrapped around the head in such a way that one strip went beneath the chin, as can be seen in both these figures. In the sources clothes are depicted or described as dyed chiefly in bright colours, predominantly reds and blues of most shades. Striped clothing of the type worn by 54, popularly associated with Arabs, only became commonplace from the 12th century. Hair was black.

Joinville also records a Bedouin belief 'that no one can die save on the day appointed, and for this reason they will not wear armour,' and that 'in battle they carry nothing but sword and lance', which basically repeats William of Tyre's comment that 'according to their custom' they 'fought with lances only'. Burchard of Mount Sion, who wrote c.1270, adds that 'they do not use arrows, saying that it is base beyond measure to steal away a man's life with an arrow.' The lance was usually of cane ('reed'). The sword was generally suspended from a baldric across the right shoulder, the Bedouins apparently adhering to this traditional Muslim custom rather than following the prevalent habit of girding the sword at the waist; other than the Bedouins only Nur ed-Din's army appears to have regularly used baldrics.

The Byzantine Scylitzes ms. of c.1200 depicts Muslim horsemen in dress identical to that worn by these figures, and likewise armed with lance, sword and shield (most of the shields resemble that of 30, though a few apparently carry crescent devices).

55 & 56. MAMLUKS

These figures are based on the Baptistère de Saint Louis of c.1300. Both wear 'Tartar coats' (qaba al-Tartariyyah) which, as is obvious from the name, were of Mongol origin and followed the Mongol practice of having the muqallab flap cross the chest from left to right as opposed to the Turkish fashion of right to left. (The left-over-right Mongol-style muqallab also features in Rumi and Persian sources in the 13th century.) Such coats were often worn under a longer topcoat (see 57).

In 1283 some 1,500 Mamluk guardsmen are described as wearing red satin or silk coats, undoubtedly uniforms such as are sometimes mentioned in other contemporary sources (Fatimid Sudanese guardsmen appear to have been uniformed, and certainly as early as 1177 Saladin's personal mamluk regiment is recorded by William of Tyre wearing yellow uniforms). Red was

the most common uniform colour under the Mamluks, though Ayyubid yellow was still sometimes worn. Red was also the usual colour for the kalautah cap, usually worn with a kerchief wound round it as by figure 55. Yellow kalautahs were worn under the Ayyubids and also by the early Mamluks up to the reign of Khalil (1290-1293). They were sometimes embroidered. The kalautah itself appears to have been padded with cotton, probably to increase its defensive value.

Both wear sashes of coloured silk round the waist, sometimes yellow but probably more often red. Amirs, and even a few ordinary mamluk troopers, instead wore decorated mintaqa belts, which comprised gold and silver links mounted with precious stones according to rank. Usually a black leather belt-pouch was suspended at the right.

Footwear consists of knee-length khuff boots with coverings called saq al-muza worn over them. A slipper-like shoe could also be worn over the boot. The boots themselves had a clear seam down the side (see 47 and 57) and were usually of yellow or black leather in winter, white leather in summer. Red boots are also recorded.

The dress of amirs is recorded as being much richer than that of ordinary mamluks. The ceremonial dress of Amirs of 100, for instance, consisted at one time of an outer coat of red satin embroidered in gold and trimmed with miniver, and a fringed inner coat (probably a qaba al-Tartariyyah) of yellow satin. The kalautah was of gold brocade, with a muslin kerchief striped in white and other colours wrapped round it. Finally a beaver cloak might be worn.

Though 56 wears a helmet both appear to be otherwise unarmoured, but it should be noted that Muslims often wore body-armour beneath their outer garments in the same way that they wore helmets beneath turbans and caps (William of Tyre, for instance, records Saladin's bodyguard wearing armour under their yellow silk uniforms at Montgisard). In addition Usamah, Ibn Hudayl and other authors record how armour was often carried on pack mules and only donned immediately prior to battle.

57. MAMLUK

This figure, from a 'History of Outremer' of c.1280, is typical of those appearing in the mss. executed in Acre in the second half of the 13th century, so can be assumed to be a fairly reliable representation of a Mamluk warrior of that time.

He wears khuff boots, a small turban (big turbans were banned at least in Syria in 1291) and a long outer robe, the 'Islamic coat' (qaba al-Islamiyya). The qaba could be wool, satin, silk or cotton and was apparently most commonly either white or striped in red and blue. By the 15th century only winter topcoats appear to have been coloured and decorated thus, most Mamluks' outer garments (as well as their boots) being white in summer. Another type of coat sometimes worn was the sallari, an outer garment with elbow-length sleeves.

He is armed with a mace, a favourite Mamluk weapon, used principally to crush helmets and, consequently, heads. It was called either dabbus or 'amud (Persian curz) depending on whether it was entirely of iron or had a wooden handle. Some were flanged or spiked. When not in use it was normally tucked beneath the knee and stirrup strap to the right of the saddle, mamluks being recorded carrying their maces 'from the stirrup' in this way at least as early as the mid-12th century. Another typical Mamluk weapon related to the mace but only recorded in later sources is the ghaddara, a steel staff kept in a case at the saddle and capable of cutting off a man's arm. One figure in the

Baptistère de Saint Louis seems to be carrying such a weapon, where it appears to be about 30 inches long.

Although the Mamluks adopted the kite-shield (see 31) the turs clearly remained far more popular. Like the main figure, 57a-f are all from the Acre mss. so are fairly typical of the heraldic charges carried by Mamluks. Most noticeable are the large number of crescent devices. It has been claimed that the crescent was not widely adopted amongst Muslims until the Ottomans adopted it in the 15th century, but the frequency with which it appears in these mss would seem to disprove this, the crescent being, alongside the rosette, the most common shield device depicted. See also 64.

58. MAMLUK IN FULL ARMOUR c.1290

Mamluks in full armour appear only rarely in the sources of this era, though as mentioned above many probably wore similar body-armour to that depicted here but concealed it beneath their topcoats.

He wears a mighfar helmet, with plume and solid neckguard, and a long lamellar djawshan. (By the end of this era at the latest the term djawshan could also be applied to a mail corselet reinforced with small tin plates called teneke, as depicted in 58a; being of more expensive construction than either mail or lamellar this type was generally restricted to amirs.) The mail coif covering all but his eyes is taken from the Baptistère de Saint Louis; similar coifs are to be occasionally seen in other Muslim sources at least as early as c.1200, sometimes worn without a helmet. His arms consist of lance, bow, sword (with tasselled hilt – see also 36 and 40) and circular shield charged with an heraldic lion.

a

58   59

59. MAMLUK TABARDAR

This figure probably represents one of the infantry guardsmen called Tabardariyyah, named after their distinctive weapon, the tabar (axe). How big this unit actually was does not seem to be altogether clear – it may have comprised no more than the ten Tabardariyyah who accompanied the Sultan on parade. Their commander was the Amir-Tabar. The axe was also employed by other troops, Joinville recording 30 al-Halqa in 1250 'with drawn swords in their hands and Danish axes hanging at their necks'; the shape of the axe blade was apparently very similar to the traditional Scandinavian design.

Al-Tartusi describes the shape of the nagin, a smaller, cavalry version of the tabar, as like a half-moon. The haft of the tabar could be of wood or metal. The blades of ceremonial axes were usually decorated with inlay and perforated patterns.

60. MAMLUK ENGINEER WITH MIDFA

A certain al-Hassan al-Rammah describes and illustrates the midfa in a work of c.1280-1290. It was clearly an early firearm, made of wood with a barrel only as deep as its muzzle width, used to fire bunduks (bullets) or feathered bolts. The charge filled a third of the barrel and consisted of a mixture of 10 parts saltpetre (barud), 2 parts charcoal, and 1½ parts sulphur.

The actual discovery of gunpowder is a dubious distinction that has been variously claimed for Chinese, Indians, Byzantines, Arabs, Germans and Englishmen, but the name of the discoverer and date of actual discovery remain uncertain. The date of the application of gunpowder to a projectile-firing weapon is even more hazy, but if the dating of this Mamluk ms. is correct then this source is certainly amongst the earliest pieces of evidence

outside of China. This weapon was probably no more than an experimental device of the Royal Arsenal and may never have seen active service, though the late 13th-century chronicler Ibn 'Abd al-Zahir remarks that for the siege of al-Marqab in 1285 'iron implements and flame- throwing tubes' were issued by the royal arsenals, and one wonders whether any of the Mamluk engineers armed with 'naptha tubes' at Salamiyet in 1299 (apparently mounted), or storming the breaches of Acre in 1291, might have actually carried such weapons. It has to be admitted that hand-siphons like those used earlier by the Byzantines seem more probable.

'Midfa' was also the name applied to the earliest known Mamluk cannons, dating to 1366 or possibly 1340 (late dates considering the apparent earliness of the weapon described here).

61. ASSASSIN

The dress of the Assassin was, like that of his modern-day counterpart, in no way remarkable. Disguises are often mentioned, however; the Assassins who killed Conrad of Montferrat, for instance, were dressed as monks, and other incidents see the dress of merchants, Frankish soldiers and Syrian Christians being worn. In their own strongholds Assassin brethren wore white cloaks and red caps.

They normally operated singly or in pairs, though on occasion considerably larger groups appear, perhaps to be doubly certain of success. Il-Bursuqi of Mosul was murdered by a band of ten Assassins in 1126 and Caliph al-Mustarshid by as many as 15 or 17 in 1135.

Their weapon of execution was exclusively the dagger, sometimes poisoned and apparently sometimes engraved with the name of the intended victim, an early instance of 'if it's got your name on it...'! Usamah even records battle anecdotes where Assassins appear to be armed only with daggers, but normally sword, spear and shield would have been added in combat, and fully-armed Assassins would have been indistinguishable from ordinary Muslim warriors.

A ceremonial dagger described by Joinville consisted of three daggers of which the top two had their blades sheathed in the handles of the lower two. This was carried by one of the three envoys sent to Louis IX at Acre in 1252; another carried a funeral shroud wrapped round his arm, to be presented to the king for his own burial should he reject the Assassin demands! Another ceremonial weapon recorded by Joinville was a long-handled axe carried before the Old Man of the Mountain, the haft of which was covered in silver and had daggers fixed to it in some way.

62 & 63. MUSLIM MUSICIANS

Mounted bands accompanied most Muslim armies in battle during this era, the Muslims believing that the more noise they made the bolder their spirits became and the more fear they struck into the hearts of their enemies (the Bedouins in particular were sensitive to the noise of drums); the Itinerarium Regis Ricardi records of Arsuf that 'before the amirs there went men clanging away with trumpets and clarions; others had drums, others pipes and timbrels [tambourines], rattles, gongs, cymbals, and other instruments suited to making a din. To raise these noises was the special duty of certain men; and the louder their din the fiercer their comrades fought.'

Probably most important of all were the nakers and kettle-drums. The nakers were great drums that accompanied the Sultan, or his commanders-in-chief, and could only be beaten at his personal command, to transmit orders on the battlefield. The Sultan's band, commanded by the Amir-'Alam, comprised four nakers, 40 kettle-drums, four hautboys, and 20 trumpets; some must have also carried cymbals and other instruments.

The importance of the bands can be judged from the fact that an 'amir with drums' (Amir al-Tablkhanah) was one of the highest ranks in the Mamluk military hierarchy, only 'amirs with drums' and amirs of 100 being permitted bands at all. Those of amirs of 100 consisted of eight or ten kettle-drums, four trumpets, two hautboys, two timbrals, plus other instruments. Amirs of 40 (i.e. 'amirs with drums') had three kettle-drums, later two kettle-drums and two flutes. In Saladin's day the amirs commanding Tulbs were each accompanied by at least a single trumpeter.

Though they are often shown carried on mules (but only rarely on horses), it was camels that were most commonly used for carrying drums, the drums of the Mamluks besieging Acre in 1291 being carried on as many as 300 camels.

The Mongols used nakers in an identical capacity to the Mamluks, the roll of the Khan's or army commander's nakers being the command to attack, 'for the Tartars,' reports Marco Polo, 'do not dare to start a battle till their lord's drums begin to beat.' Those of the Mongols appear to have averaged about one metre across, and were likewise usually carried on camels, though Kublai Khan had some which appear to have been considerably bigger and were carried on elephants.

Though on the battlefield they normally transmitted orders by trumpet calls, even the Franks appear to have used drums in this capacity under Muslim influence, William of Tyre relating how at Ascalon in 1125 the king 'ordered that his men be recalled by the sound of trumpet and roll of drum.'

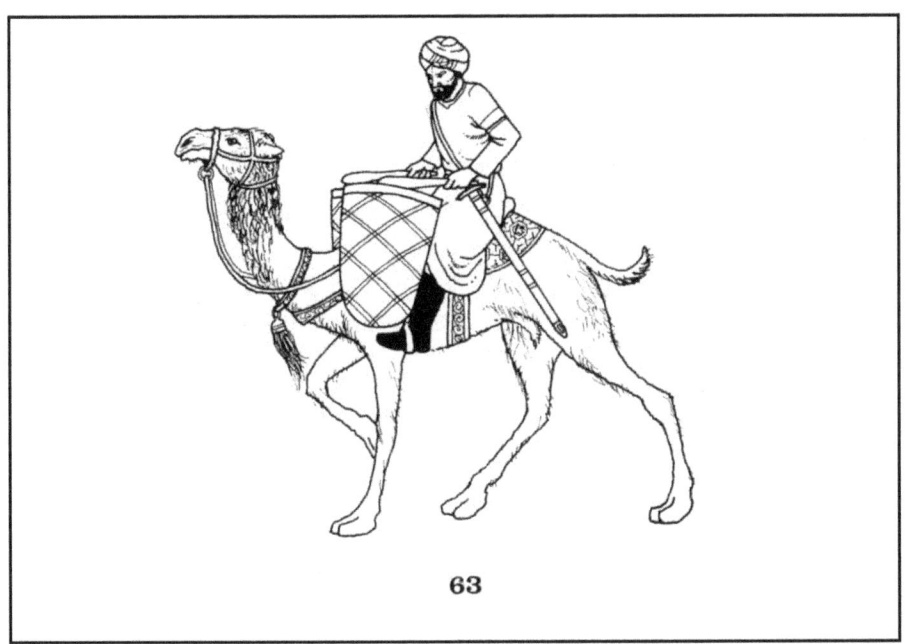

63

64. SARACEN HERALDRY

In the Muslim world heraldry played only a secondary role amongst the military elite. Only the Sultan and his amirs could have coats-of-arms (called runuk), Qalqashandi recording c.1412 that it was customary for every amir to have a special blazon 'according to his choice and preference', this to be borne on the caparisons of their horses and camels, on their shields, their ships, their swords and other property. Such devices were hereditary only to such descendants as followed military careers. They were probably originally granted by the Sultan himself and usually represented the office which the bearer held at the time that he was made an amir, but during the Crusades period were more probably chosen by the amirs themselves. Abu'l Fida, who died in 1331, records that 'the emblem of the Secretary is the pen-box, and of the Armour-bearer the bow, and of the Superintendent of Stores the ewer, and of the Master of the Robes the napkin, and of the Marshal is the horseshoe, and the emblem of the Jawish is a golden saddle.'

Of those depicted here, 64a is the pen-box of the *Davadar* (Secretary), 64b is the napkin of the Master of the Robes, and 64c and d the sword of the Armour-bearer, the latter also including a napkin. As mentioned by Abu'l Fida, the Armour-bearer's device could also be a bow (sometimes accompanied by arrows), or even a crossbow, though no examples of the latter survive. 64e is a device usually described as a crescent, though in his *'Saracenic Heraldry'* L.A. Mayer plausibly suggests that it is a Saracen horseshoe, and therefore the device of the Marshal (see also note 57).

Other officers' devices not listed by Abu'l Fida included the table of the Taster (64f) and the cup of the Cup-bearer (64g and h), one of the most common devices in Mamluk heraldry. Other devices indicative of their bearers' offices were polo-sticks (Polo-master, 64i), standard ('Alamdar, or Standard-bearer), drums and drumsticks (Tabldar, or Drummer) and horn. 64j, a device very common amongst the 13th-century Bahriyyah Mamluks, Mayer suggests as the device of the Dispatch-rider.

Animal devices were unusual, and the only animals to appear in Saracen heraldry are the lion, the eagle and occasionally the horse. The most famous during this period was the lion of Sultan Baibars (64k), and one source speaks of Saladin's standard and that of his brother el-Afdal as carrying pairs of lions at Acre in 1191. However, Saladin's device may have been an eagle, a device that appears to have been particularly popular amongst the Seljuks;

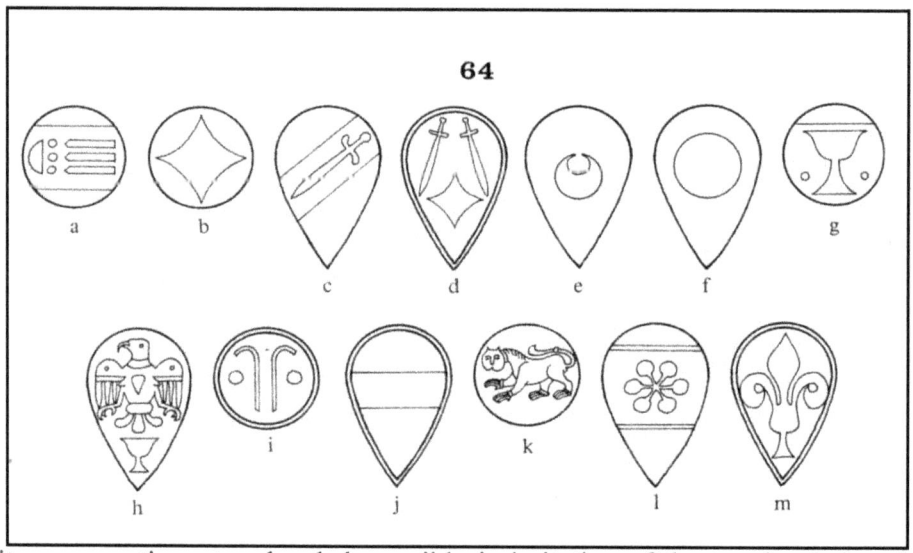

it was sometimes two-headed, possibly in imitation of the two-headed eagle adopted by the Byzantines some time during this era. Zengi and the Ortoqids appear to have used this device. The banner of the vizier Fakr ad-Din, the Muslim commander at El Mansurah, also bore an eagle.

64l and m were also popular during this era. 64l, usually described as a rosette, was a common device under both Ayyubids and early Mamluks, usually six-pointed as here but sometimes with five or eight points. The fleur-de-lis (64m) was the device of Nur ed-Din and also features on a large number of Ayyubid coins. The Saracen fleur-de-lis differs slightly from that used in Frankish heraldry in that the three leaves grow from a common stem; in Frankish heraldry the leaves are individual and are joined together only by a band in the middle.

Some other devices represented tamghas, the tribal symbols used as brands by many Asiatic peoples and introduced into the Near East by Turkish mamluks.

From the evidence of surviving examples it would appear that the colours used consisted of white, yellow, red, blue, green, brown and black, and clearly the formal regulations of European heraldry, forbidding the use of colour on colour or metal on metal, did not apply. Indeed, the choice of colours was entirely up to the coat-of-arms' owner.

65. SARACEN STANDARDS

Under the Ayyubids and early Mamluks the royal standard was of gold-embroidered yellow silk or damask. Their Royal Mamluk units also carried

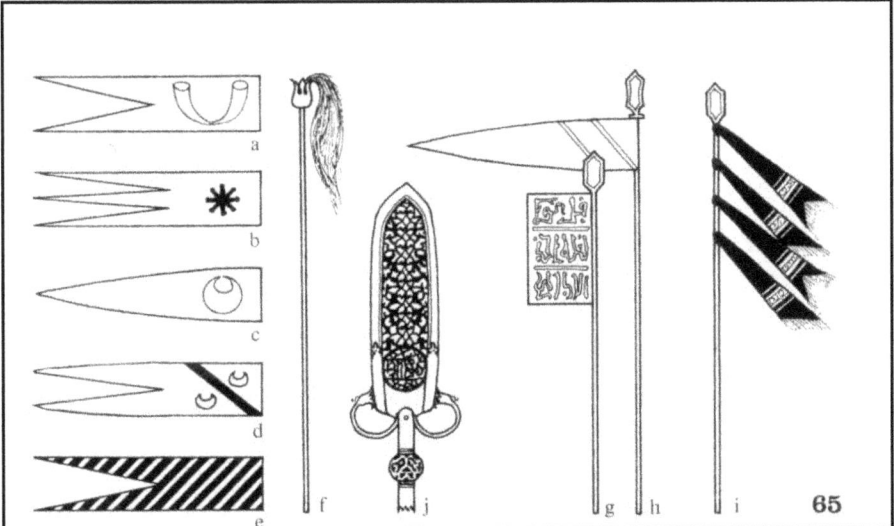

yellow standards, each one embroidered with the heraldic device of its unit commander. Joinville records these devices to have been in crimson, mentioning roses, 'bends' and birds as examples. This practice may also be intended by a remark in the Itinerarium Regis Ricardi that at Arsuf Taqi ad-Din commanded 700 of Saladin's mamluks, each unit of which carried a yellow standard together with 'a pennon [device?] of a different colour', especially since this source also refers to the use of emblems on standards. Taqi's own standard resembled 65a; the Itinerarium describes it as 'a pair of trousers'.

The Itinerarium mentions banners and pennons of 'countless' shapes and sizes, other sources noting many different colours in use. Imad ad-Din records red as well as 'jasmin' standards in Saladin's army at Hattin, while green standards are recorded in the Seljuk army at Dorylaeum. The Abbasid Caliphs continued to use black standards up until the destruction of the

Caliphate by the Mongols in 1258, though in 1057 purple banners decorated with gold script are also recorded, probably similar to 65g. In 1171 the Abbasid Caliph sent black banners to both Saladin and Nur ed-Din.

The standards given here are characteristic of those depicted in contemporary

66   67   68

sources. Most date to the 13th century. The devices on 65b and c of c.1250, and on 65d and e which date to 1287, are heraldic. 65f is a horsetail banner of Turkish design such as was probably carried by many mamluk units of steppe origin, as well as by Seljuks and Turcomans; see also 90b. The Fatimid vizier al-Afdal's standard at Ascalon in 1099, described as having a golden ball atop a silver-plated staff, was probably just such a banner, as were the Khwarizmian lances recorded by Joinville on which were fashioned 'heads with hair, that seemed like the heads of devils.' Joinville also speaks of Khwarizmian standards which were 'red and indented up towards the lance', presumably swallowtail pennons.

65g, h and i depict a type of standard called a tu, an ornamental metal blade atop a wooden shaft. It was usually perforated or damascened, often with inscriptions or heraldic devices. These particular examples are from Hariri's 'Maqamat' of 1237, while 65j shows an actual Mamluk tu in detail. In the source the ribbons of 65i are black with gold band and fringe, while the flag of g is black, blue, red or crimson with black or white lettering. The tu was used in Rum, Persia, Syria and Egypt.

66, 67, 68 & 69. BYZANTINE HEAVY INFANTRYMEN

In their armour, as in many other respects, the Byzantines (or 'Romans' as they persisted in calling themselves) clung tenaciously to their classical heritage throughout this era, the evolution of armour basically stagnating after the 11th century so that most soldiers depicted in sources of the 11th-13th centuries differ from one another only in detail. Unfortunately there are no military manuals other than the somewhat Machiavellian 11th-century Strategicon of Cecaumenus, so we are almost entirely dependant on such contemporary illustrations for information regarding arms and armour.

Basic equipment clearly consisted of corselet, helmet, shield, sword and spear. The corselet was most frequently of lamellar or scale, less often of mail, usually reaching only to the hips and shoulders with hanging pteruges still protecting the thighs and upper arms. Helmets were of three main types. The most common variety was pointed, with the neck protected by a scale or mail aventail or hanging leather lappets (66-68); the other two varieties were conical with the back extended into a nape-guard (72, 73); or brimmed like a kettle-helmet, also sometimes with a neckguard of leather lappets or mail. Shields could be circular or kite-shaped, though some infantry still carried the old oval shield in the late 11th century. The kite-shield appears to have been in general use amongst heavy infantry and cavalry by the mid-12th century (but see note 75-78), though the circular shield prevailed amongst light infantry. Flat-topped heater shields like those of the Franks were also in use by the 13th century, though the kite remained more common; that carried by 69, quartered in red and black, is from a late 13th-century wood-carving.

The infantryman's spear was now usually of about 8-10 feet, though the old 12-foot kontarion may have remained in limited use throughout this era. The sword was most commonly suspended from a baldric.

Other items of armour to be found in use included mail coifs; woollen or linen hoods such as that worn by 69, probably the same as that described as laced at the back of the neck in Leo VI's Tactica; the old traditional leather harness of breastbands and shoulder pieces (67, 69, 72 etc.); tubular upper-arm guards; and greaves and vambraces (both of these mentioned only very occasionally during this era).

Uniforms, where worn, were still mainly of various shades of red and blue, usually with heavily embroidered borders and hems, often brocade. Officers and noblemen wore much more elaborately embroidered tunics and trousers of brocade. Embroidery was often gold. Boots, a standard part of Byzantine military equipment, were chiefly red, black, white or yellowish leather; the markings, consisting of two or three dark bands at the top and round the ankle, were fairly standard. Some men, however, appear to have worn shoes

supplemented with similarly marked gaiters in place of the boots (see figure 76).

Hair was generally long enough to cover the ears, but was neatly trimmed, while short beards were characteristic of the Byzantines throughout this era and are often recorded in anecdotes (such as when Richard I of England captured Cyprus in 1191 and obliged the Greek population to shave off their beards 'in token of their change of masters').

Of the four figures depicted here, 66 dates to the latter part of the 11th century while 67 and 68 are from illustrations in the famous Scylitzes ms. which probably dates to c. 1200 (note the shield devices of these two figures, which closely resemble Bayeux Tapestry types). Figure 69 dates to the 14th century and is probably representative of Byzantine infantry as they appeared at the time of the 'Catalan Vengeance' and the early Ottoman wars.

70, 71, 72 & 73. BYZANTINE LIGHT INFANTRYMEN

Light infantry continued to constitute a fair percentage of Byzantine foot-soldiers, some continuing to resemble the traditional types described under figures 9, 10 and 11 in the second edition of *'Armies of the Dark Ages'* (Anna Comnena, for instance, describes light infantry armed only with bow and small shield). Others were slingers and some were crossbowmen (called tzangratoroi). After apparently falling out of favour in the 10th century the crossbow (tzangra) was reintroduced under Frankish influence during the 12th century; when Anna wrote her Alexiad c.1140-1150 she still described the crossbow as 'a weapon of the barbarians [Franks], absolutely unknown to the Greeks' and felt it necessary to give a detailed description of it, which would suggest that its use was not widespread even then (though she is describing Frankish crossbowmen of the First Crusade). However, it is mentioned in use during Manuel's reign (1143-1180) and certainly it was in general use by the end of the century, Isaac of Cyprus' army in 1191 apparently including a considerable number of crossbowmen. It frequently occurs in 13th-century sources.

Most light infantry, however, were archers or, to a lesser extent, javelinmen. Figures 70 and 71 are both armed with composite bows, though 70 (c.1100) carries in addition a spear. Figure 71, from the Scylitzes ms., carries no shield; he is probably one of the light-armed Anatolian provincial troops (Paphlagonians and Bithynians in particular) held in high regard by the Byzantines during this period, especially in Nicaean armies of the 13th century – there were Bithynian archers at Pelagonia in 1259, for example, and at Galata in 1260, while 800 elite Bithynian archers were the nucleus of the army with which Alexius Strategopoulos recaptured Constantinople in 1261. His cap is characteristic of both Bithynians and Phrygians (that of 70 is similar).

The spearmen depicted in 72 and 73 are probably fairly representative of the light-armed ex-Thematic provincial levies and the infantry contingents of the stratiotes. These two date to the 12th and 13th centuries respectively, but similar figures are to be found throughout this era. Both wear helmets of similar design and carry circular shields about two feet in diameter. Figure 72 in addition wears a leather corselet with reinforcing breastband and pteruges at the shoulders. Scylitzes shows many such unarmoured infantry spearmen with kite-shields in place of round ones.

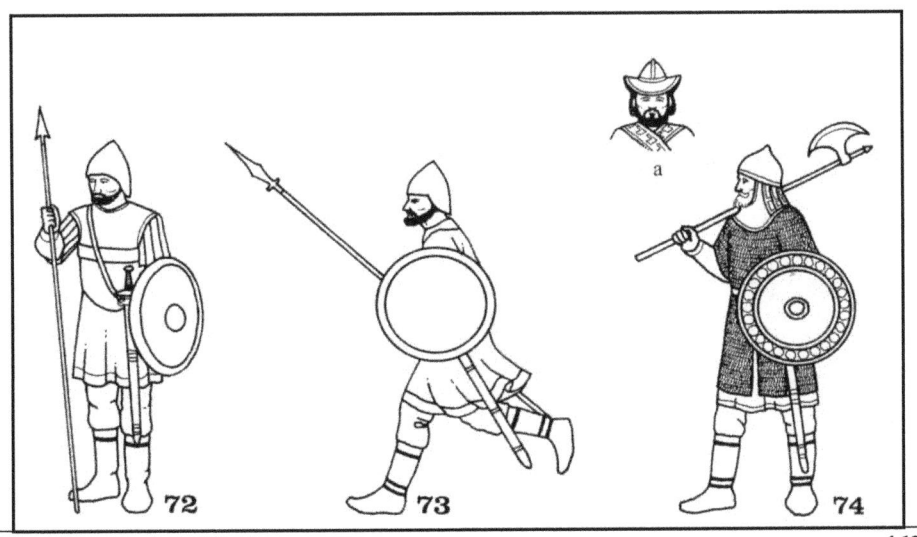

74. VARANGIAN GUARDSMAN

The axe remained the principal weapon of the Varangians, John VI Cantacuzenus writing of 'Varangians with their axes' as late as 1329. The usual blade-shape can be clearly seen in this figure, from the Scylitzes ms. A spear could also be carried. The illustration from which he is taken indicates that some at least continued to carry the round shield as late as 1200 or perhaps even later, though Niketas (who wrote in the early 13th century) describes Varangians with axes and 'long' (i.e. kite) shields at Eski Zagra in 1122.

74a depicts the head and shoulders of a Varangian Guardsman in state dress from a portrait representing John VI in 1351; in this source hats are white with gold trim and tunics are blue. 'Sky-coloured' silk tunics are also recorded by Haroun ibn Yahya as being worn by guardsmen in the 10th century, presumably Varangians since they carried gilded axes.

Their armour was generally heavy – we hear from Anna Comnena, for instance, that 'the weight of their arms' soon brought on fatigue at Durazzo in 1081. Quite what should be made of an alternative source for the same battle referring to a lack of mail corselets amongst the English (i.e. Varangians) I do not know. The Guard probably ceased to exist towards the end of the 14th century.

75, 76, 77 & 78. BYZANTINE HEAVY CAVALRYMEN

Byzantine cavalry were generally less heavily armoured than their

Frankish counterparts, and Frankish chroniclers as a result almost invariably describe them as 'sergeants'.

There was little uniformity of armour, probably only guard units now maintaining any degree of uniform appearance. Of these four figures, two wear mail corselets with breastbands (plus shoulder pieces in the case of 78), one a scale corselet with pteruges, and the fourth an apparently quilted corselet, probably over mail or lamellar. Taken from Scylitzes pictures, he wears in addition splint greaves. Most heavy cavalry in Scylitzes in fact resemble 68 and 76.

All four carry kite-shields decorated in almost Western fashion. The kite-shield appears to have been invented by the Byzantines in the first half of the 10th century (see *'Armies of the Dark Ages'*) and by the 11th century was in widespread use, particularly amongst horsemen. Cinnamus, however, contains a passage which seems to imply that prior to the beginning of Manuel's reign (1143) most cavalry were 'armed with round shields' and that long shields 'reaching to their feet' were only introduced during army reforms of c.1150. Quite how this statement should be interpreted is open to debate, but it is worth noting that al-Tartusi refers to the kite-shield quite specifically as 'the shield used by the Franks and Byzantines'. Nevertheless, some late sources still occasionally show round shields used by Byzantine cavalry.

At the beginning of this era some heavy cavalry units still included archers as well as lancers (the Immortals, for example, included bows amongst their equipment) but these seem to have steadily disappeared in the course of the 12th century. Manuel's reforms were basically responsible for their final demise though we still occasionally hear of heavy cavalry horse-archers even

78   79

at the end of the 12th century; Isaac of Cyprus' army included heavy horse-archers in 1191, including Isaac himself. Most cavalry, however, were lancers. The 12-foot kontos was still in use during much of this era (the Muslim quntariya, and probably the rumh too, were derived from it) but Frankish and Italian lances were also used. Officers still seem to have carried the bardoukion or mace.

79. BYZANTINE LIGHT CAVALRYMAN

Scylitzes and various other illustrated sources often show bands of unarmoured horsemen similar to this figure, armed only with sword, lance, shield and helmet, apparently representing native light or medium cavalry such as are occasionally recorded in the written sources. It may have been troops of this type that constituted at least a part of the contingents of the quasi-feudal stratiotes. It is probable that many of the ex-Thematic cavalry as still served were also of this type. They were possibly uniformed, and some may have been bow-armed.

However, most light cavalry of this era were Asiatic mercenaries, particularly Pechenegs and Cumans (the Pigmatici or Pincenati and Comans of Frankish sources, both described under figures 115-117 in *'Armies of Feudal Europe'*; see also figure 80 below) and subsequently – in numbers that steadily increased during this era – Turks, generally referred to as Turcopouloi. (One point of interest is that Pechenegs and Torks recorded fighting for the Byzantines in the Manzikert campaign were indistinguishable from their Seljuk enemies, which indicates a close affinity in their dress).

80. CUMAN CAVALRYMAN

At various times during this period the Cumans (also called Kipchaks, or Polovtsy by the Russians) fought either as allies or mercenaries for the Byzantines, Georgians, Mongols and Romanian Franks as well as for the Russians, Bulgarians and Hungarians, and as slave-soldiers in Ayyubid, Mamluk and Khwarizmian armies. They may also, towards the end of the 11th century, have served with the Khazars during the twilight years of their Khaganate.

They wore trousers, boots, long Arab-style tunic and kaftan. Brocade, fur, wool and linen predominated, but goatskins were also worn and Robert de Clari, recording the events of the Fourth Crusade, speaks of the Cumans wearing a sheepskin garment that may have been intended to serve as light armour. Other forms of armour including scale and lamellar were also worn depending on wealth and social status; for such richer warrior types see figures 115-117 in *'Armies of Feudal Europe'*. They shaved their chins and scalps but wore long moustaches.

Robert de Clari implies that the Cumans were armed only with their bows, but Byzantine and Russian sources also record sabres, lances, lassoes, maces and javelins in use, the Cumans being noted for their accuracy with the last. Most shields were small circular ones, but some Cumans carried a small version of the kite shield. They also included some foot-soldiers on occasion. These probably rode camels on the march.

The Cumans' Russian name 'Polovtsy' and German name 'Falven' both originated from words meaning yellow, which is fairly certainly a reference to skin colour. In the 12th century they absorbed some of the remnants of several other Turkish peoples, most notably the Torks and Pechenegs.

81. ALAN CAVALRYMAN

The nomadic Caucasian Alans (also called Ossetians) survived well beyond the close of this period, albeit only in small communities round the Black Sea coastline, particularly round Cherson, after their crushing defeat by the Mongols in 1239. Although they could include a large number of infantry their main arm was cavalry and the 14th-century Catalan chronicler Muntaner records that the Alans were 'held to be the best cavalry there is in the East', which explains why Alans serving in the Byzantine army received double the pay of the best native troops.

Archaeological finds prove that they were still principally bow-armed; the Byzantines, who continued to hire Alans in large numbers in the 12th and 13th centuries, usually brigaded them alongside their Turkish troops and used them as skirmishers. Cinnamus records one instance in 1156 when they were brigaded with Georgian troops, and certainly this figure from Daghestan could equally well be a Georgian.

Other equipment would have included sabre, dagger, shield (probably of wicker and/or leather) and a light lance, though finds of spearheads are comparatively few in number. Most wore little if any armour, but there were at least some heavy cavalry; 3,000 'Agulani' – Alans or possibly neighbouring Albanians – recorded in the Seljuk army at Antioch in 1098 were armoured all over 'with plates of iron' (probably indicating lamellar) as were their horses, while mail-armoured Alans are also mentioned during the Mongol conquests.

Their infantry fought principally with a heavy, long-handled battle-axe. As with most steppe peoples they were accompanied on the march by their families and wagons, forming the latter into the characteristic defensive laager when they encamped and pitching their tents within. They were generally blonde with blue eyes.

82. GEORGIAN CAVALRYMAN

Jacques de Vitry tells us that the Georgians were 'very warlike and valiant in battle, being strong in body and powerful in the countless numbers of their warriors', adding that they were 'much dreaded by the Saracens ... on whose borders they dwell.' Marco Polo similarly relates that 'the Georgians are a handsome race of doughty warriors, good archers and good fighters on the battlefield.' Of their appearance during this era we know little and this figure is based largely on 14th-century sources. Arms and equipment appear to have been principally of Persian design and the composite bow was one of their main weapons, though lance, mace and sword or sabre were also carried. De Vitry records that they wore their hair and beards 'about a cubit long', while Polo says they wore their hair short, so we are obviously not the only ones uncertain of their appearance!

83 & 84. MONGOL LIGHT CAVALRYMEN

Mongol costume and equipment is described fairly thoroughly in contemporary sources. William of Rubreck records that in summer the Mongols wore silks, rich brocades and cottons from China and Pema, and Friar John de Plano Carpini probably intends the same materials when he speaks of buckram, 'purple' and baldequin. Marco Polo also speaks of cloth of gold (brocade) and silk, lined or decorated with sable, ermine, squirrel and fox fur. One type of Chinese shirt, first recorded in 1219, was of raw silk worn as a type of armour since arrows could not penetrate it, instead being driven into the skin so that by tugging on the shirt the arrowhead could be extracted from the wound cleanly.

In winter fur coats and breeches were worn, usually two of the former, the inner coat with the fur on the inside and the outer with it outside. The outer coat was of wolf, fox, monkey, badger, dog or goat skin depending on the social status of the wearer. Sheepskin and stuffed silk were also worn, plus felt, which served as a type of light armour.

Carpini mentions white, red and blue-purple tunics as well as baldequin. H.H. Howorth, describing the dress of mid-19th-century Mongols, says the usual colours for the outer summer coat (the kalat) were blue or brown, over a bright blue or grey shirt; trouser colours appear to have been similar. The flap-opening of the kalat went from left to right, as opposed to the right-over-left opening of the Turks (see note 55-56). An ornamental belt, round fur or plush-trimmed cap and leather boots with felt soles completed the costume. Howorth adds that at that late date the cap had two 45cm ribbons hanging down at the back, and these appear to be mentioned in at least one contemporary source of our period. The alternative hat worn by 84 is a saraquj.

Polo records basic Mongol equipment as bow, mace and sword (other sources describe the last more accurately as a curved, one-edged sabre). Apparently two or three bows were carried, or else one particularly good one, and three large quivers of arrows. Polo speaks of only 60 arrows being carried, '30 smaller ones for piercing and 30 larger with broad heads for discharging at close quarters'; armour-piercing arrows were also in use. All had eagle-feather flights. Carpini's report indicates that the arrows were 28-30" long; another

83   84   85

source says they were longer than European arrows and had iron, bone or horn heads 3" broad. The bow was both longer and capable of greater range than the type in use with the Turks and Mamluks.

Other arms were lasso, dagger, and lance, the last often with a small hook below the head to pull enemy horsemen from the saddle. Vincent de Beauvais, however, says few Mongols carried lances and Carpini seems to confirm this. Polo records shields in one passage and Carpini says that wicker shields were carried, though he adds that they were not used much because they interfered with the use of the bow and that he only saw them in use in camp at night by guardsmen such as the Keshik. Meng Hung (a Chinese general contemporary to Genghis Khan) seems to disagree since he lists four types of Mongol shield: large, of hide or willow wood (the latter possibly meaning it could be of interwoven osiers); a smaller type used by front rank light troops to deflect arrows; large 'tortoise' shields for use in siege-work; and apparently a type of face-visor.

84a depicts how the Mongols wore their hair. The crown was shaved right round, leaving just a long lock of hair on the very top of the head which hung down to the eyebrows. The back of the head was also shaved. At the sides they grew their hair long 'like women', plaiting it behind the ears. Rubreck indicates that there could also be a plait at the back of the head. Compare to the hairstyle of figure 50. Moustaches could be grown to extravagant length, though Carpini says only a few grew hair on their top lips. All the sources agree that beards were scanty

85. MONGOL HEAVY CAVALRYMAN

Contemporaries offer a fair number of descriptions of Mongol armour, albeit generally vague. Carpini records iron or steel helmets with leather coifs or aventails, mail corselets, and leather body-armour of overlapping strips; he also gives an accurate and detailed description of lamellar armour used for both men and horses. Marco Polo says they wore a very strong armour 'of leather that has been boiled', i.e. cuir bouilli. Matthew Paris also records leather armour, of oxhides strengthened with iron plates, adding the improbable but amusing detail that only their chests were protected, their backs being left unarmoured to discourage them from running away. Thomas of Spalato describes 'armour of buffalo hides with scales fastened on it' (possibly lamellar) as well as iron or leather helmets. The Emperor Frederick II records 'untanned hides of oxen, horses and asses' reinforced with plates of iron which were somehow stitched in. He also mentions that there were many considerably better-equipped from the spoils of their defeated enemies (he actually says 'Christians', therefore Franks). Into this category fall iron helmets and armour of 'iron plates' of

Persian origin and mail hauberks of Alan origin recorded in addition to hardened-leather armour by Rubreck. Metal armour was polished to a high shine.

Quite clearly leather was the commonest form of body-armour, constructed from 'overlapping pliable strips' according to Carpini. He records that the hide strips – about 3½ inches wide – were tightly sewn together three layers thick, then softened by boiling and shaped to fit. He adds that the hide was stiffened with bitumen, which would also have served to protect it from humidity. The whole armour consisted of front, back, arm and leg pieces, the front and back being joined at the shoulder (and sides, one assumes) by iron plates and buckles; see also 89.

The standard Mongol battle-formation required that 40% of the army were heavy cavalry, but William of Rubreck says only the officers and picked men wore armour and this is reiterated by Vincent de Beauvais, who adds that no more than 10% of the Mongols were armoured.

86. MONGOL INFANTRYMAN

Although early Mongol armies were exclusively cavalry they gradually came to include a large percentage of infantry recruited from the subject populations of conquered territories, principally Chinese but also Turks, Arabs, Khwarizmians, Russians and others.

Main weapons appear to have been a long thrusting spear (principally as a defence against horsemen), javelins, bow or crossbow, and a shield could also be carried. Others were engineers. This particular figure, from the Mongol Invasion Scroll of 1293, is probably a Chinese auxiliary. He wears helmet and quilted body-armour,

86   87

probably of felt.

87 & 88. ILKHANID LIGHT CAVALRYMEN

These two figures and the next all come from illustrations to the 'World History' of Raschid al-Din, executed between 1306 and 1315. It was undoubtedly the Ilkhanids to whom Marco Polo was referring when he wrote that 'those [Mongols] who live in the Levant have adopted the manners of the Saracens', though it is apparent from these figures that it was the traditions of Persia rather than Egypt or Muslim Syria to which they had succumbed. The dress of both these figures (particularly that of 87 with his short-sleeved jacket and baggy trousers) betrays considerable Persian influence and is fairly characteristic of that worn by Persians and Moghuls over the next several hundred years, the only apparent concession to Mongol fashion being the saraquj hat worn by 88. Turbans were also frequently worn from Ilkhan Ghazan's time (1295-1304) onwards, while some of Raschid's illustrations also show the sharbush in use (see 41a-d). Clothing colours were bright, with reds and blues predominating, often richly embroidered.

The circular device on the chest of 87 may be a badge of office called a paizah; those of the Ilkhanids were marked with one to five lions depending on seniority, probably one lion for a commander of 100 men, two for 1,000, three for 10,000, four for 100,000 and five for princes and commanders-in-chief.

Judging from the illustrations bow and sabre were the principal arms, the latter a long, narrow weapon with only a very slight curve. Probably a small shield like that of 89 was also carried. 87a depicts an

88   89   a   b   c 90

alternative type of shield that was also in use, ultimately derived from the Frankish kite-shield; one illustration shows such a shield slung at a warrior's back by a guige-strap.

89. ILKHANID HEAVY CAVALRYMAN

The armour worn here is typical of that depicted in many late 13th century sources and throughout Raschid al-Din's mss., comprising a long, lamellar corselet (often completely covered by a heavily embroidered 'surcoat') and a spiked helmet with aventail. Buckles and laces are very clearly depicted across the shoulders and down the chests of some corselets in Raschid's illustrations, indicating that they were constructed of several different pieces as described under 85. The arm-pieces are flaps rather than short sleeves. On many corselets alternate rows of lamellae are sometimes shown painted or decorated, much like later Japanese armour. The helmet, with its cloth or leather aventail, is almost invariably depicted a blue colour (probably indicating iron) with the spike coloured gold.

Other items of armour in use before the end of the 13th century included tubular vambraces, knee-guards, greaves and 'mirror' armour (i.e. plates on chest and back secured by straps). Note the clever if somewhat impractical method of stowing away the lance when both hands are needed, stuffing it through the waist-belt and passing the foot through a small loop near the butt. Lances seem to have varied in length between about 9 and 12 feet, or sometimes more, and were held in a variety of ways including the underarm couch and the two-handed overarm thrust. A bow was also carried, together with a sabre and frequently a mace. Shields seem to have been mostly 12-20" in diameter, apparently held by a single central grip.

90. MONGOL STANDARDS

There appear to be no contemporary illustrations of the Khan's nine-tailed tuk standard. All we know of it is that it consisted of nine white yak tails, Meng Hung adding that it had a 'black moon' in the middle, probably referring to a ball or crescent atop the staff. John Greer has suggested to me in correspondence that in fact there was no set arrangement for the tails, but that probably it was the number of tails that indicated rank. The number nine itself was sacred to the Mongols, and Howorth thinks that the nine yak-tail tuk of the Khan probably resulted from the original division of the Mongols proper into nine hordes (by Genghis Khan's time represented by the Orlok). 90a is my own interpretation of its appearance.

Most other standards were like 90b. Thomas of Spalato describes Mongol standards as short, made of black or white yaks tails with balls of wool at the top, while other sources also refer to standards made 'from the black horse's tail', one of four black horsetails apparently being another of their main battle standards. The Mongol standard at the Battle of Leignitz in 1241, described by German chroniclers as a demon with 'a grey head and a long black beard', was undoubtedly of this type. The Mongols at 'Ain Jalut in 1260 appear to have had white standards, but others may have been dyed red or other colours. Other standards might be of cloth, as was Kublai's, described by Marco Polo as carrying a sun and moon device. These may have resembled 90c, from Raschid al-Din's ms. of 1306, the main part of which is red with blue centre, plus a yellow-brown pennon with blue border and a black horse-tail.

91. FRANKISH HORSE

Because the Franks depended so heavily on the charge of their mailed knights horses were extremely valuable in Outremer, even more so than in Europe because of the constant danger of injury or loss in battle as a result of Turkish archery tactics. Restor, the custom of replacing a vassal's horse if killed or injured in battle (see page 6 in *'Armies of Feudal Europe'*), may have actually evolved in Frankish Syria in the early 12th century; Usamah records in an anecdote how Tancred, told by his men during a battle of c.1110 that they feared for their horses, promised to replace all those hurt in the fighting ('The horses are my property. Whosoever of you loses his horse shall have it replaced.'), and this appears to be the earliest recorded instance of Restor.

Horses in Outremer came chiefly from Syria and Cyprus. Arab steeds were particularly highly prized, and high prices were also paid for Kurdish and Persian horses, 'fine steeds' of 'great value' according to Marco Polo. Turcoman (Turqueman or Turquan) horses were also used but these were clearly smaller, like the hardy horses of Cilician Armenia, both therefore being ridden mainly by sergeants (though Templar statutes indicate that Commanders, as well as the Grand Master and other officers, also had a Turqueman each).

European horses also found their way to the Holy Land with the various crusading armies but if the sources are to be believed most of them did not last long, the majority of those that came overland dying of exhaustion, starvation or wounds long before they reached Syria. In addition the Military Orders frequently had horses sent out to them by ship from their European Convents: their regulations also specified that no brother was allowed to take a horse from Outremer back to Europe if he should be 'posted'.

The Muslims, incidentally, did not think much of European horses, despising them as 'overlarge in the body and lacking spirit'. Most knights were expected to serve with two or three spare horses, and even sergeants sometimes had to have one remount.

92 & 93. MUSLIM HORSES

One of the characteristic features of Muslim harness was the collar (mishadda) worn at the throat, usually with a plume of horsehair suspended from it as in figure 92. It has even been suggested that this may have been coloured as a means of (unit?) identification. A second plume was often suspended from the breast-strap together with other pendants; 92 has in addition three pendants hanging from long straps on either side of the saddle, apparent in many illustrations of Turkish horses throughout this era.

The saddle itself was often very ornate; Usamah describes one as black and quilted, and another as gold with a black centre and the rider's name in black lettering round the edge. The saddle-cloth (zunnari), which usually covered about half of the horse's back, also tended to be richly decorated.

Figure 93, a Seljuk mount dating to c.1225, is interesting in that it wears a housing, called kanbush by the Muslims (compare to that of figure 7). These were probably in use by the 12th century and were fairly common by the end of the Ayyubid era. The Mamluk sultan Baibars had a horse with a black housing at his coronation in 1260, and at Acre in 1291 the Templar of Tyre reports of the Mamluks that 'they had their mounted men all armed, and their horses in housings.' At Homs too, in 1281, many of the Mamluk horses appear to have worn housings. Probably such housings sometimes concealed armour.

Horse-armour was in use amongst the Muslims even before the Crusades but owing to the predominance of light cavalry in their armies it appears only rarely in the sources. There were at least 3,000

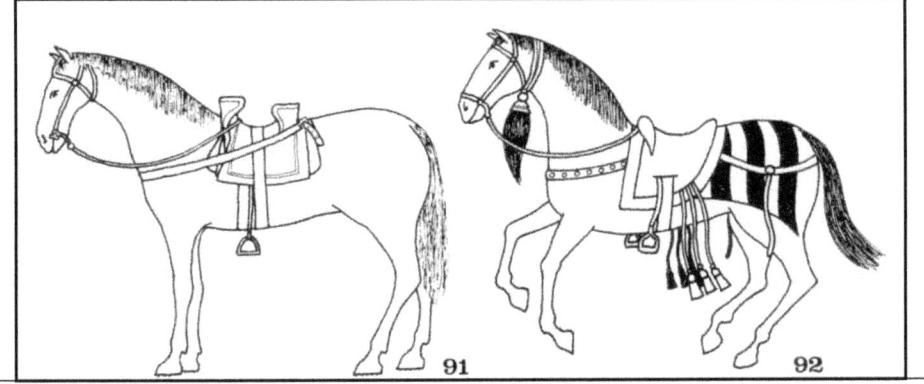

91   92

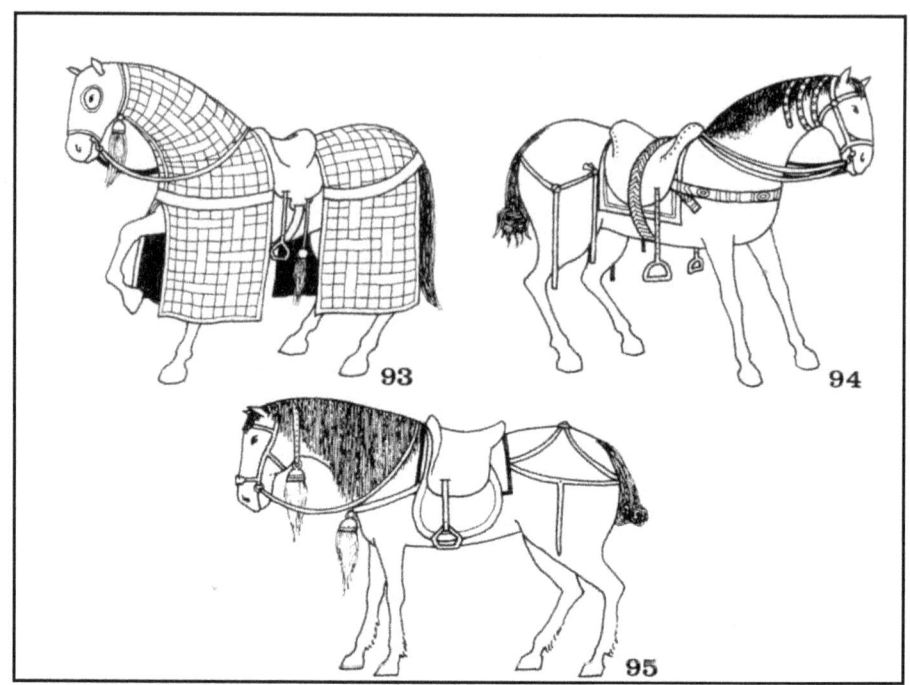

93

94

95

armoured horses in the Seljuk army defeated at Antioch in 1098, and Sultan Kilij Arslan I rode an armoured horse at the Battle of Khabar in 1107. In his *'Raymond III of Tripolis'* M.W. Baldwin implies that there were armoured horses in Saladin's army at Hattin in 1187, apparently citing Ibn al-Athir and Abu Shamah. Muslim terms for horse-armour were barasim (bard), baraki (chanfron) and tigfaff (quilted armour). The Franks adopted horse-armour in the late 12th century, and its use steadily increased throughout the 13th century; for Frankish horse-armour see figures 120 and 121 in *'Armies of Feudal Europe'*.

94. BYZANTINE HORSE

This is typical of Byzantine harness throughout the 11th, 12th and 13th centuries. It appears to have most commonly been dyed red or black. Horses were mostly from Anatolia and Syria – Anna Comnena mentions Damascene, Edessan and Arab horses being bought for the army, and the Byzantine word for horse (pharrhi) itself derives from the Arabic. Another type held in high regard for its speed was called the 'Wild Horse' by the Byzantines, apparently the same as the Turcoman or Frankish 'Turqueman' horse. Thessalian horses were also of good quality.

The Byzantines wore their stirrups shorter than the Franks. Spurs are absent from most contemporary illustrations, but they do occasionally occur, as, for instance, in one or two pictures in the Scylitzes ms.

Some Byzantines (possibly those of Turkish ancestry or extraction) appear to have followed the Turkish custom of controlling the horse by means of a small whip suspended at the wrist. I know of no Byzantine sources of the Crusade era that depict or mention the use of horse-armour by Byzantines, though this does not prove that it had completely disappeared. It seems more probable that its use simply became less widespread with the gradual deterioration of the military establishment, and that only those wealthy enough (or with access to Imperial armouries) were able to obtain horse-armour after the end of the 11th century or the early part of the 12th. Two armoured horses, ridden by the Emperor and an aide, do occur in a mid-14th-century illustrated 'Romance of Alexander the Great' ms.

95. MONGOL PONY

Mongol ponies were short-legged and stocky and stood only 13-14 hands high but they were, in the Emperor Frederick II's words, 'swift and at need long-enduring.' Each man had at least two and possibly as many as 18 horses, these apparently being ridden in rotation from day to day. They were mainly geldings and mares. The harness depicted here is fairly typical, most horses having a plume suspended at throat or chest. The tail was normally tied or shortened and the stirrups were worn short. The saddle was made of wood, rubbed with sheep's fat to protect it against the rain. Some were armoured or half-armoured. Carpini records leather horse-armour of two or three layers protecting the horse down to its knees, also describing horses 'with their shoulders and breasts protected', apparently with metal armour. In addition he records lamellar horse-armour and iron head-pieces. Without citing a source Harold Lamb, in his *'Genghis Khan'* (1927), says that the 'shock divisions' had horses 'encased in lacquered leather – red or black', by which he may be referring to Keshik units.

Solid-coloured horses were generally preferred since they concealed the blood of both their own and their rider's wounds, white horses being generally shunned for the same reason (white horses were in fact sacred amongst the Mongols). The Baatut rode black horses, while greys, chestnuts, bays, sorrels and skewbalds are also recorded. The Ilkhanids appear to have mainly ridden large Arab steeds. Like all Asiatic nomads, the Mongols directed the horse with a whip rather than spurs. Such a whip can be seen suspended from the wrist of figure 84.

96. CAMEL

Camels were the main means of baggage transport in the Middle East and accompanied most armies – Muslim, Mongol or Frankish – in

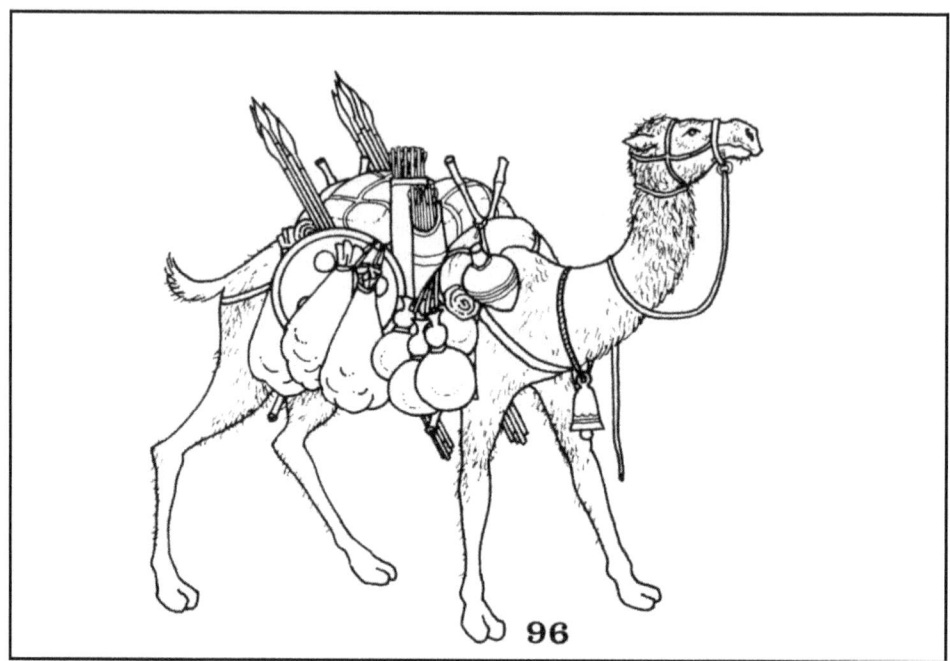

96

large numbers; Beha ed-Din records the Franks capturing as many as 3,000 camels from one of Saladin's supply caravans in 1192 (the Itinerarium claims the even higher figure of 4,700) in addition to mules and asses, also used in large numbers, and this was only one of three similar convoys. In addition to carrying baggage the camels often doubled as infantry mounts on the march, but they do not seem to have been ridden in battle except by some Arabised Sudanese tribes, such as the Bega. Mamluks usually had at least one camel each, more often two, while non-mamluks of the al-Halqa received three per two men.

Muslim caravans generally had their own escorts, composed of cavalry, in addition to which the drivers were usually armed, Fulcher of Chartres describing how the drivers of the Fatimid supply column at Ramla in 1102 'carried staves and missiles in their hands for fighting.' Of the three caravans reported in 1192, two were escorted by Bedouins; in all these three caravans seem to have had a combined escort strength of 2,000 cavalry (including 500 elite mamluks) plus 'numerous footmen', probably the camel drivers.

APPENDIX 1 MILITARY SERVICE OWED TO THE KINGDOM OF JERUSALEM AS RECORDED BY JEAN D'IBELIN

Jean d'Ibelin wrote c.1265 but appears to have recorded military service as it probably existed in the reign of Baldwin IV, therefore some time between 1174 and 1185. There are several versions of his lists extant in which, inevitably, certain discrepancies have been introduced; these are noted where they appear. A later list by Marino Sanudo shows certain other differences, and these too are noted. D'Ibelin's 'Livre des Assises de la Haute Cour', from which this data is taken, is quoted in full in Volume I of *'Recueil des Historiens des Croisades, Lois'* published in 1841 (a facsimile edition was published in the UK in 1969).

KNIGHT SERVICE

The Barony of the Count of Jaffa and Ascalon, including Ramla, Mirabel and Ibelin, owed 100 knights (one version gives the improbable figure of 500) thus:
Jaffa 25
Ascalon 25
Ramla and Mirabel 40
Ibelin 10

The Barony of the Prince of Galilee owed 100 knights (the same one version again says 500) thus:
The lands to the east of the River Jordan 60 (one version says 40)
The lands to the west of the River Jordan 40

The Barony of Sidon, including Beaufort, Caesarea and Beisan, owed 100 knights (one version again says 500, while Sanudo does not list this Barony at all) thus:
Sidon and Beaufort 60
Caesarea 25
Beisan 15

The Seignory of Kerak, Montreal and Hebron owed 60 knights thus:
Kerak and Montreal (Oultrejourdain) 40
Hebron 20

The Seignory of Count Joscelyn owed 24 knights (one version says 50) thus:
Château dou Rei (Mi'iliya) 4
Saint George (Lydda) 10
The lands of Geoffrey le Tort 6

The lands of Philip le Rous 2
The Chamberlain 2

Next d'Ibelin lists the knight service 'which the bishops of the kingdom of Jerusalem owed' (one version includes these as part of the Seignory of Count Joscelyn; they are not listed at all by Sanudo) thus:
The Bishop of Saint George of Lydda 10
The Archbishop of Nazareth 6 (one version says 10)

(The Seignory of) Toran and Maron 18 (one version says 15) thus: Toran 15
Maron 3

D'Ibelin then moves on to the knight service owed by the cities of the kingdom. Of these, Jerusalem, Nablus, Acre and Daron composed the royal demesne at this time.

The service which 'the Holy City of Jerusalem' owed was 41 knights (43 in three versions, but 41 in Sanudo) thus:
Lorens de Francleuc 4
Ansel Babin 5
The wife of Jean Comain 4
Raymond le Buffile 3 (5 in three versions)
Henry des Mons 1
Nicholas d'Artois 1
Simon the son of Peter l'Ermin 2
Andrew of the Temple 2
Peter d'Antil 1
Amalric the son of Arnold 3
Baldwin de Saint-Gilles 3
Simon of Bethlehem 1
Engeram de Pinquegni 2
Lady Gille, the wife of Jean de Valence 1
Peter le Noir 2
Fulk le Noir 1
Ansel le Borgne 1
Hugh le Petit 1
The children of Robert de Pinquegni 2
Eustace Patric 1

The city of Nablus (Neapolis) owed 85 knights (one version says 80, another 102, but 85 in Sanudo) thus:
The Viscount 10 (50 in one version)
Renier Rohart and his mother 8
Jean Belarnier 5
Eudes dou Merle 4
The wife of Hugh de Mimars 4

The wife of Baldwin le Prince 3
The wife of Raymond 1
Jean de Saint Bertin 1 (3 in four versions)
Constantine the brother of Raymond 1
William le Queu 1
Henry the son of Guy Rays 1
The wife of Baldwin of Paris 1
Isaac de la Pessine 1
Roger l'Asne 1
Aubrey de Roi 2
Bernard Fouchier 1
Richard of Nazareth 1
Raymond Babin 1
Baldwin de Rotrines 1
The wife of Robert Salibe 1
The wife of Michael le Grant 1
Gerard Passerel 1
Baldwin of Ibelin 4
The Lady of Caesarea 2
Henry the Crossbowman 1
Guy of Naples 1
Arnold of Tripoli 1
Reynald de Soissons 1
Amalric de Landre 1
Philip of Nazareth 1
George l'Escrivain 1
Balian d'Ibelin, 'for the land which he holds in Nablus' 15
Simon de Darrian 2

The city (or seignory in one version) of Acre owed 80 knights (three
versions say 72, but Sanudo – who calls the city by its classical name
of Ptolomais – also says 80) thus:
The Constable (Amalric de Lusignan) 10
Balian of Jaffa, the Chamberlain 7 (6 in one version)
Pagan of Haifa 7
Raymond of Scandelion 7
Philip le Rous 1
The wife of Eudes 2
Gerard Espinal 1
Lady Gille 3
William de Molembec 2
The wife of William of Antioch 1
Walter de Saint Denis 2
Robert Tabor 1
Raoul of Nazareth 1

Simon des Moulins 1
Count Joscelyn 1
Jordan de Terremonde Michael of Mount Sinai 1
Dreux the bother of Gilbert de Flor 1
Walter of Blanchegarde 9, of whom Arnold de Brie supplied 1
The wife of Adam Coste 1
Walter le Bel 1
Eudes de la Midi 1
Gace the son of Robert Gille de Calavadri 4
The Seneschal 3 (4 in one version)
Quastrin Benoit 2
Arnold de Difoille 1
The Viscount (William de Flor) 1
Jordan Harenc 1
Jean de Rains 1

The city (or seignory) of Tyre owed 28 knights (25 in one version) thus:
The Venetians 3 (1 in one version)
Simon de Marrini 3 (1 in one version)
The wife of William le Grant 2
The wife of Gilbert Vernier 1
Fulk de la Falaise 2
Ansel the son of Charles Gerard Gazel 2
Henry de Machelin 1
Adam of Arsuf 1
Denis the son of Geoffrey 1
Raoul de Boutellier 2
Roger Sauveri 7
Simon des Moulins 1
Roger le Gast 1

The city (or seignory) of Daron owed 2 knights thus:
Gerard de Douai 1
Reynald of Montgisard 1

The city (or seignory) of Beirut owed 21 knights
(No details given. Neither Daron nor Beirut appear in Sanudo's list).

D'Ibelin adds up his own figures to a total of 577 knights; of the other versions one gives 567, two give 677, and three give 666, while Sanudo – who, as noted above, omits several figures – gives 518. However, d'Ibelin's arithmetic is at fault in several places (Nablus adds up to only 81, Acre to 76) and his sum total is likewise wrong. Adding the figures for yourself, you will arrive in fact at 675. Smail, in his *'Crusading Warfare'*, says that 'however the figures are added, their total cannot be less than 647', but in fact by taking each minimum total (40 instead of 60 for Eastern Galilee, 15 instead of 18 for Toron/Maron, 80 instead of 85 for Nablus, 72 instead of 80 for Acre, and 25 instead of 28 for Tyre) the total can be reduced a little further, to 636. Conversely by taking the highest figure in each case (except for the impossible 500 of the 3 great Baronies, therefore 50 instead of 24 for Count Joscelyn, 10 instead of 6 for Nazareth, 43 instead of 41 for Jerusalem, and 127 instead of 85 for Nablus, including 50 instead of 10 for the Viscount) it is possible to increase the total to as much as 749. However, as noted the figures are clearly incomplete; d'Ibelin himself admits his lack of knight service data for Banyas and **Subeibe** (both captured by Nur ed-Din in 1164) and Château Neuf, and it is known that other fiefs (such as Arsuf, which owed 6 knights and 21 sergeants – i.e. 16½ knights – in 1261) have also been omitted.

SERGEANT SERVICE

This service appears to have been owed only by church lands and the burgesses of the cities. Like the list of knight service, it is almost certainly incomplete (we know, for instance, that Magna Mahomeria provided 65 'light-armed youths' – undoubtedly a contingent of sergeants – at Gaza in 1170). D'Ibelin lists the following:

The Patriarch of Jerusalem 500
The Chapter of the Holy Sepulchre 500 (Sanudo says just 5)
The Abbey of St Mary of Jehosaphat 150
The Abbey of Mount Sion 150
The Abbey of the Mount of Olives 50 (150 in three versions. Not listed by Sanudo)
The Templum Domini 50 (three versions say 150, as does Sanudo)
The Latina 50
The Bishop of Tiberias 100 (500 in two versions)
The Abbey of Mount Tabor 100 (500 in two versions)
The City of Jerusalem 500
The City of Acre 500
The City of Tyre 100
The City of Nablus 300
The City of Caesarea 50
The Bishop of Bethlehem 200
Ramla, Mirabel and Ibelin 150 (Sanudo says 100)
The Bishop of Saint George of Lydda 200
Arsuf 50
The Bishop of Sebastea 100 (500 in two versions, 150 in another)
The Bishop of Acre 150 (550 in one version)
The Bishop of Hebron 50 (550 in one version)
The Archbishop of Tyre 150

The Archbishop of Nazareth 150 (Not listed in two versions. Sanudo says 50)
The Bishop of Sidon 50
The Archbishop of Caesarea 50 (Not listed in one version)
Ascalon 150 (100 in three versions, and in Sanudo)
Jaffa 100 (Not listed in three versions, nor in Sanudo)
Le Lyon (Lajjun) 100
Le Gerin (Janin) 25
Haifa 50
Tiberias 200

This time d'Ibelin adds up his figures correctly to a total of 5,025, though one version miscounts to 5,175. Those versions with variant figures add up to 4,975, 5,075, 6,125 and 7,025 though three versions give their own totals inaccurately as 7,075. Sanudo's total of 4,280 is much lower than any of these.

APPENDIX 2 ROGER DE FLOR AND THE CATALAN GRAND COMPANY 1302-1311

Catalan mercenaries are first recorded in Byzantine service in 1279, during the campaign leading up to the Battle of Negroponte. Corsairs of Catalan origin also appeared on occasion in the fleets of the pirate Megas Duces Licario and John de lo Cavo, but it was not until 1302 that the Byzantines employed Catalans in particularly large numbers.

The previous year the Sicilian wars that had commenced with the so-called 'Sicilian Vespers' of 1282 had finally been ended by the Peace of Caltabellotta, and Frederick III of Aragon, King of Sicily, could finally dispense with the service of the mercenary Grand Company of Catalans under Roger de Flor – not without a sigh of relief. They left his service some 18,000 strong, in addition to true Catalans including at that time Italians, Frenchmen, Germans, and some Aragonese; when first raised by Peter of Aragon in 1281 the company had even included Moors.

Roger de Flor (whose real name was Rutger von Blum) is described by a 14th-century Florentine chronicler as 'the father of all Condottieri'. He was an apostatized Templar sergeant who had made his fame and fortune at the fall of Acre in 1291, when he had commandeered a Templar galley and charged exorbitant prices for passage to the safety of Cyprus! After a period of piracy as captain of a Genoese ship he had joined the mercenary troops of Frederick III and become commander of the Catalan Grand Company, and it was he who, after the Company had been made redundant by Frederick, managed to extort considerable privileges from the Byzantine Emperor Andronikos II in exchange for the promise of its service against the Turks of Asia Minor. Byzantine sources record the strength of the Company when it sailed from Sicily for Constantinople as 2-8,000 men (8,000 men in 18 galleys and four great ships), while the more reliable Muntaner, de Flor's secretary, records them as 36 ships and 6,500 men, composed of 1,500 cavalry, 4,000 Almughavari (Aragonese mountaineers – see figure 64 in *'Armies of Feudal Europe'*) and 1,000 other infantry. This total does not include the seamen, who probably account for the difference between Muntaner's 6,500 and Pachymeres' 8,000. (The latter, however, records the size of de Flor's fleet as only 18 galleys and four 'great ships'; since Genoa supplied a number of his ships this figure may represent only those that were his own.) Either way, by the spring of 1303 the Catalans numbered about 6,000 men.

On his arrival at Constantinople de Flor was created Megas Dux by Adronikos (this being one of the terms of their agreement) and, following scuffles with Genoese colonists in the city, the Catalans were promptly shipped over to Asia Minor for a campaign against the Turks, of whom they subsequently killed more than 50,000 in engagements at Cyzicus, Philadelphia, Ania and the Iron Gates. Unfortunately these successes went to de Flor's head, and he became openly hostile to Andronikos, seeing himself as ruler of a suzerain Byzantine state that he had plans to carve out in Anatolia. Despite his elevation to the rank of Caesar, an official request to reduce the numbers of his troops to 3,000 was ignored, and incidents continued until Michael IX, Andronikos' son and co-Emperor, resorted to having de Flor assassinated in 1305, and in the ensuing carnage some 2,300 or more of the Company were hunted down and killed; Muntaner records that their numbers were reduced to 3,307 men and 206 horses.

Leaderless and demoralised the majority of the survivors then disbanded. But 1,500 of them, a mixture of Almughavari and Frenchmen (the latter, together with Catalan knights, undoubtedly providing the cavalry element) fortified themselves in Gallipoli, from which they successfully repulsed two Byzantine attacks. They were gradually reinforced by motley bands of adventurers plus some 3,800 Turcopoles and Turks (1,800 cavalry and 2,000 infantry) who had deserted from the Byzantines.

Ultimately internal dissension forced them to abandon Gallipoli and split up. The largest part, some 8-9,000 men including 3,000 Turks, marched inland into Thessaly in 1308, finally heading towards the Frankish Duchy of Athens, where Duke Walter de Brienne employed them against the Byzantines and the Duchy of Neopatras, from whom they seized over 30 fortresses for him within six months. However, as soon as he concluded peace with his Byzantine enemies the Duke had no desire to retain such a vast number of unmanageable mercenary troops; he consequently granted lands to just 500 of them (200 cavalry and 300 infantry) and dismissed the rest without pay, which was four months behind anyway. Understandably, the Catalans were not content to leave it at that, and events ultimately culminated in the decisive Battle of Kephissos or Almyra in 1311.

All too aware of the Catalans' capabilities, Duke Walter had mustered a large army against them drawn from all Frankish Greece. As usual the sources differ regarding numbers, but probably there were 2,000-4,000 cavalry – including many Turkish mercenaries and 700 knights – and some 4,000-8,000 infantry, largely composed of Almughavari but including some Byzantine prisoners-of-war pressed into service because they were good archers. (The Catalan chronicler Muntaner's claim of 24,000 infantry can be dismissed.)

Encountering the Catalans on the banks of the Kephissos with their right flank on Lake Capais, Walter's cavalry were tricked into charging headlong into a carefully camouflaged marshy plain where their horses became bogged down. The Catalans then all but exterminated the Frankish army – so thoroughly that only four or five noblemen are known to have escaped with their lives. Of the 24,000 Frankish infantry present according to Muntaner, 20,000 were allegedly killed. Thereafter the Duchy of Athens became a Catalan state, which lasted down to 1388.

SELECT BIBLIOGRAPHY

The following is a list of those books that I found to be the most useful during the course of my original research back in 1978. Although fairly extensive, it is a very long way from being comprehensive, even as regards books available at the time that I wrote. Readers who wish to delve deeper into the Crusade era are strongly recommended to consult the bibliographies and follow up the references that many of these books contain, as well as looking at online booklists and catalogues for newer publications, in which books on the Crusades and Crusading warfare have proliferated pretty much exponentially over the past few years. The bibliography in *'Armies of Feudal Europe'* should also be consulted. Where it isn't clear from the title of a modern translation which source it is that's been translated the name of the original author(s) is given in brackets afterwards. Translated passages in the main text are based largely on these modern translations.

Allen, W.E.D. *'History of the Georgian People'* 1932.

Angold, Michael. *'A Byzantine Government in Exile'* 1975.

Archer, T.A. *'The Crusade of Richard I 1189-1192'* (extracts from various contemporary sources) 1888.

Archer, T.A and Kingsford, Charles Lethbridge. *'The Crusades: The Story of the Latin Kingdom of Jerusalem'* 1894.

Ayalon, David. *'The Wafidiya in the Mamluk Kingdom'* Islamic Culture XXV, 1951.

Ayalon, David. *'Studies on the Structure of the Mamluk Army'* Bulletin of the British School of Oriental and African Studies XV, 1953 and XVI, 1954.

Baldwin, Marshall Whithed. *'Raymond III of Tripolis and the Fall of Jerusalem (1140-1187)'* 1936.

Barthold, W. *'Turkestan down to the Mongol Invasion'* 1928.

Beeler, John H. *'Warfare in Feudal Europe 730-1200'* 1971.

Benvenisti, Meron. *'The Crusaders in the Holy Land'* 1970.

Berry, Virginia G. (trans). *'De Profectione Ludovici VII in Orientem'* (Odo of Deuil) 1948.

Blondal, S. *'Nabites the Varangian'* Classica et Mediaevalia II, 1939.

Boase, T.S.R. *'Kingdoms and Strongholds of the Crusaders'* 1971.

Bradford, Ernle. *'The Shield and the Sword – The Knights of St John'* 1972.

Bradford, Ernle. *'The Great Betrayal: Constantinople 1204'* 1974.

Bradford, Ernle. *'The Sword and the Scimitar: The Saga of the Crusades'* 1974.

Brand, Charles M. *'Byzantium Confronts the West 1180-1204'* 1968.

Brand, Charles M. (trans). *'Deeds of John and Manuel Comnenus'* (Cinnamus) 1976.

Buchthal, Hugo. *'Miniature Painting in the Latin Kingdom of Jerusalem'* 1957

Buckler, Georgina G. *'Anna Comnena: A Study'* 1929.

Budge, Ernest A. Wallis (trans). *'The Chronography of Gregory Abu'l Faraj'* (Bar Hebraeus) 1932.

Cahen, Claude. *'La Campagne de Mantzikert d'après les Sources Musulmanes'* Byzantion IX, 1934.

Cahen, Claude. *'Un Traité d'Armurerie Composé pour Saladin'* (Murda al-Tartusi, in French) Bulletin d'Etudes Orientales XII, 1948.

Cahen, Claude. *'Pre-Ottoman Turkey. A General Survey of the Material and Spiritual Culture and History, c.1071-1330'* 1968.

The Cambridge Medieval History (8 volumes) 1911-1936.

Campbell, G.A. *'The Knights Templars, Their Rise and Fall'* 1937.

Chabot, J.-B. (trans). *'Chronique de Michel le Syrien'* (Michael the Syrian, in French) 1905.

Cirac Estopanan, Sebastian. *'Skyllitzes Matritensis, Tomo I Reproduciones y Miniaturas'* 1965.

Conder, C.R. *'The Kingdom of Jerusalem 1099-1291 AD'* 1897.

Dawkins, R.M. *'The Later History of the Varangian Guard: Some Notes'* Journal of Roman Studies XXXVII, 1947.

Donovan, J.P. *'Pelagius and the Fifth Crusade'* 1950.

Encyclopaedia of Islam (4 volumes) 1913-1929, second edition 1954-2005, third edition 2007- (in progress).

Finlay, George. *'History of the Byzantine and Greek Empires from 716 to 1453'* (2 volumes) 1853-1854.

Folda, Jaroslav. *'Crusader Manuscript Illumination at Saint-Jean d'Acre 1275-1291'* 1976.

Gabrieli, Francesco (trans). *'Arab Historians of the Crusades'* (extracts from various contemporary sources) 1969.

Gardner, Alice. *'The Lascarids of Nicaea: The Story of an Empire in Exile'* 1912.

Geanakoplos, D.J. *'The Emperor Michael Palaeologus and the West 1258-1282'* 1959.

Geanakoplos, D.J. *'Graeco-Latin Relations on the Eve of the Byzantine Restoration: The Battle of Pelagonia 1259'* Dumbarton Oaks Papers VII, 1953.

Gibb, H.A.R. (trans). *'The Damascus Chronicle of the Crusades'* (Ibn al-Qalanisi) 1932.

Gibb, H.A.R. *'The Armies of Saladin'* in 'Studies on the Civilization of Islam' 1962.

Gibb, H.A.R. *'The Life of Saladin, from the Works of 'Imad ad-Din and Baha' ad-Din'* 1973.

Glubb, John Bagot. *'The Course of Empire: The Arabs and their Successors'* 1965.

Glubb, John Bagot. *'The Lost Centuries: From the Muslim Empires to the Renaissance of Europe 1145-1453'* 1967.

Glubb, John Bagot. *'Soldiers of Fortune: The Story of the Mamlukes'* 1973.

Hill, G. *'A History of Cyprus'* (3 volumes) 1940-1948.

Hill, John Hugh and Hill, Laurita L. (trans). *'Raymond d'Aguilers: Historia Francorum Qui Ceperunt Iherusalem'* 1968.

Hill, Rosalind (trans). *'The Deeds of the Franks and the Other Pilgrims to Jerusalem'* (Gesta Francorum) 1962.

Hitti, P.K. (trans). *'An Arab-Syrian Gentleman of the Crusades' (Usamah ibn Munqidh)* 1929.

Hodgson, Marshall G.S. *'The Order of the Assassins'* 1955.

Howorth, H.H. *'History of the Mongols'* (4 volumes) 1876-1888.

Hubert, Merton Jerome (trans). *'The Crusade of Richard Lion-Heart'* (Ambroise) 1941.

King, Edwin James. *'The Knights Hospitallers in the Holy Land'* 1931.

Komroff, Manuel (trans). *'Contemporaries of Marco Polo'* (William of Rubreck and John de Plano Carpini) 1928.

Krey, A.C. and Babcock, E.A. (trans). *'A History of Deeds done Beyond the Sea'* (William of Tyre, 2 volumes) 1943.

Lane Poole, Stanley. *'Saladin and the Fall of the Kingdom of Jerusalem'* 1898.

Lane Poole, Stanley. *'A History of Egypt in the Middle Ages'* 1925.

Latham, J.D. *'Notes on Mamluk Horse-archers'* Journal of the British School of Oriental and African Studies XXXII, 1969.

Latham, J.D and Paterson, W.F. *'Saracen Archery'* 1970.

Latham, Ronald (trans). *'The Travels of Marco Polo'* 1974.

Levy, Reuben. *'The Social Structure of Islam'* 1957.

Lewis, Bernard. *'The Assassins: A Radical Sect in Islam'* 1968.

Lowe, Alfonso. *'The Catalan Vengeance'* 1972.

McEvedy, Colin. *'The Penguin Atlas of Medieval History'* 1961.

McNeal, E.H. (trans) *'The Conquest of Constantinople'* (Robert de Clari) 1936.

Martin, H. Desmond. *'The Mongol Army'* Journal of the Royal Asiatic Society 1943, Parts 1 and 2.

Martin, H. Desmond. *'The Rise of Chinghis Khan and his Conquest of North China'* 1950.

Martin, Michael E. *'An Adriatic Hastings, 1081'* History Today XXVII, 1977.

Marzials, Frank (trans). *'Memoirs of the Crusades'* (Geoffrey de Villehardouin and Jean Sire de Joinville) 1908.

Mayer, H.E. *'The Crusades'* 1972.

Mayer, L.A. *'Saracenic Heraldry: A Survey'* 1933.

Mayer, L.A *'Saracenic Arms and Armor'* Ars Islamica X, 1943.

Mayer, L.A. *'Mamluk Costume'* 1952.

Miller, William. *'The Latins in the Levant: A History of Frankish Greece 1204-1566'* 1908.

Miller, William. *'Essays on the Latin Orient'* 1921.

Miller, William. *'Trebizond, The Last Greek Empire'* 1926.

La Monte, John L. *'Feudal Monarchy in the Latin Kingdom of Jerusalem 1100 to 1291'* 1932.

La Monte, John L. and Hubert, Merton Jerome (trans). *'The Wars of Frederick II against the Ibelins in Syria and Cyprus'* (Philip of Novara) 1936.

Munro, Dana C. *'The Kingdom of the Crusaders'* 1935.

Nicholson, Robert L. *'Joscelyn I, Prince of Edessa'* Illinois Studies in the Social Sciences XXXIV No. 4, 1954.

Nicholson, Robert L. *'Joscelyn III and the Fall of the Crusader States, 1134-*

1199' 1973.

Nicol, Donald M. *'The Despotate of Epirus'* 1957.

Nicol, Donald M. *'The Last Centuries of Byzantium, 1261-1453'* 1972.

Nicolle, David. *'Early Medieval Islamic Arms and Armour'* Gladius, Tomo Especial, 1976.

Norgate, K. *'Richard the Lion Heart'* 1924.

Norman, Vesey. *'The Medieval Soldier'* 1971.

Oldenbourg, Zoe. *'The Crusades'* 1966.

Oman, C.W.C. *'A History of the Art of War in the Middle Ages'* (2 volumes) 1924.

Ostrogorsky, G. *'History of the Byzantine State'* 1952.

Pernoud, Régine. *'The Crusades'* (extracts from various contemporary sources) 1962.

Phillips, E.D. *'The Mongols'* 1968.

Poliak, A.N. *'The Ayyubid Feudalism'* Journal of the Royal Asiatic Society, 1939.

Poliak, A.N. *'Feudalism in Egypt, Syria, Palestine and the Lebanon 1250-1900'* 1939.

Prawdin, M. *'The Mongol Empire'* 1940.

Prawer, Joshua. *'The Latin Kingdom of Jerusalem'* 1972.

Prawer, Joshua. *'The World of the Crusaders'* 1973.

Recueil des Historiens des Croisades, Lois (16 volumes in French, including translations of the Estoire d'Eracles, Jean d'Ibelin, Abu Shamah, Ibn al-Athir, Matthew of Edessa and many other Muslim, Frankish, Greek and Armenian chronicles and sources) 1841-1906, facsimile reprint 1969.

Rice, David Talbot and Gray, Basil. *'The Illustrations to the "World History" of Rashid al-Din'* 1976.

Rice, Tamara Talbot. *'The Seljuks'* 1966.

Richard, Jean. *'An Account of the Battle of Hattin referring to Frankish Mercenaries in Oriental Moslem States'* Speculum XXVII, 1952.

Riley-Smith, Jonathan. *'The Knights of St John in Jerusalem and Cyprus c.1050-1310'* 1967.

Riley-Smith, Jonathan (trans). *'Ayyubids, Mamlukes and Crusaders'* (Ibn al-Furat) 1971.

Riley-Smith, Jonathan. *'The Feudal Nobility and the Kingdom of Jerusalem, 1174-1277'* 1973.

Robinson, H. Russell. *'Oriental Armour'* 1967.

Runciman, Steven. *'A History of the Crusades'* (3 volumes) 1951-1954.

Ryan, Frances Rita (trans). *'A History of the Expedition to Jerusalem'* (Fulcher of Chartres) 1969.

Salibi, Kamal S. *'The Maronites of Lebanon under Frankish and Mamluk Rule (1099-1516)'* Arabica IV, 1957.

Schlumberger, G. *'Sigillographie de l'Orient Latin'* 1943.

Setton, Kenneth M. (Editor). *'A History of the Crusades'* (6 volumes) 1969-1990.

Seward, Desmond. *'The Monks of War – The Military Religious Orders'* 1972.

Sewter, R.A. (trans). *'The Alexiad of Anna Comnena'* 1969.

Shepard, Jonathan. *'The English and Byzantium: A Study of their Role in the Byzantine Army in the Later Eleventh Century'* Traditio XXIX, 1973.

Simon, Edith. *'The Piebald Standard: A Biography of the Knights Templars'* 1959.

Smail, R.C. *'Crusading Warfare 1097-1193'* 1956.

Smail, R.C. *'The Crusaders in Syria and the Holy Land'* 1973.

Stevenson, W.B. *'The Crusaders in the East'* 1907.

Stewart, Aubrey (trans). *'The History of Jerusalem'* (Jacques de Vitry) 1896.

Stewart, Aubrey (trans). *'Burchard of Mount Sion'* 1896

Tritton, A.S. (trans). *'The First and Second Crusades from an Anonymous Syriac Chronicle'* 1933.

Vasiliev, A.A. *'On the Question of Byzantine Feudalism'* Byzantion VIII, 1933.

Vasiliev, A.A. *'History of the Byzantine Empire'* (2 volumes) 1971.

Verbruggen, J. F. *'The Art of Warfare in Western Europe during the Middle Ages'* 1977.

Vryonis Jr, Speros. *'The Decline of Mediaeval Hellenism in Asia Minor and the Process of Islamization from the Eleventh through the Fifteenth Century'* 1971.

Wilson, C.W. (trans). *'Life of Saladin'* (Beha ed-Din ibn Shedad) 1897.

Yewdale, Ralph Bailey. *'Bohemond I, Prince of Antioch'* 1917.